Handmade Jewelry

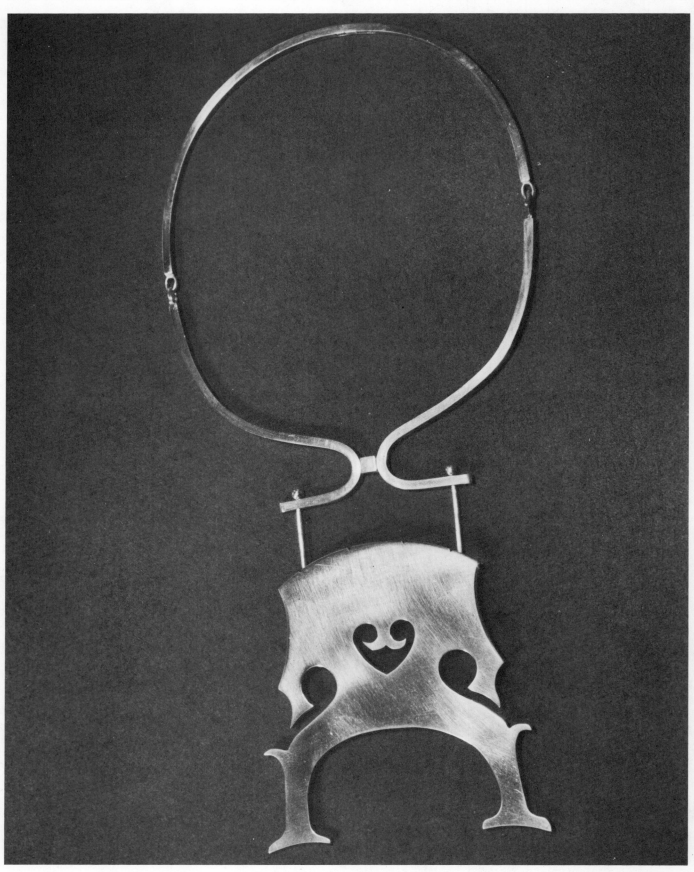

Example of pierced work. Cello Bridge neckpiece for Ellen Etkin, cellist with Maggio Musicale, Florence, Italy. (L.W.)

Third Edition

Handmade Jewelry

A Manual of Techniques

Louis Wiener

VNR Van Nostrand Reinhold Company
New York Cincinnati Toronto London Melbourne

In memory of my parents,
Rae and David Wiener

Thanks are due Dudley Shannon, of Allcraft, for his kindness in providing certain auxiliary equipment and corresponding photographs wherever needed.

And to Sid Dorfman, for his generosity in providing expert photographic aid for this new edition.

And to Mary Ann Scherr and the Parsons School of Design, for access to the work of their gifted pupils.

And last, but not least, to my wife, Betty, for her patience and multifaceted aid in the preparation of the manuscript.

The photograph on page 144 first appeared in *Egyptian Jewellery* by Milada Vilimkova (Paul Hamlyn, 1969).

Printed in the United States of America
Design by Loudan Enterprises

Published in 1981 by Van Nostrand Reinhold Company
135 West 50th Street, New York, NY 10020

Van Nostrand Reinhold Limited
1410 Birchmount Road, Scarborough, Ontario MIP 2E7, Canada

Van Nostrand Reinhold Australia Pty. Limited
17 Queen Street, Mitcham, Victoria 3132, Australia

Van Nostrand Reinhold Company Limited
Molly Millars Lane, Wokingham, Berkshire, England

First edition published 1948 by D. Van Nostrand Company, Inc.
Second edition published 1960 by D. Van Nostrand Company, Inc.

16 15 14 13 12 11 10 9 8 7 6 5 4 3 2 1

Library of Congress Cataloging In Publication data (CIP)

Wiener, Louis, 1912-
    Handmade jewelry.

    Includes index.
    1. Jewelry making.   I. Title.
TT212.W53   1981   739.27'028   81-50773
ISBN 0-442-29308-9   AACR2

Contents

Preface to the Second Edition

It is now twelve years since the first edition of this work was published. In a manual such as this, where so much ground must be covered and a vast number of possible constructions might be discussed, I have found it necessary to be carefully selective in determining the material worthy of inclusion. I have stressed technique and construction because it is basic to all jewelry design, regardless of taste, fad, and fashion. Consequently, I have reviewed all chapters in this manual with great care, and where required have made changes and additions.

Hand Made Jewelry, in this revised and enlarged edition, features improved techniques in soft soldering, an expanded section on enameling, additional stone-setting techniques, new and up-to-date sources of supplies, more new photographs and drawings, and a much augmented section on miscellaneous constructions with added suggestions for items of jewelry. The index has been completely redone.

This amount of new material would seem to require the addition of a relatively large number of pages. By resetting some pages and utilizing empty space at chapter endings, as well as by cropping and rearranging several plates, the generous increment has been made with a comparatively small expansion in book size.

Preface to the Third Edition

Since the last edition of this book, the world has witnessed a renaissance of handcrafts unprecedented in modern times. A major part of this revived interest has been in the field of handmade jewelry. Increased experiment on the part of the craftsman/designer has been matched by increased availability and variety of equipment and materials.

Such activity has resulted in my revision of the section on enameling, which reflects the convenience of preground enamels and ready-mixed chemicals; inclusion of electrosoldering; and a treatment of electroplating technique—of particular importance now, since the prices of precious metals have soared in recent years.

The daring creations involving combinations of techniques have justified my emphasis on matters of construction. Therefore, the section on miscellaneous constructions has been further amplified. Additional pieces of jewelry have been photographed with the aim of clarifying and suggesting specific details applicable to designs of entirely different conceptions.

As in previous editions, *all* material has been carefully reviewed and changes or additions made when considered of value to the craftsman, whether novice or expert.

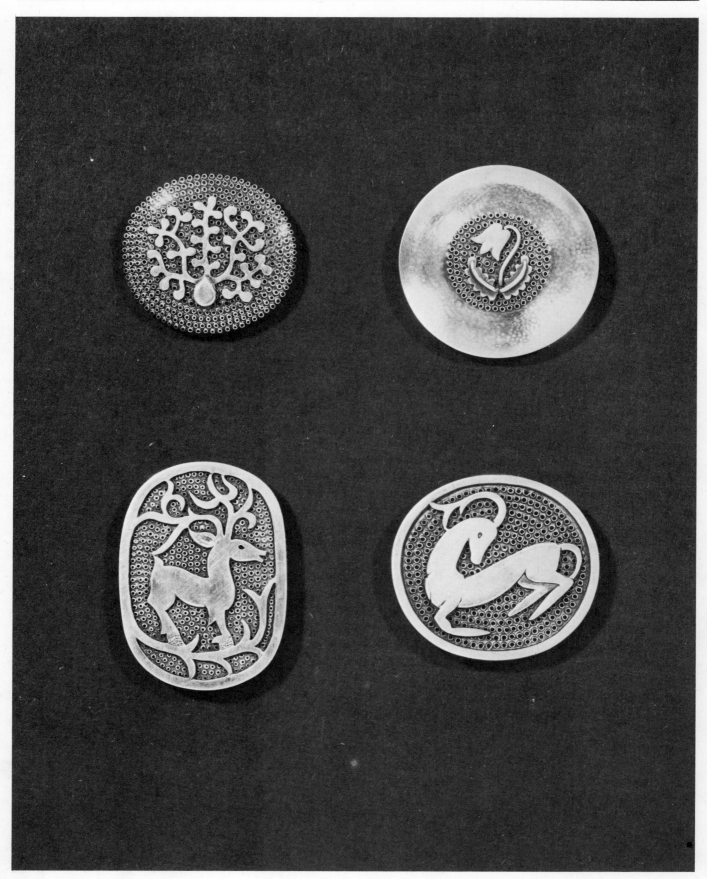

A group of brooches illustrating use of jeweler's saw. (Anna Halasi)

Introduction

All creative effort in the jewelry crafts can probably be classed in either of two categories: (1) the enrichment of a metallic surface and (2) the manipulation of its form or contour. These two larger divisions may be broken into a series of basic techniques. The purpose of this book is to review these techniques so as to enable the aspiring craftsman to master them fully.

Just as the musician must master the difficulties presented by his instrument before he can divulge the innermost meaning of his music, so may the craftsman, by mastery of the techniques of his art, fully achieve creative expression without the limitations of a partially understood technique.

Years of teaching the art of the craftsman have made it possible for the writer to observe at first hand the habits and errors of the novice. In the text, therefore, it has constantly been the aim to supply those necessary hints and suggestions that are frequently so tantalizingly missing at other sources. Nowhere has the writer assumed the reader to be the informed, experience-equipped craftsman in search of mere suggestions for designs. Where deemed advisable, several methods of procedure have been supplied, as different experienced workers have their individual preferences. Any one of these suggestions may be the answer to the novice who is dissatisfied with the results of the method he has been using.

Projects, as such, have been included only where they serve to illustrate a technique. A book of projects has a limited value; tastes change with time and differ with individuals. A mastery of the techniques presented here, however, will make it possible to understand as well as plan the procedure for limitless numbers of objects of jewelry.

To study a technique, the author suggests the following procedure:
1. Read with care the information presented in any unit
2. Apply the reading to actual practice
3. Reread the text immediately after the practice

This procedure has been found to be the most effective means of completely assimilating the text.

Consider how many circumstances must favorably unite before the beautiful can emerge in all its dignity and splendor.
—Robert Schumann

Inside of every musician there exists two people. One is the technician, the other the interpreter. Until the first person is in total control, the second cannot start to have a full life.
—Mstislav Rostropovich

1

The Jeweler's Saw

Probably the most often used tool in the field of hand jewelry is the jeweler's saw. This tool consists of a saw frame and a fine-toothed blade.

The Frame

The frame resembles somewhat a fretsaw or coping saw. It is made of a good grade of steel, tempered properly so as to have some degree of "spring" to it. A good quality frame should be used. These saw frames vary in depth—that is, the distance from the saw blade to the back of the frame. Depths vary from about 2¼" to 12". A 3" frame is a good size for jewelry. For work on bracelets made of 6" to 8" strip, a 4" frame may be desirable. The distance between the two clamps on the frame is variable, making it possible to utilize blades that have been made shorter through breakage. The standard blade length is 5". The clamps on the frame are made tight by thumbscrews, and it should *not* be necessary to use pliers on them.

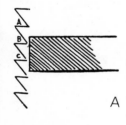

A

The Saw Blade

Jeweler's saw blades are available in various sizes. The size refers to, though it does not literally indicate, the number and size of the teeth on the blade. The length is always 5". Sizes used by jewelers run from about No. 4 to No. 8/0. No. 4 is the coarsest, 8/0 the finest, numbers running 4, 3, 2, 1, 0, 2/0, 3/0, etc.

These blades should be of fine, tempered steel. The two end portions without teeth are tempered differently from the cutting portion. The end portions are somewhat softer, in order to withstand the strain and flexing stress at the clamps. The middle cutting portion is tempered very hard, so as to cut metal, and is rather brittle. When the end portions of the blade break, many users shorten the frame and continue to use the remaining saw

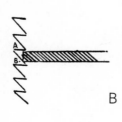

B

Fig. 1.

Fig. 2. Holding the saw frame for the insertion of a blade.

blade. This may be done, but the frequent breakage that then occurs is due to the breaking of the *brittle* cutting portion of the blade, which is now in the clamp.

The choice of blade size depends upon the thickness of the metal to be cut and, to some extent, on the intricacy of the design. For No. 18 gauge metal, a No. 1 blade will suffice. This is probably the most commonly used blade size. Actually, although this practice is not assiduously followed, blades are selected according to the following rule (note *A* and *B*, Fig. 1):

In Figure 1*A*, teeth *B* and *C* are in contact with the metal being cut. This means the metal cannot become caught between teeth since, when tooth *C* leaves the metal, teeth *A* and *B* are in contact.

In Figure 1*B*, which shows incorrect practice, the blade size selected allows the metal to become caught between teeth *A* and *B*. Operation of the saw then becomes very jerky, with frequent blade breakage and coarse results.

Using the Saw

To mount the blade, loosen the thumbscrews on the clamps one or two turns. The frame should be set so that the distance from the center of one thumbscrew to the center of the other is about equal to the blade length. The frame is then held as shown in Figure 2, and one end of the saw blade is clamped in the upper clamp. The blade should be held so that the teeth point outward from the frame and toward the handle. This permits the teeth to do their cutting on the down, or pull, stroke. When one end of the blade is tight, lean the body forward against the handle so as to bring the two clamps on the frame toward each other. The lower end of the blade is quickly set into its clamp, which is made tight, and body pressure is released. Plucking the blade lightly with the finger should produce a clear musical tone if the job has been properly done.

If a blade persistently slips out of the jaws of the clamp, do not condemn the saw frame until you have opened the clamp entirely and inspected the inner surfaces. A piece of saw blade from a previously broken blade sometimes lodges in the clamp and prevents the application of full pressure on the new blade. If this is so, remove the obstruction and repeat the mounting procedure.

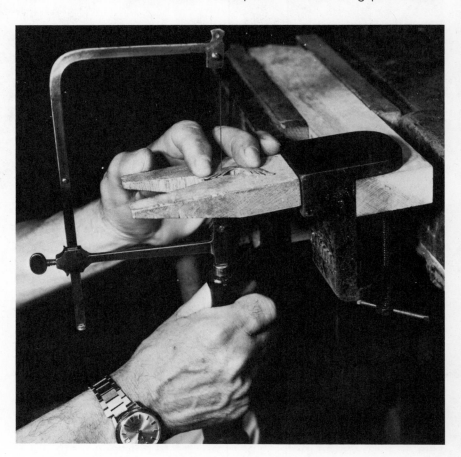

Fig. 3.   Correct position for sawing

With the jeweler's saw properly rigged, attention must be paid to the **V** block, or bench pin. This should be mounted at a height which will allow the forearm to be approximately horizontal or parallel to the floor when the saw is held against the work, with the work at the blade's midpoint (Fig. 3).

If the bench height is not exactly right, remember that the stool upon which the worker is seated may be varied in height. The work should be held against the **V** block with the fingers, striving for fullest possible support and rigidity.

The blade should be perpendicular to the work. The saw motion should be up and down, with the faintest emphasis on the down, or pulling, stroke, since this is the stroke that cuts. Avoid forward pressure—the saw will seemingly feed itself. Additional pressure will only clog the teeth and make sawing more difficult and breakage more frequent. The spaces between each of the teeth determine approximately the amount of removed metal the blade will accommodate.

Forcing the blade forward will only choke the saw. Maneuver around curves naturally, just as one maneuvers a bicycle. *Angular* changes in the direction of sawing are more difficult and require a special technique. When a cut is to be made at a right angle, for example, cut down along the line until the point is reached where the change in direction is to occur. In Figure 4, this is point *X*. If one mentally likens this procedure to a boy marching in a gymnasium, assume the boy to march in the direction of the arrow. Stop at point *X*, and "mark time" in place. This means the saw will be moving up and down at this point without forward progress. Now the boy, continuing to "mark time," slowly turns a full 90 degrees until he is facing the new direction squarely. He then marches off. The saw, likewise, is *slowly* turned toward the new direction, continuing its *normal* up-and-down motion without, however, any forward progress. When facing the new direction, the saw progresses along this new path in the usual manner. The author has found that by actually using a pupil marching on a chalk line in the classroom a most effective demonstration of this technique is made.

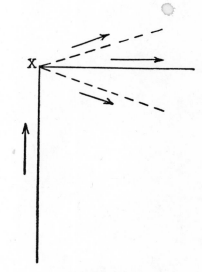

Fig. 4.

Sticking Saw Blade

If the saw seems to stick at some particular point during sawing and resists all efforts to dislodge the blade, abandon all forcible attempts to free it. It will usually be found that the saw frame is not pointing in the same direction as the saw kerf. This results in wedging the corner of a saw tooth diagonally in the kerf (see Fig. 5). To free the blade, exert a slight upward pressure and move the frame through an arc until the saw tooth, facing the proper direction, frees itself. If necessary, free the lower end of the blade from its clamp.

Delicate Trimming

Mention of the saw blade's "tooth-corner" action brings up an important usage of the blade. When delicate sawing is done and it is impossible to find files small enough to trim up the final results, a fine-toothed blade can be utilized in the following manner: insert the blade as usual and utilize the blade as a fine file by bringing a slight sideways pressure against the kerf. If the saw is turned very slightly so that the tooth corners tend to cut against the metal, a very delicate job of trimming can be accomplished. By using a blade somewhat finer than the one used for the original job, the tendency for the teeth to wedge in the kerf will be eliminated.

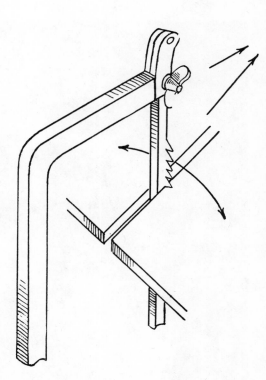

Fig. 5.

Piercing

When metal is to be removed from inner portions of a design, small holes must be drilled in the portions to be cut out. These holes are drilled after they have first been located away from the line of the design and punched lightly with a center punch and a light hammer. The work should be placed on a steel plate or anvil, and the punch mark should not be so deep as to leave a noticeable mark on the reverse side. The slight dent made by the punch will prevent the drill from "walking" off the design and making a hole at the wrong location. The work is then removed from the steel surface and the holes drilled. Assuming the frame to be rigged, release one end of the blade, thread through the hole, and move the work close to the tightly clamped end. The other blade-end is reset in the usual manner. This type of "internal" sawing is called *piercing* (Fig. 6 and Frontispiece).

Additional Hints

As a lubricant on the saw blade, use beeswax or paraffin. Soap is sometimes used, but because it holds moisture, it may cause rusting and consequent weakening of the blade. Draw the saw once down the cake of wax. Repeat when the saw seems to

Fig. 6. An example of saw piercing as well as a means of decorating a plain silver spoon.

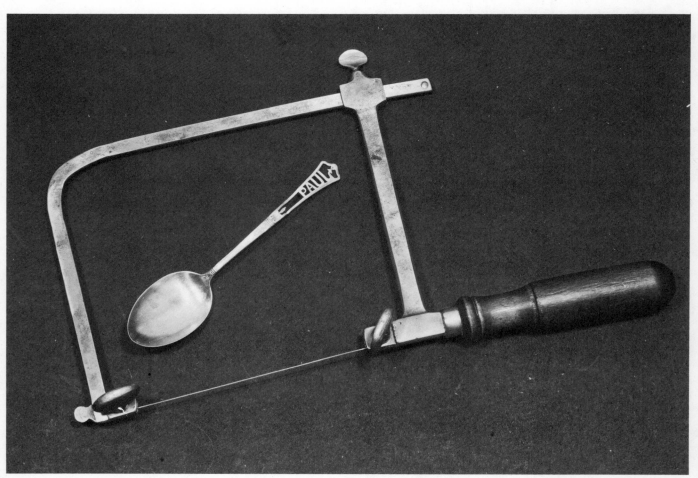

"stick" frequently. A blade used with wax will pick up tiny particles of metal. The metal and the wax will fill the spaces between the teeth. This will give the appearance of a blade with no teeth. Do not be fooled by this appearance, as a blade in this condition will continue to cut quite well.

It is not necessary to rest the blade to allow it to cool.

When cutting out a design, the saw kerf (as the actual cut is called) follows *alongside* the line of the design. It is not necessary to leave a space between the blade and the line. The line must *not* be removed, however, and should readily be seen on the work after sawing is completed. Good saw work necessitates only the slightest use of the files for smoothing. Space left between line and blade means actual *hours* wasted filing to the line.

When a zig-zag or jagged outline is to be sawed, first saw to a curve around the points of the outline, as shown in Figure 7. When this has been done, cut straight in from the edge to the bottom of the **V**. Then back out the saw blade and use *either* of these techniques:

  1. Cut from the next point in to the same **V** bottom, completely removing the portion in between the sides of the **V**.

  2. *Back* the saw blade into the first **V** cut made, and when the bottom of the **V** is reached, turn the frame slightly and saw out along the next side of the **V**. This is a useful technique to remember.

If it is necessary to stop work momentarily for any reason when sawing, bring the upper clamp down to the work and the blade will be less likely to snap when the frame is moved, either through accident or when starting to cut again. If work on a complicated design must be stopped for the day before the sawing is completed, rather than back out the blade along a lengthy and complex route, open the upper clamp so as to release the blade and pull down the frame, releasing the saw from the work.

Remember, when backing out of a cut line, move the saw frame up and down just as if forward sawing were going on, only pull backward and follow the kerf carefully.

Always sit directly behind the saw frame. Turn the *work* when necessary, *not* the saw frame.

The beginner will find that fingers holding the work will tire before the sawing arm. Rest the fingers. Never clamp the work. It is not necessary to grasp the frame handle tightly. This tires the forearm and makes cutting no easier.

There is a tendency to use the middle portion of the blade, actually utilizing about an inch of blade. Remember that 2" of blade will cut twice as much metal, and the blade has about 4" of cutting edge available!

Path of first saw cut

Fig. 7.

2 Transferring the Design to the Metal

Several methods are available when it is necessary to transfer a design to the surface of a piece of metal. The most satisfactory of these involves the use of white tempera paint, carbon paper, and tracing paper.

Most of the work in jewelry will necessitate transferring a design to a flat sheet of metal. Two methods are recommended. Method 1 calls for a perfect drawing of the design. This may be done with the help of thin, hard, tracing paper and a sharp-pointed, medium-grade pencil. The completed drawing or tracing must be glued to the metal surface. Before this is done the metal surface should be thoroughly cleaned with steel wool. Select a good hide glue or fish glue. Pharmacists use an excellent glue to attach their labels to bottles. Such a glue is useful, for the nonporous surface of a glass bottle is somewhat similar to the surface of smooth metal. Having selected the glue, apply it *very thinly* to the underside of the *paper drawing* or *tracing.* Apply the drawing to the metal and smooth. If too much glue is applied, the design will require much time for drying, and more important, the applied drawing will later curl off the metal surface. The use of rubber cement is inadvisable. Designs applied with such cement will not remain in place, but will "creep" over the metal surface and occupy another position.

When the glue is dry, carefully go over the penciled lines of the drawing with ink, preferably waterproof. If this is not done, the drawing will rub off the paper during handling. Later, the paper may be removed by using hot water.

The first method has its limitations when designs are to be transferred for etching purposes. In such circumstances, the design must be applied directly to the metal surface. This may be accomplished by first coating the surface with white tempera paint or Chinese white. Coat the surface only after it has been scrubbed with steel wool. When scrubbed, dip the finger in a thick, white tempera paint, or rub the dampened forefinger on a cake of

Chinese white. The paint-carrying finger is then rubbed firmly over the metal surface. The object is to deposit a *thin,* dull layer of paint to the metal. Do not be disturbed by a streaky appearance so long as the metal is completely covered.

When the paint has dried *thoroughly,* place a piece of fresh carbon paper over the coated metal. Over this, position the drawing to be used and fasten both pieces of paper with small tabs of masking tape. Go over the drawing with a hard pencil. When the papers are removed, a perfect tracing will be found on the coated metal surface. This tracing must now be transferred to the metal, as the paint is to be washed off before the etching ground is applied. Using a well-sharpened scriber, the carbon lines are traced through, so that they are carried by the metal surface. Wash the paint away with water. The clearly cut design is now ready to be worked upon or painted over with asphaltum if etching is to be done.

NOTE: The use of carbon paper over a bare metal surface is rarely completely successful.

A somewhat similar method can be used when the craftsman is artist enough to draw directly on the coated metal with a scriber or when a pattern is to be applied with a scriber and steel ruler. This method eliminates the carbon paper. The metal is merely coated with a layout stain, such as that used by machinists. The stain, usually methyl violet in a cellulose solution, is available at machinists' supply houses. It can be made by adding methyl violet to a solution of metal lacquer that is considerably thinned with lacquer thinner. This solution is brushed on and dries in a few moments. Lines are scratched on the metal, through the stain, and will appear in bright contrast with the stain used. When all drawing is done, the stain can be removed by wiping with cotton dipped in lacquer thinner. Some types of layout stains can be removed with alcohol.

3

Files, Filing, and Abrasive Tools

Selecting and utilizing the proper file for a piece of work are important factors in hand jewelry making that are too often only partially understood. Although the file does shape the metal to some extent, it is not usually used for that particular purpose. Rather it is used for finishing and smoothing and for slight changes in metal objects.

Files, other than jeweler's or needle files, consist of a toothed cutting portion ending in a pointed tang, which is driven into a wooden handle of proportionate size. Needle files and escapement files have a rounded, smooth, unpointed metal end which replaces the tang and forms a convenient handle. Files come in a variety of sizes and cuts. The length of a tanged file is designated by the *cutting length*. A self-handled needle file is measured according to overall size. The cut may be either single or double cut (see Fig. 8), and the tooth size is also considered when referring to the cut, *e.g.*, No. 2 double-cut (see Fig. 9).

Files are available with a variety of cross-sectional shapes. These shapes make it possible to reach portions of the work otherwise inaccessible and also to smooth out a shaped portion with maximum efficiency. A file is always fitted to a curve as closely as possible, except for convex curves, which require the flat surface of a file.

Riffle files are used to reach depressed or otherwise inaccessible areas. These files are double-ended and bent. If a riffle file is unavailable when needed, it can be made by taking a needle file of the required cross section, heating it in a flame until orange in color, and pressing the heated point against a steel block, bending it to the required curve. Do *not* attempt to bend the file if it loses its heated color, but instead, reheat. When the required curve is achieved, heat to red heat and plunge the file quickly into cold water. The resulting riffle file will not be as fine a tool as the commercial riffle file, but it will serve well in an emergency.

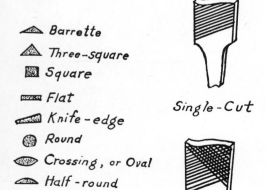

Barrette

Three-square

Square

Flat

Knife-edge

Round

Crossing, or Oval

Half-round

Single-Cut

Double Cut

Fig. 8.

18

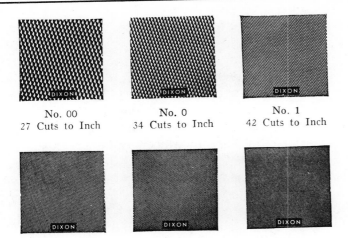

No. 00	No. 0	No. 1
27 Cuts to Inch	34 Cuts to Inch	42 Cuts to Inch

No. 2	No. 3	No. 4
98 Cuts to Inch	110 Cuts to Inch	144 Cuts to Inch

Permission of Wm. Dixon Inc., Newark, N. J.

These Cuts Compare with the Regular American Files as Follows:

GLARDON	No. 00	No. 1	No. 2	Nos. 3 or 4
REGULAR AMERICAN	Bastard	Second Cut	Smooth	Super Smooth

NOTE: For cuts numbered from No. 4 to No. 6 there is no equivalent in Regular Files.

Fig. 9.

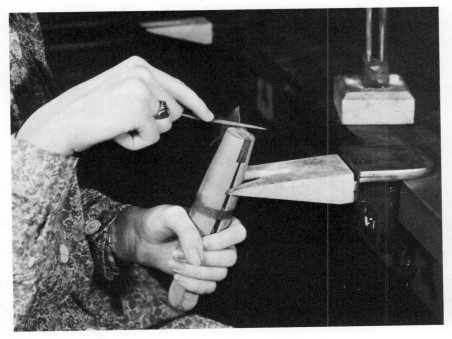

Fig. 10. One method of holding work for filing.

Fig. 11. Another method of supporting work for filing.

Filing is the removal of metal by passing a series of short, chisel-shaped teeth over it. Because of the angle of the teeth, a file will cut *only* on the *push* stroke. This is very important, because *pulling* the file back over the work accomplishes very little cutting and quickly dulls the file. The work may be held in the hand, in a ring clamp (Fig. 10), or in a hand vise, depending on the nature of the job. Sometimes the work is mounted in a bench vise. A convenient method of filing small work is to rest the work on the **V** block and file downward, removing the pressure on the upward, return stroke (see Fig. 11).

Chalk, rubbed lightly into a file, reduces the tendency of the file to fill with metal particles. It also makes it easy to remove the particles with a file card or a stiff brush for fine-cut files. Do not oil files. Oil may be removed from a file by washing it with benzene (*beware of fire*). Files have a tendency to fill most rapidly when used on copper, lead, or similar soft metals. It is unwise to use your choice files on lead if they are generally used on sterling silver. Remember that minute particles of lead on a silver surface will pit the surface when the silver is heated to a red heat.

If a file is in particularly bad shape due to filling in with soft particles, it can still be redeemed, even when a file card fails. Take a piece of No. 18 brass or copper about ⅜" × 1" and rub the ⅜" edge slowly and hard against the file, near the tang. Rub it in the *same direction* as the slanting cuts on the file. In a short time, the copper edge will be so shaped as to be a reverse pattern of the tooth cuts. This prepared metal edge, rubbed on any filled portion of that file *in the same slanting stroke,* will remove stubborn particles that previously yielded to no other method.

When a borax flux has been used on a soldering job, pickle the work before filing, as the hard borax glaze which remains after soldering is difficult to cut and may dull the file.

If the portion of an article being filed is wider than the file, move the file in such a way so that it travels not only forward, but also sideways to some extent. This will prevent cutting a depressed section in the work equal to the width of the file.

As with the jeweler's saw, a file can remove only a certain amount of material. Additional pressure may break the file, which, though hard, is very brittle. A coarse file can be used to remove large quantities of metal, but a finer file must be used to finish up the job.

A last note on files: keep them separate from each other and from other steel tools—rubbing them together will dull their sharp but brittle teeth very quickly.

The Scotch Stone

After a file has been used on the surface of a piece of work (but not the edge), it may be necessary to remove the faint marks left by the file. These marks become very noticeable when the work has been buffed or polished. To remove such marks and other marks made by scrapers and other tools, the Scotch, or water-of-ayr, stone is used. This is a slatelike material available cheaply in stick form, 6" in length and in cross-section sizes from ⅛" × ⅛" to ½" square. The stone is rubbed against the work, or in angles formed by the juncture of a bezel and a surface, or around applied ornaments. The stone must be kept well moistened with water while in use. It will wear itself quickly to fit the particular shape against which it is worked. If marks are particularly deep, small Carborundum abrasive sticks can be used before the Scotch stone to hasten the work. The Scotch stone is not intended for use on large areas, on which one of the many abrasive cloths or papers can be used, but only on small, scratched, hard-to-reach areas, where the application of other abrasive materials is impracticable.

Abrasive Cloths and Papers

When a piece of metal is selected for use in making an article, it is generally cleaned with a piece of fine steel wool. This removes dirt from the surface but does *not* clear away marks or imperfections in the metallic surface. For the removal of these imperfections prior to working the article or polishing its surface, abrasive cloths and papers are used.

Emery cloth or paper is used for smoothing metal. The cloth sheets are usually 9″ × 11″ and consist of emery grains coated on a blue jean cloth. The grit range for metal finishing runs from No. 3, which is coarse, to No. 3/0, fine.

The sheet can easily be torn to smaller-size squares or strips. (Never cut abrasive papers or cloths with scissors or shears. The hard, abrasive grit will spoil cutting edges.) To remove scratches, a grit size is selected capable of removing the particular flaw in the metal, and successively finer grits are applied until the surface is quite clear and polished.

Emery polishing paper comes in a sheet size measuring 9″ × 13¾″. The grit range differs from emery cloth and the numbers run from No. 3 to No. 4/0. This paper imparts a very fine surface to a piece of metal when the finest grit size is used.

A faster cutting abrasive that is available on cloth is aluminum oxide. This material is available in sheet form or in narrow rolls, in which form it is very economical for hand jewelry work. This product, available on lightweight cloth referred to as "J" weight, runs in grit range from No. 80 to No. 180, with two very fine grits, No. 240 and No. 320.

Crocus cloth and rouge paper are two other abrasive sheets used. Both have a reddish-appearing abrasive surface and are extremely fine in grit size, enabling these abrasives to be used for final finish purposes—final as far as hand abrasives are concerned. The buffing or polishing machine is the next step.

4 Soft Soldering

Soft soldering is the process of joining two metals by the use of a third metal known as "soft solder." This metal is an alloy generally composed of 60 percent lead and 40 percent tin. Proportions vary and should be known, as melting points will vary. (For alloy 60 tin, 40 lead, 370° F is the melting point. For 50-50 alloy, melting point is 414° F. For 40 tin, 60 lead, it is 460° F.) The metal is available in wire, ribbon, or bar form. Some forms of wire solder are hollow, or tubular, and contain a flux in the core. Fluxes are generally of the rosin or acid types.

Because of the low melting point, soft soldering has several important applications. It can be used extensively in repair work, particularly of moderate-priced or cheap jewelry, or it can be used in repair work on enameled jewelry. Where repairs are to be made on work containing stones, soft solder may be used when it is impracticable to remove the stones. Where the high temperatures necessary for hard soldering are not available—for example, in camps or other locations where gas or compressed air are not available—soft soldering may be done by electric soldering irons, alcohol burners, or propane torches.

Soft soldering, however, is not used on better grades of jewelry. Wherever possible, particularly when working with silver and other precious metals, hard soldering should be used. Soft soldering, properly understood, can be accomplished easily by young children who are attempting the easier types of copper jewelry.

The same general rules apply to all types of soldering—hard or soft—and they are as follows:

1. The work or surfaces to be joined must be perfectly clean. This can be accomplished by means of a scraper or clean steel wool. Very dirty work may be previously pickled.

2. The surfaces to be soldered must be protected against oxidation by means of a flux—for jewelry work (soft soldered), a rosin-base flux in paste form is recommended, rather than reliance on core-containing solders.

Fig. 12. Soft-soldering a pin-back.

3. The work being soldered must be brought to the degree of temperature necessary to melt the solder. Solder will not adhere to a cooler surface, even though the solder is in a molten state.

4. Contact between the two surfaces being soldered must be good. Solder will not flow into a wide gap.

Figure 12 shows the method used to apply a pin-back of the soft-solder type. Where available, a Bunsen burner or an alcohol lamp will do the best job. Note the locking-type tweezers, which are a convenience of particular interest to occupational therapists who work with patients whose hands tend to tremble. They are also helpful for young children who are likely to relieve the pressure on ordinary tweezers before the solder has solidified sufficiently.

To do this job, clean the back of the work thoroughly, using steel wool. Bend the bar on the pin-back, if necessary, to make good contact with the work, and then clean it. Both surfaces to be joined should be coated with a thin smear of rosin paste flux. With the extreme tips of the locking tweezers clamp the two pieces of metal in position so that good contact is maintained. Cut soft solder in wire form into ⅛-inch pellets. If the pin-back has two spaced holes, place one pellet of solder over each hole. If a pin-back without holes is used, place two spaced pellets of solder on the back of the brooch, *touching the edges* of the pin-back bar. Hold the work over a soft blue flame until the pellets melt into the holes, or in the second case, until the pellets melt against the edges of the pin-back and flow under the bar. If the contact is good, the solder will be drawn under the bar by capillary action, and an excellent job will result, with a minimum of solder visible. When this action is completed, remove the work from the flame without disturbing the tweezers, and allow it to cool.

NOTE: The solder will melt before the flux has begun to carbonize or turn brown if the work has been properly prepared. Take care to avoid the presence of flux or solder *in the joints of the pin-backs.*

Cooling may be hastened by resting the work on a cool metal surface. The heat will be drawn out of the work more quickly in this way. Do not chill the work by dipping into water. A chilled joint has a tendency to part more easily because of crystallization of the solder.

Sweat soldering may be done on soft-soldering jobs as well as on hard soldering. The rooster pin shown in Figure 16B has been sweat-soldered. If soft solder is to be used, coat the upper pieces of the work with solder at the points of juncture. This may be done with a soldering iron or with a small gas or alcohol burner. Clean the work, coat with flux, and hold over the flame until a little solder melts over the proper area. Then clean the main portion of the work to which the previously prepared pieces are to be joined, and coat thinly with flux. Now apply the solder-coated pieces in position over the flux-coated piece that has been prepared to receive them. The work can then be heated with a flame while it rests on a large asbestos pad. The pieces will flatten out as soon as the solder underneath each piece melts. If the pieces are designed so that they will not lie properly without some form of pressure, use locking tweezers or cotter pins at each point of juncture (see Fig. 16A). When the solder melts, the tweezers will press the parts together and hold them firmly until cool. Remember that the heat of a Bunsen flame is all that is needed.

Using the Soldering Iron

While the soldering iron is not as handy as a Bunsen flame for doing the work previously described, it is frequently valuable in doing repairs on finished pins. Prepare the iron for use by coating its tip with a thin, bright layer of solder. The tip is made of solid copper and must be made bright before "tinning" with solder. Secure a small, bright square of tinplate. Place a small amount of rosin paste flux in the center of the tinplate, which should be on an asbestos pad. In the flux, place a small piece of soft solder. The brightened, hot tip will later make contact with this flux and solder. The tip must also be hot enough to melt solder when bright, so the tinning should be done rapidly. Heat the iron sufficiently, file a bright face on the tip, and bring the brightened face in contact with the solder, flux, and tinplate. When the tip of the iron is removed, it will be coated with solder. A small wiping cloth may be used to keep the tinned surface bright.

It is sometimes undesirable to use a file on the copper tip, as this necessitates occasional replacement. A solution to brighten the tip may replace the file. Prepare this solution by mashing a 1″ cube of sal ammoniac and adding it to a glassful of water. Stir well. Keep in an earthenware container. Dip the tip of the *hot* iron in this. When bright, apply to tinplate as previously described.

The tinned surface will pick up small amounts of solder. The solder may be applied where necessary, but it must be remembered that the *work* must also be hot enough to melt the solder. Therefore, hold the tip in contact with the joint until it is obvious that the solder between the soldering iron and the work is completely "liquid." Remember also that a small iron will solder small work and may not suffice for large pieces of metalware. An electric iron of 60 to 100 watts, with a fairly narrow tip, will do very nicely for hand jewelry repairs.

Repairing White-Metal Jewelry

Much popular-priced rhinestone jewelry is made of a tin-alloy metal. These metals are of the pewter or Brittania metal type. The metal has a bright silvery appearance, but in contrast to sterling silver, it melts at a low point from 425° to 450° F. The metal is easily identified by testing with a pocket knife. It is easily cut or dented. Such metals are largely tin—as high a content as 90 percent. Good grades contain no lead. Other metals in the alloy are small quantities of copper and antimony. The copper makes the metal ductile and is generally present in amounts up to 1.5 percent. The antimony adds hardness and tends to make the metal expand slightly on cooling. This is desirable in cast products for finer detail. The antimony also adds whiteness to the metal. About 7 or 8 percent of this metal is used in the Brittania alloy.

To solder pin-backs to such a low-melting-point metal requires care. A rosin paste flux will serve. A small-pointed electric soldering iron, well tinned, may be employed, applying the usual 60-40 solder. Watch carefully, however, for signs of the melting of the Brittania metal, as this will take place soon after the soft solder is brought into contact with it.

Damaged pins of this metal can be carefully restored by building up with solder, using the electric iron. The solder, however, should be lacquered if in a visible location, as it will dull on exposure to air.

Pin-backs are sometimes attached with various cellulose cements. This is highly undesirable and not at all workmanlike. It is a means of saving time and labor on cheap work. If this method has been employed on a pin that is to be repaired, remove all signs of the cellulose cement with a small scraper or knife blade before applying any heat to the work.

Bismuth Solder

When a solder of a particularly low melting point is needed, bismuth solder may be used. This alloy consists of lead, tin, and bismuth. It will melt at less than 300° F. A rosin flux in paste form can be used. If a pewter pin (or Brittania) is being repaired, another flux of value may be made by adding ten drops of hydrochloric acid to an ounce of glycerin. Bismuth solder and an appropriate flux can be purchased at large craft or jewelry supply establishments. Consult catalogs.

Silver-Colored Solder

Because the common lead-alloy solders quickly become gray in color, they are sometimes found undesirable for repairing silver jewelry. Therefore, if the use of hard solder is not being considered as an option, the use of pure tin as a solder is another choice. A solder advertised as silver-colored is available from some jewelers' supply firms. This is usually either pure tin or largely so. Pure tin in bar form is available from some scientific supply firms if unavailable elsewhere. This metal, used with the ordinary soft-solder paste flux, will give a much brighter joint than the lead-bearing solders. It also does not oxidize to a dull gray very readily. Techniques for use are the same as for ordinary soft soldering.

Copper-Coloring Soft Solder

Sometimes, particularly when working with copper jewelry, the use of a lead-alloy soft solder creates a problem because of the contrast in color between copper and solder. Industrially, this is sometimes taken care of by electroplating a thin coating of copper over the entire finished piece. The individual craftsman can obtain some success by a simpler means, without resorting to electroplating equipment.

Cut up about 1 ounce of clean scrap copper into small pieces. In a separate container—a pyrex bowl is suitable—mix 1 ounce of nitric acid with 2 ounces of water. (Always add *acid* to *water*!) Add the copper scrap to the mixture, where it will dissolve. When effervescence stops, the solution is ready for use.

Make certain all flux has been cleaned from the soldered joint. Make a small swab from absorbent cotton and a swab-stick, obtainable at any pharmacy. Wet the cotton swab with the copper solution and coat the joint. Immediately touch the still-wet joint with a piece of freshly cleaned steel (a clean, large nail will do). A film of copper will appear on the joint. Repeat if necessary.

After a brief interval, rinse the work under running water and allow to dry. This copper film will not withstand buffing or polishing, but it is useful for many ordinary repairs on copper jewelry. The joint may be clear-lacquered.

NOTE: Acid fumes are hazardous. Work with care. Keep such mixtures in clearly labeled, well-stoppered bottles.

Hard Soldering and Electrosoldering

5

The Solder

Hard soldering is used in all high-grade jewelry work when several pieces of metal are to be permanently joined. Hard solder consists of a piece of the same metal used in making the piece of jewelry alloyed with a base metal, such as zinc or brass. The amount and kind of alloy in the hard solder will determine its melting point.

Sterling silver, which is 925 parts silver and 75 parts copper, becomes liquid, or flows, at 1640° F.* Therefore, an alloy of silver must be used as a solder, which will flow at a temperature *safely below 1640° F.* Several alloys are available, each melting at a particular temperature. William Dixon, for example, stocks hard solders melting at four different temperatures. The usual range of melting points for hard solders is from 1200° F to about 1450° F. Handy and Harman, dealers in precious metals, produce four grades of silver solder for jewelry work, in addition to many varieties of solders for various purposes. The four grades are: "Easy," melting at 1325° F; "Medium," 1390° F; "Hard No. 1," 1425° F; and "Hard," 1450° F. The last is recommended for enameling work.

The purpose of using a variety of such solders is to permit a piece of jewelry to be built up in several soldering operations. Thus, by using a higher temperature alloy on the first soldering operation and lower temperature solders on subsequent operations, the danger of melting the solder used on the previous operation is lessened. The writer, however, has frequently relied upon the use of protective substances, such as yellow ochre or loam, on previous joints and has had complete success using one grade of solder. Solder is available in wire form, sheet form, or

---

*Coin silver is 900 parts silver, 100 parts copper. Foreign silver varies in content and is as low as 700/1000. "German silver," or nickel silver, contains no silver; it is an alloy of nickel, copper, and zinc.

cut form. In cut form, it is supplied as tiny squares (about 1/16"). These may oxidize, however, when stored and are difficult to clean. Wire form is of particular value in link soldering, which will be discussed in soldering techniques. For all-around use, sheet form is preferable, and it is cut as needed, in 1/16" squares, as shown in Figure 13. The sheet of solder should be cleaned first with clean steel wool.

The Flux

In the heating of a metal, an oxide is rapidly formed, and this oxide prevents solder from flowing over the metals being joined, thus preventing their union. Therefore, a substance known as a *flux* (derived from the Latin, meaning "to flow") is used. The flux, coated over a previously cleaned surface, will not prevent the flow of the solder or its contact with the metals being joined, but flux will prevent a metallic oxide from forming, absorb oxides formed in preheating, and help solder to flow. The flux itself must form a protective film before the melting point of the solder is reached and must not be rendered useless by excessive temperatures. This means that fluxes especially prepared for hard soldering must be used.

The flux most widely in use is common borax. Mixed with water, it obtains the consistency of cream. It is prepared by rubbing a piece of borax in stick or lump form in a borax slate into which a small amount of water has previously been poured. The flux is ready when the mixture takes on the consistency mentioned. Sometimes borax is used mixed with boric acid. These mixtures range from 75 percent borax and 25 percent boric acid to 75 percent boric acid and 25 percent borax. In general, the addition of boric acid raises the point at which the flux becomes fluid. Borax flux becomes fluid at about 1400° F. Other fluxes prepared for hard soldering become fluid at different points, generally lower; this is a fact to remember when working on jobs requiring a number of soldering operations. Also remember that the point at which the flux flows does not affect the point at which the solder flows. Borum junk is also used as a flux and is a good one. It is prepared and used in a similar manner to borax.

The writer has found liquid *commercially prepared* fluxes particularly suitable for those who have only moderate experience in hard soldering for the following reasons: when common borax is used as a flux, the water in the mixture tends to displace the pieces of solder when the water boils in preheating. This can be avoided by careful preheating so as to gently evaporate the water, leaving a film of borax. However, when this film of borax is heated to form a protective glaze, it "blows up" into a frothlike foam, lifting the solder with it. When continued heating melts the borax so that it subsides together with the solder, the solder is frequently found to be displaced.

Fig. 13.

TECHNIQUES

A variety of techniques is used in hard soldering, each technique having a particular value in a specific case. General rules, however, are the same in all cases and are dealt with at this point before going into specific cases.

The first step to remember in hard soldering is that all parts involved in soldering must be *clean*—free of dirt, grease, oxides, and other foreign materials. Cleaning can be accomplished by various methods, depending on the condition of the metal. Badly oxidized pieces are cleaned first by heating in an acid pickling solution (see *Pickling*). Such pieces are then rinsed in cold water. Work may be scraped with a scraper at the point where soldering is to be done, cleaned with a small, clean file, or rubbed with clean steel wool. Any residue from the steel wool should be blown away before applying the solder and flux. Soldering is impossible unless work is perfectly clean at the area being soldered.

Fitting

Hard solder *will not* bridge a gap between two pieces of metal, so the work must be fitted perfectly. Seams must be snug, and all junctions of any nature must be perfectly fitted if it is intended that solder flow into these junctions. In soldering, a phenomenon known as capillary action takes place. This means that the solder, when reaching a fluid state, will flow readily between two tight-fitting surfaces, joining them securely, whereas an imperfect union will result if the fitting is uneven. This point cannot be over-emphasized. Solder will not hide the mistakes of poor fitting. It will refuse to flow into a gap. When such a gap exists in a job and it is impractical to make a part over, fit the edge of a small piece of the same metal as that being worked upon into the gap so that it fills the gap properly, and solder into place. File the excess metal away after the soldering has been completed.

Applying Flux and Solder

The flux is applied with a camel's hair brush to the *freshly* cleaned sufaces, and then the solder is applied, using the flux-dampened tip of the brush to pick up the small pieces of solder. Flux also covers the solder. Experience will aid in determining the amounts to use, but in general, one should try to roughly estimate the amount of solder required to flow between the surfaces being joined. If, during a soldering operation, it has been found that insufficient solder has been used, the tang of an old needle file dipped in flux may be used to convey additional pieces of solder to the work being soldered. During this time, the flame is momentarily removed.

The Heat

To heat the work for soldering, a source of heat is used that is able to bring the work up to the proper temperature. In very small work, a mouth blowpipe can be used together with a Bunsen burner or an alcohol lamp. The use of such a blowpipe requires practice. To solder the joint on a small bezel or wire ring, a Bunsen burner alone will give sufficient heat, and the beginner will be less likely to melt the entire bezel.

Proper heating requires judgment. Remember these points: some indication of the temperature can be had by observing the glow emitted by the work being soldered. This is made easier by shielding the work from any direct light. The first visible red will then occur at about 900° F. At about 1200° F this will turn to an even, dull red. Bright or cherry red appears at about 1400° F, and a pink appearance—the danger point—at 1600° F.

Before attempting to melt the solder, the work should be pre-heated. If using a gas-and-air torch, use a moderate flame and move it slowly over the entire surface of the work. When the work is dull red, begin to concentrate on the joint. Remember: solder flows to the *hottest point*. Therefore, finally concentrate the heat *on the joint* and allow *the metal of the work to melt the solder*. If the soldered joint occupies a small place on a large mass of metal, heat the whole mass first before attempting to solder the joint. Melting the solder first will cause it to assume a ball-like shape, and when this happens, it will not flow out until the main body of the work reaches the temperature required to melt the solder. Melting solder first will frequently cause a pitting of the

Fig. 14. Joining the ends of a bangle using wire solder (hard).

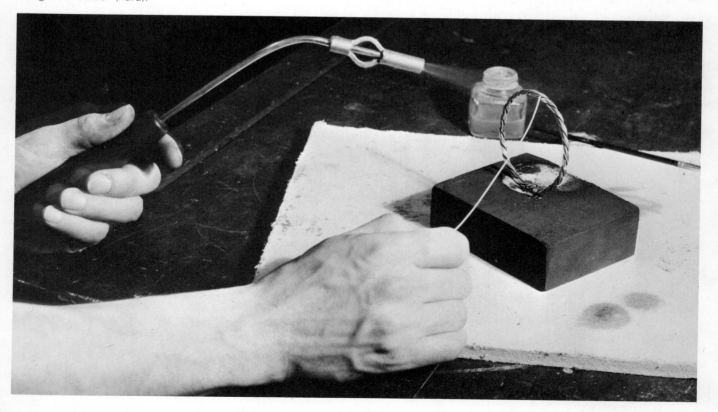

surface at the joint. Other causes of pitting are dirt and the presence of small quantities of lead, generally due to using files previously used on lead or to residue from lead blocks upon which the work was shaped. When solder persistently balls, either the heating methods are incorrect, the fluxing is insufficient, or dirt of some type is present. Drafts of air sometimes delay heating when work is done near an open window.

When using the gas-and-air torch, remember to have the gas and air tubes connected to their proper terminals—they are not interchangeable. Avoid a roaring blue flame. A roaring noise and a bright blue cone at the base of the flame indicate too much air. Such a flame may cool work faster than it may heat. Subdue it by reducing the air intake. The greatest heat is generally near the point of the flame. Never allow yellow to appear in the flame—a purplish color is about best. There should be some relationship between the size of the flame and the size or mass of the work, so observe this point carefully.

A torch is available that requires *no* compressed air supply and gives a flame satisfactory for hard soldering. This torch operates on ordinary illuminating gas and provides sufficient heat for good work on rings and brooches of moderate size. In Figure 14, it is shown in use while the ends of a bangle bracelet are soldered. Wire solder is being used in a technique similar to that used in joining the ends of links for chain making.

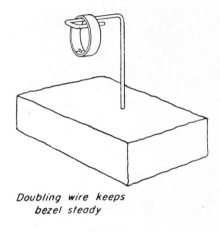

Doubling wire keeps
bezel steady

Fig. 15.

Soldering Aids

In hard soldering, the work is generally supported on a charcoal block. Additional soldering aids are iron staples, cotter pins, binding wire, and nails. With experience, uses for such items will suggest themselves, but a start can be made by remembering these procedures: a "gallows" formed by a piece of heavy wire—No. 16 to No. 14—can be used when working on flat rings or bezels (Fig. 15). Iron binding wire can be used to hold joints tight fitting, but avoid its use when possible. Solder will sometimes flow along such a wire, leaving ridges. Also, overheating the wire may cause it to burn portions of the work. The binding wire is oxidized to avoid the possibility of solder sticking to it (this accounts for its black color), although solder may sometimes flow over it. A magnesium block may be substituted for a charcoal block and will probably last longer. Portions of some pieces of work can be imbedded in the magnesium more easily than on charcoal, affording protection to the portion imbedded. An asbestos pad, at least 12" × 12", should be placed underneath the soldering block to protect the bench. Some work may be soldered directly on this pad, but care should be taken to have the pad in a clean condition with no stray filings or other waste materials on its surface. Staples are valuable when soldering lengths of wire together side by side, as in making ring shanks or bracelets (see Fig. 95). Cotter pins act like tiny clamps to hold work closely together during soldering. Figures 16A and B show a "rooster" pin assembled by the sweating process described later in this chapter. The main parts of the

Fig. 16A.   A method of securing parts of a job during sweat soldering.

Fig. 16B.   The completed rooster pin.

Fig. 17.   Full-size pattern for rooster pin.

rooster are held in position with cotter pins during heating. Normally the joint and catch are applied last. The model in the photo, however, has already been completed. It is being used only to show the application of the cotter pins.

Protection of Stones During Soldering

Remember that in hard soldering, either during the fabrication or repair of jewelry, ornaments other than metal—stones for example—will be affected by the heat and should be removed. In some cases where a stone cannot be removed from a ring, the following procedure is frequently successful, although some element of danger will exist with the inexpert: a somewhat oval potato is mounted upright. A tripod may be formed by the insertion of three long nails at the base. A slot is cut in the potato and the stone with its setting is carefully worked into the potato until it is shielded. A broken ring shank can then be hard-soldered. Use a small flame and do not dwell upon the operation too long.

Soldering Filigree

When soldering the assembled pieces of coiled wire that compose filigree work, solder is used in a granular form. This is made by filing solder into a small amount of flux. The combined flux and solder filings are deposited at the junctions of the assembled work with a camel's hair brush. The work is then heated in the usual manner. Links are sometimes soldered in this way.

Multiple Soldering Jobs

Sometimes different "grades" of solder are used in multiple soldering jobs. For example, a bezel may be soldered to a piece of silver, then some form of metal ornament, such as a dome, soldered to the work, and, finally, a catch and joint soldered to the reverse side of the work. The procedure in such cases is to do the heavy soldering first, using a solder with a high melting point. If the ornament to be applied to the work is larger in mass than the bezel, it is soldered first. Then the bezel can be done, using a solder with a somewhat lower melting point. If the ornament will not be dislodged by the melting of the solder used in its application, a similar grade of solder may be used in mounting the bezel. When this work is completed, the joint and catch are applied to the reverse side, using a solder with a somewhat lower melting point. During this work, the previous joints have no protection. Sometimes they are coated with a borax flux, which has a tendency to keep the joints together. The differences in melting points of the solders used may be deemed sufficient protection against the disintegration of the work done. For the inexperienced, all previous joints can be coated with a mixture of water and yellow ochre or loam, or a mixture of water and jeweler's rouge in powder form. These substances are mixed to a mud consistency. They are painted evenly over the finished joints and can usually be relied upon to hold the work together, even though a single grade of solder is used for all work. When substances such as ochre are used for protection, the mixture is slowly heated after it has been applied to the work to evaporate all the water and to prevent the flux from the new joint from mingling with the ochre or loam. When all soldering is completed, the loam is cleaned off with hot water and an old toothbrush before pickling. This will keep the acid pickle in a clean condition, usable again for further work.

Using Investments

A method used by dentists for protecting built-up bridgework involves the use of shredded asbestos fiber and plaster of Paris. This "investment," as it is called, can be utilized by the jeweler for excellent protection of soldered work during heating processes. Shredded asbestos fiber is available at jewelers' supply houses. One part of asbestos fiber is mixed with two parts of plaster of Paris in water. The asbestos eliminates the tendency of the plaster to crack during heating. Complicated pieces of work can be treated with investment and heated as soon as the investment is dry. The compound is applied fairly heavily and can be broken off by chipping with a knife when soldering is completed. Remember that large masses absorb heat, so consider this when judging the preheating of a job treated with investment.

Surface Protection and Fire Scale

It is sometimes necessary to hard-solder polished or engraved work. The heat causes enough oxidation to require repolishing. This is particularly undesirable on engraved work, as the engraving is affected.

To avoid this oxidation, an antioxidizer can be made. In 4 ounces of distilled water add as much boric acid (powdered) as will dissolve. To this, add about ¼ ounce of powdered borax. Mix thoroughly. Gently warm the article to be protected. Then apply the solution thinly with a camel's hair brush. Wait until dry.

Fig. 18. Cuff link. Thirteen separate pieces are joined with one grade of silver solder. (L.W.)

The work can now be hard-soldered following the usual procedure, beginning with application of flux. Joint protection with ochre may be used as needed.

Fire Scale. In certain lights a polished surface sometimes shows a grayish film which is difficult to remove. (See *Pickling to Remove Scale*). This "fire scale," as it is called, can be avoided by the use of an antioxidant throughout the construction of the article.

Another form of antioxidizer useful for this purpose is made by adding to alcohol as much boric acid (powder) as will dissolve. Dip or paint the job with this solution. Ignite the coating on the work with a match, and the alcohol will burn off, leaving a protective coating against fire scale.

SOME SPECIFIC HARD-SOLDERING JOBS

To Solder a Joint on a Bezel

Small bezels are frequently made of fine silver rather than sterling for two reasons. First, the fine silver is softer and can be easily burnished over the edges of a stone, thus keeping the stone set in its place. Second, the melting point of the fine silver is somewhat higher, and there is less danger of melting the delicate bezel. Because the beginner is liable to melt a bezel during the soldering of the joint, the use of a Bunsen burner will be safer. Otherwise, a very gentle blue flame from the gas-and-air torch may be used. Some prefer to bind the formed bezel with a light binding wire, such as No. 24, to keep the joint closed. If, however, the two edges of the joint are alternately bent past each other—first one over and past the other and then the reverse procedure—it will be found that the two edges of the joint will tend to spring against each other without the use of the wire. These edges should show *no light* between them. The bezel can be hung from a "gallows" of heavy binding wire, such as shown in Figure 15, with the joint down. Then put flux and one or two pieces of solder on the seam, depending on the size of the bezel. Preheat gently, and then concentrate the flame on the joint. It should solder at red heat. The use of binding wire is usually unnecessary, and its use will introduce the danger of marring the bezel's surface should the wire be overheated.

To Solder the Bezel to a Ring or Flat Base

The bezel must first be trued at its base. This is done by placing a piece of No. 0 emery cloth on a flat steel plate or sheet of plate glass, with the abrasive side up. The bezel is then gently moved to and fro over the emery cloth until a check shows that no light comes between the underside of the bezel and the plate. The surface to which the bezel is to be soldered can be trued in the same manner. Avoid bearing down at any one point. The bezel and the work should then fit perfectly with no need for binding. A flat piece of work is then laid on the charcoal block, and the bezel is set upon it.

A ring can be set up by pressing the edge of a five-cent piece straight down into a charcoal block or magnesium block for a distance of about one-half its diameter. The shank of the ring is then worked into the resulting groove with the ring faceup (Fig. 19). The bezel is then placed flat on the ring. Flux should be applied to the seam around the bezel, as well as on the joint previously soldered. Small squares of solder are placed on the inside of the bezel at intervals of about 3/16". The solder is handled with a camel's hair brush moistened with flux. The work is gently preheated, then the main body or mass heated to a dull red. Now the portion bearing the bezel is concentrated upon until it is dull red, and finally the flame is played over the bezel. A characteristic gleam at the point of the bezel's junction with the work should be ap-

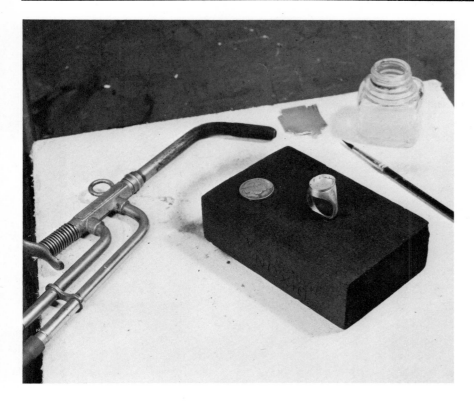

Fig. 19. Bezel ready to be hard-soldered to a cast ring.

parent when the solder flows. Become familiar with this gleam of molten solder, as it indicates the precise moment at which the flame can be safely removed. As soon as the red color dies out of a piece of soldered work, the work can be moved without danger of spoiling the soldered joint. The fashioning of various types of bezels is further discussed under *Stone Setting*.

To Solder Links on a Chain

Here the use of wire-form hard solder is recommended. The links can be divided into two groups. One group can be set aside temporarily while the other group is soldered. The links are placed on a flat, clean, charcoal block. The joints should be snug fitting. A drop of flux is applied, and then a small, somewhat intense flame. When the joint is at bright-red heat, the flux-moistened end of the wire is touched to the joint. The link should melt enough solder from the end of the wire to seal the joint. If necessary, keep the flame on the joint an additional moment to make a clean job. This procedure will work best if the wire solder is no heavier, or somewhat lighter, than the wire used in forming the link. If necessary, the solder may be reduced in diameter by means of a drawplate. Also remember that the solder must be clean before it can be successfully used. Clean with steel wool. Now one-half of the links are complete. Open the joints of the remaining links, *not* by springing them away from each other, but by moving the wire ends to the side (Fig. 20). Join a soldered link, an open link, a soldered link, etc. Bend the wire links closed again and repeat the soldering process in a manner similar to the first operation (see *Wire Working—Links*).

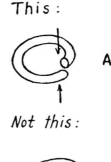

Fig. 20.

Soldering Two Domed Pieces Together

If two domes of equal diameter are to be soldered together, true their bottom surfaces with surface plate and emery, as previously described, and coat with flux. Now hold the two, properly positioned, with a long soldering tweezers. Heat in the flame of a torch that is secured by vise or clamp, and touch the edges of the seam with wire solder moistened with flux when the work has reached red heat. The solder will rapidly flow around the seam at the proper temperature. When doing such a job, select a soldering tweezers sufficiently strong to hold the work but not so heavy as to absorb most of the heat. Avoid too much pressure on the domes, as at red heat the work is soft and may be dented.

When two hollow pieces are joined, or a hollow to a flat, the trapped air expands and will try to escape at the seam. Sometimes this will result in a persistent pinhole at some part of the seam where the air escapes. If the presence of a tiny drilled hole (either on the dome which is to be in the rear or on the flat of the work) is of no consequence, then the pinhole difficulty can be done away with by drilling. In joining the two hollowed sections of a heart-shaped locket, a hole is permissible at the top for the insertion of a loop.

When domes as small as ³⁄₁₆″ or less are to be mounted on a surface, the procedure is as follows. True the bases of the domes, clean under their surfaces (concave) thoroughly, and coat with flux. Now melt four or five tiny squares of solder in the cup-shaped hollow of the dome. The amount of solder needed will decrease with the size of the dome. Clean the surface to which the dome is to be applied, drill a tiny hole to correspond with the center of the dome, and coat with flux. Now place the domes in position over the tiny holes and heat the large mass of the work on a charcoal block. At dull red heat, concentrate on individual domes, and the solder inside will flow down to the closely fitted seam or joint. A gleam at the junction of the two pieces of metal will show when the solder has run around the seam.

Application of Small Ornaments (Sweating)

If small ornaments, such as leaves, small, shaped pieces of sheet metal, etc. (Fig. 21), are to be soldered to a surface, the procedure is somewhat similar to the soldering of small domes. To the clean underside of the ornament are applied flux and a few pieces of hard solder. The ornament is heated until the solder has melted over its underside, which at this point is faceup on a charcoal block. The major portion of the work is now cleaned at the point to which the ornament is to be affixed, and flux is applied. The ornament is now placed on the work in its normal position, and the work is heated. Both work and ornament are carefully brought to a dull red together, and then the flame is applied to the ornament. The gleam at its base will tell when the solder has taken hold. Sometimes slight pressure is applied at this point with a long, thin, soldering tweezers to make the junction perfect. This

Fig. 21.   Group of Victorian English pieces illustrating appliqué work as well as engraving.

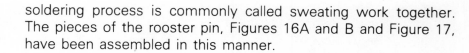

soldering process is commonly called sweating work together. The pieces of the rooster pin, Figures 16A and B and Figure 17, have been assembled in this manner.

Soldering on Sloped or Curved Surfaces

Sometimes pieces of jewelry are so shaped that applied ornaments have a tendency to roll off rather than stay in position for soldering. To prevent this, mix gum tragacanth with water to a thin pastelike consistency (see Chapter 17). This substance is available from jewelers' supply houses. The mixture is applied to the ornaments in just sufficient quantity to secure them in position. The flux and solder can then be applied. Preheat work, from underside if possible, bring to red heat, and concentrate flame on joints. The gum tragacanth will not interfere with the soldering process. This same mixture, incidentally, is used to keep enamels in place during firing in inverted positions.

Soldering Joints and Catches

The cleanest and most effective method for soldering a joint and a catch to the back of a brooch may be accomplished as follows: establish the position of the pin. The novice is advised to mark the path of the pin on the back with a scriber to avoid mounting the catch or joint incorrectly. The position of the pin should be slightly above the center of gravity of the brooch. If the pin is set too low, the brooch will hang awkwardly. Remember that a pin may pass over a space in the design of the brooch, as it will not be visible when worn on an article of clothing. Mark a small **x** with the scriber where the catch is to be placed. Make two short parallel lines where the joint is to be, directed toward the catch. The pin itself must not be inserted in the joint until the soldering is done. The point of the pin should project about 1/8" to 3/16" past the catch but not past the edge of the brooch.

Next, clean the two places to be occupied by joint and catch. Apply flux and two pieces of solder to each point. Preheat the work, then concentrate on each spot in turn until the solder becomes fluid. Remember that all soldered work on the reverse side should be carefully protected with jeweler's rouge, loam, or ochre. Carefully clean the bottom of the joint and coat with flux. Take a long soldering tweezer and hold the joint. Find a comfortable

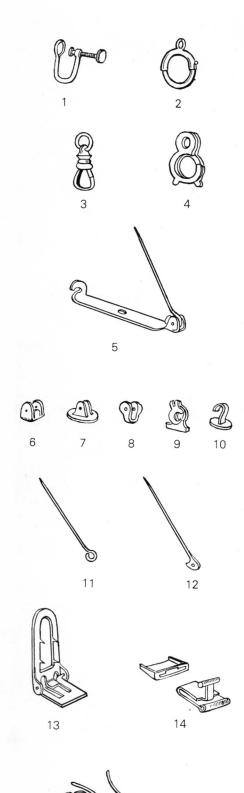

Fig. 22.

Some Common Findings

1. Ear-back or ear-wire; 2. Spring ring; 3. Swivel; 4. Sister-hook; 5. Pin-back (also available with safety catch); 6. Joint (self-riveting); 7. Joint, patch-type (for soft soldering); 8. Joint; 9. Safety catch; 10. Catch, patch-type (for soft soldering); 11. Coil-pin (for self-riveting joint); 12. Pin-tong (used with rivet on No. 8); 13. Clip attachment; 14. Clasp; 15. Barrette attachment.

NOTE: Better grade findings are made in the precious metals—gold, platinum, etc. Other findings are usually available in brass, nickel-silver, or nickel-plated brass.

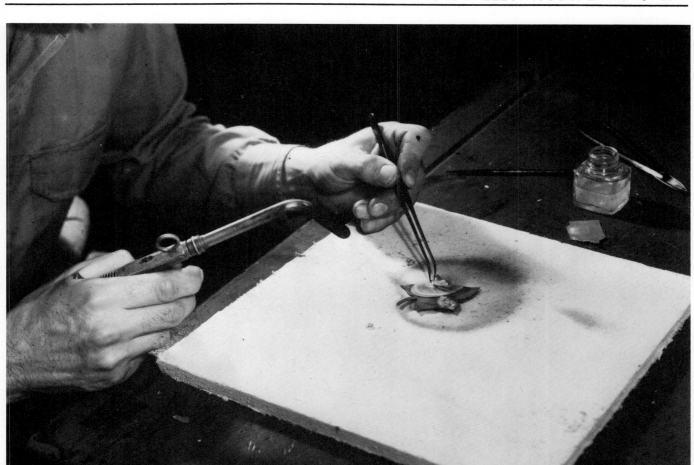

Fig. 23. Applying a catch by hard soldering.

position to rest the right hand, and holding the torch in the left, heat the *spot on the brooch* where the solder was melted for the joint. When this solder becomes fluid again, lower the joint into place, keep the flame on the joint and brooch at the junction for another five or ten seconds until the gleam of the melted solder shows a union, and then remove flame (see Fig. 23). Release the work when the red glow dies down. This requires coordination but should be quickly mastered. The catch is applied in a similar manner. Keep flux out of the moving parts of the safety catch, as the solder tends to follow the flux and the catch will then become inoperative. Be sure to mount the catch with the "mouth" down, or facing the bottom portion of the brooch.

The foregoing procedure can be modified somewhat. Hold the cleaned and fluxed joint in the tweezers, and heat to red heat. Apply a bit of solder from the end of wire solder to the bottom of the joint. Then heat the brooch at the proper point, which should have been previously cleaned and fluxed. When that portion of the brooch reaches bright-red heat, lower the joint, hold down until the gleam of molten solder shows, remove flame, and release when the red glow dies down. Follow same procedure for the catch.

Protecting Findings Against Overheating

Situations may exist where physical coordination is not of the highest order. This is particularly true when jewelry craft is a part of an occupational therapy program. Inexperience can also make coordination less perfect in soldering operations. The result may be overheating the "finding," such as an ear-wire, catch, or joint.

An overheated ear-wire will result in a loss of "spring." The annealed metal will make the ear-wire practically useless. Joints and catches are sometimes melted. Although it is not advocated that the path of least resistance be taken, *when no other recourse is offered,* findings may be protected by loam.

The loam should be coated fairly liberally over the finding, excluding the area that is to be soldered. Dry the loam gently and use the usual soldering procedure. Should it be necessary to apply heat from the torch for a lengthy period, the coated finding will generally survive this operation with no damage. The loam can later be scrubbed off with an old toothbrush and hot water.

Soldering Gold and Silver in Combination

When soldering gold and silver in combination, silver solder is used, since gold solder generally melts at a temperature past the melting point of the silver portion. Gold and gold solders are rendered fluid at ranges between 1550° F and 2000° F. A table of gold melting points will be found in the Appendix.

Gold solders are available in three standard colors—yellow, white, and green. These solders are alloyed in varying degrees so that they can be matched for soldering different karat gold alloys. If, for example, a 14-karat job is being soldered, a 14-karat solder of the required color is specified. The designation of 14-karat on the solder does not mean that the solder is 14-karat gold, but that the solder is safe—will melt at a lower point—for 14-karat gold.

The temperatures vary with different-colored golds because of the varying alloys. White golds, because of their nickel content, melt at higher temperatures. Gold to be used for enameling purposes must be so specified when purchasing, because such golds must be free of zinc. The melting point of 24-karat (pure) gold is 1945° F.

Providing a Source of High Velocity Air for High Temperature Flame

A major problem confronting the home craftsman is the difficulty in providing a source of compressed air for hard soldering and metal melting. This problem can be solved wherever an electric vacuum cleaner is available. All that is necessary is to remove the dust catcher—usually the bag at the rear of the machine. Turning on the motor will then produce a strong blast of air at the opening where the bag was connected (Fig. 24).

To harness the air for crafts purposes, this opening must be covered with a plate containing a length of metal tubing to conduct the air to rubber tubing, which in turn leads to a torch or small furnace.

The best form of closure would be a large funnel. In probably the easiest construction, a brass plate, *A,* Figure 24, is made to fit tightly over the bag opening. This can be secured by the thumb screws normally used to hold on the dust bag. A cork or rubber gasket, *B,* can be used between the machine and brass plate. A commercial cement can be used to cement the gasket to the plate. In this brass plate a hole is cut, of large diameter. Over this opening can be soldered a tin funnel, *C.* Thus, a unit consisting of a funnel-shaped air passage with a flat, brass, cork-covered flange results.

With this unit clamped in place, turn on the motor. A blast of air will emerge from the funnel end. Route this air to the air barrel of a gas-air torch. The gas tube leads, via separate rubber tubing, to its own source.

If the use of this device is contemplated in a kitchen, a handyman or a plumber can make provision for a gas outlet where a gas stove is used with very little labor and material—in some cases only the addition of a gascock.

NOTE: If the vacuum cleaner has a revolving brush, disconnect belt from pulley when using as an air source. Either tip machine on its side or raise about an inch off the floor to allow free intake of air.

Using the cleaner as an air source in *no way* injures the machine, or prevents quick rearrangement for normal vacuum cleaner use. Tank-type vacuum cleaners are also adaptable for this purpose using similar methods.

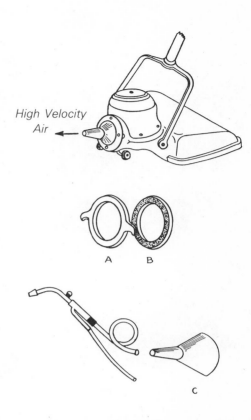

Fig. 24. Vacuum cleaner and parts for converting it into an air turbine.

The Electric Soldering Machine

Soldering by electrically produced heat has certain advantages as well as limitations. It does not have the flexibility of the flame, which can change from broad, general area coverage to an instant, intensely focused pinpoint. Such flame-type soldering is a necessity for "constructed" jewelry, as it is now termed. As a means of intense, high-temperature, pinpoint, hard soldering, quickly accomplished, however, the electric soldering machine is very valuable. Because there is no flame and because the intense heat required for hard soldering is produced in about one second, surrounding metal areas are relatively unaffected by the heat. Thus, rings containing stones can have nearby soldering done safely. Links and chains can also be hard-soldered quickly, accurately, and without danger to adjoining links. The machine, which operates from the standard AC wall outlet, is safe to handle. The hand-held accessories themselves operate at a *very low* voltage, and the user can handle the various implements without fear of shock and in complete safety.

The machine and its accessories are pictured in Figure 25. It has two electrical cords emerging from the front panel. These are the cords used for the soldering operation. A selection of different-

Fig. 25. Electric soldering machine and accessories.

shaped carbons is supplied. A large, tapered carbon on a low stand is generally used for holding a ring during soldering. Another large carbon with a flat upper surface fits the same stand and can be used for soldering chain link as well as ring joints. The stand, which has a special connector on its base, can be adjusted to hold either large carbon horizontally, vertically, or at any desired angle. In use, the stand, with its carbon, is connected to the *left-hand* cord on the machine.

A variety of smaller-diameter carbons is also supplied. These too can be connected to the *left-hand* cord. They are used to make contact with large articles where using the stand is not practical. The *copper-coated portion* of the carbons is for good electrical contact with the machine and is not used for making contact with the article being soldered.

Two different-sized spring clips are also supplied. Either of these can be plugged into the holder on the *right-hand* cord. When the large carbons on the stand are not used to hold the articles to be soldered, these clips are used and can be clipped onto the article. The larger clip is preferable if the article is not too delicate.

If the article is too large or too delicate to be held by a clip, a pointed brass rod, supplied as an accessory, is to be used. This is held in the larger clip (right-hand cord) and is used to make electrical contact with the article being soldered, while a pencil-shaped carbon (left-hand cord) contacts the joint to be soldered.

Here are two possible procedures to use when soldering a ring:

1. The ring is pressed firmly in position, with joint up (Fig. 26), over the tapered carbon (left-hand cord). Directly *under* the joint, between carbon and ring, is a small square of hard solder. Work must be clean, and both hard solder and ring joint must be well fluxed. A slim, pencil-shaped carbon (connected to the right-hand cord) is touched lightly to the top of the ring joint. The foot switch is pressed. The solder should flow within a second if the heat knob on the machine has been properly set. Release the foot switch. Lift the pencil-shaped carbon. Allow to cool. File away any excess solder.

2. Grasp the ring, *joint down,* with a clip connected to the *right-hand* cord. The large carbon with a flat surface is connected (in its stand) to the *left-hand* cord. A piece of hard solder, fluxed, rests on the flat surface. The ring, also fluxed and held in the clip, is brought down so that the joint makes contact with the solder and is held steady. The foot switch is pressed. The solder soon flows. The foot switch is released.

In this procedure the ring can also be grasped with a clean, strong metal tweezer of convenient shape if this is more comfortable, but remember to attach the right-hand clip to the end of the tweezer (Fig. 27).

Flux. Do not use a borax flux. A liquid-type hard-soldering flux can be used, as can a flux specially compounded for the soldering machine. All metallic surfaces involved in the operation must be absolutely clean. This is necessary not only for the soldering process itself but also for efficient electrical flow.

Heat Control Knob. On the front of the machine is a heat control dial or knob. The amount of heat needed will depend on the kind

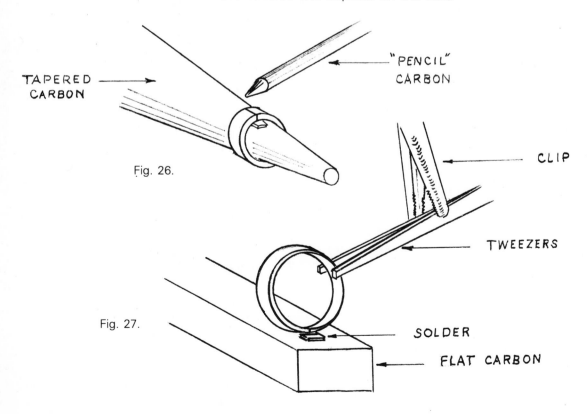

TAPERED CARBON

"PENCIL" CARBON

Fig. 26.

CLIP

TWEEZERS

Fig. 27.

SOLDER

FLAT CARBON

of solder, the area involved, and the size of the article. The knob should be set at low heat for the first attempt. If insufficient heat is produced within a second or two, release the foot switch and move the knob ahead. After some practice the user will be able to judge the setting of the knob with accuracy. Soft soldering can also be done using the proper flux and a small pellet of soft solder. The lowest heat setting is used for this, as red heat is not desired.

Use of the Brass Rod. If, because of size or shape (very large, odd-shaped, or very small), the spring clips cannot be used to hold the article, the pointed brass rod accessory can be set in the large clip on the right-hand cord. A pencil-shaped carbon should then be connected to the left-hand cord. The work must be cleaned and properly fluxed, and the proper solder should be placed at the point where the soldering is to take place. The brass rod should then be placed in contact elsewhere on the article and the *carbon* electrode placed at the joint—preferably directly behind it and as near as possible. The foot switch can then be depressed and released as soon as the solder flows.

General Suggestions

Poor Flow. Work being hard-soldered should have solder flow at red heat. If the solder balls and will not flow, fluxing or cleaning was inadequate. Do not continue heating—clean and start again. Borax flux, if used, tends to crystallize, and this breaks electrical contact. If this happens, flux must be scraped away and replaced. Avoid borax for such hard soldering.

Stones. Soft or delicate stones very near the joint (pearls, turquoise, opal) can be given some protection with a small wad of wet cotton. The article being soldered should be quickly dipped in cool water immediately after soldering if such stones are involved. The same precaution should be taken if any stone or ornament has been *cemented* in place instead of set.

Soiled Carbons. If carbons are soiled with crystallized flux or other contaminants, fine emery cloth can be used to clean them. Avoid the use of emery on the copper-coated portion of the carbons. That part should normally stay clean; if it does not, careful use of fine steel wool will accomplish the cleaning. Blow away any residue.

Pressure. Avoid excessive pressure with the electrodes, or depressions in the work may result. Electrical contact is all that is needed.

Steadiness. Set up the work so that the hands can rest on the workbench during the operation. This will assure steadiness at the moment when the solder flows and during cooling.

Practice. Practice until you feel you understand the process! The skill is quickly and easily acquired after a few experimental trials.

Final Step. Remember to pull the machine's supply plug from the wall outlet when all work has been completed and the machine is to remain idle.

Pickling, Pickling Solutions, and Annealing

Because of the oxides left by heating processes such as annealing and soldering and because of the glazes and residue left by borax and other fluxes, it is necessary to use a pickling solution to expose a completely clean metal surface. Pickling is frequently done between successive soldering jobs to enable the worker to see clearly the degree of success in the operation. The acid used dissolves the glaze and oxides and exposes the work perfectly. Pickling is frequently done just prior to the polishing processes, just as a "bright dip" is used.

When copper is pickled, it emerges from the solution clean and somewhat pink in color. The natural copper surface appears when the metal is rinsed free of pickle and then lightly scoured with fine pumice or steel wool.

When silver is pickled, it emerges pure white in color. This is because the acid has dissolved the copper ingredient used to make the sterling alloy. The resultant white is pure silver on the outer surface of the metal. This is not a durable finish and is usually removed by light scouring with fine pumice and water before the polishing process.

The Pickling Solution

Silver and copper may be effectively pickled in a sulphuric acid solution. The ratio of the ingredients is one part sulphuric acid to ten parts water. (Sparex, a commercial preparation for making pickle, is highly recommended. Its simple mixing instructions are described on the container.) A stronger solution is not recommended, as it tends to coarsen the metal surface. *The acid must be poured into* the water to avoid a dangerous reaction. The solution is stored in a covered earthenware container. In use, it is poured into a heavy copper pickle pan or a Pyrex glass bowl and heated for best results. Sometimes, after annealing, metal is put into the cold pickle. The hot metal cleans itself readily, but the reaction is somewhat more active and great care should be taken to avoid the fumes and splashing. It is safer to heat the solution. When a hard-soldering job has been done on a small piece of work, it may be dropped in its hot state into the pickle, but only if there is no iron binding wire on it or loam on the joints. The iron wire will cause discoloration. Cool the work and remove iron wire. The loam will prevent an even pickling and will make the pickle muddy. Scrub it off first with an old toothbrush. To avoid discoloration of the work, never use iron tongs for removing work from pickle. Use copper tongs. If a copper pickle pan is unavailable, a porcelain bowl or beaker or a Pyrex glass bowl can be used. Pour the pickling solution into the porcelain beaker before applying heat.

The work is immersed in the solution, which is heated just short of boiling, until it is clean. Then it is removed with copper tongs and rinsed. Keep a container of clean water next to the pickle to avoid trailing acid along the floor. Dip into this container after pickling and then rinse thoroughly under running cold water. Avoid inhaling fumes from hot pickling solutions.

Pickle may be reused until it no longer reacts with the metal. Use at least enough pickle to cover the article.

Articles made of gold that is 14-karat and over are generally pickled in a nitric acid solution. The ratio is one part nitric acid to eight parts water. Pickling procedure is the same as with sulphuric pickle, but heat the solution in a porcelain beaker or a Pyrex glass bowl. Karat golds may also be pickled in the sulphuric acid solution to which a small amount of sodium bichromate has been added. This will remove scale in cases where ordinary pickle will not do so.

A convenient device for handling small work that is to be boiled in a sulphuric acid pickle can be made. Secure a piece of fine-mesh copper screening. Cut this into a circle of required size, for example, 4″ in diameter. Work into shape with the fingers until bowl-shaped. This may be more easily accomplished if the screening is carefully annealed first. Make a circular rim of No. 8 or No. 10 gauge copper wire to fit the perimeter of the bowl-shaped copper "sieve" that has been formed. "Wire" the rim to the "sieve" with fine copper wire. Attach a copper-wire bail handle and suspend this from a wooden stick. This makes it possible to place work in the pickling solution, remove it, and keep the hands out of the acid fumes at all times. Always rinse the sieve in clean water after use to forestall its eventual destruction by the pickle.

Annealing

Annealing is the process of softening metal by heating. It is an important process to the craftsman, as the metal he works with will harden when hammered, twisted, drawn, or rolled through the rolling mill. This hardening is sometimes desirable for stiffening a piece of metal. In such cases, the portion to be hardened is usually hammered carefully with a polished flat hammer. The work rests on a steel plate during hammering, and the outline of the job may require reshaping by filing or sawing. Hardening by heat will be discussed later.

Annealing requires heat, the amount depending on the size, thickness, and type of metal in question. Usually a gas-and-air torch is employed for annealing. The work can rest on a charcoal block, which reflects the heat. Larger pieces of work are placed on a sheet of asbestos at least ½" thick or, better still, in an annealing pan. Such a pan may be improvised by securing any circular or square iron baking pan and filling it with lump charcoal or lump pumice. The work rests on the charcoal or pumice, and the heat is played over the work. It is wise to do such heating in a space shielded with asbestos or transite to prevent fire.

To anneal properly, a piece of work should be heated in a blue flame until it is evenly heated to the proper degree, which can be determined by its incandescence. Silver, gold, and brass are heated to a dull red. *Brass* should be quenched in water at 1000° F. Overheating it causes a loss of its zinc content through volatilization. *Copper* may be heated to a salmon red. When annealing *yellow gold,* the red glow should be allowed to disappear and the gold *then* plunged into cold water or pickle. This will avoid possible cracks. If it is allowed to come to a *completely* cool stage *without* quenching, it may become brittle. *White gold* being annealed is allowed to cool slowly, without *quenching. Aluminum* is heated to a dull pink. All heating should be done evenly, by keeping the flame moving over the work. This will reduce the possibility of melting one portion of the work before another part becomes red. It also reduces the possibility of warping. Silver and aluminum in particular should be annealed in a *subdued light* because the color of the metal makes it difficult to see the proper annealing color. To obtain the maximum softness of *sterling silver,* heat to 1400° F and quench immediately. Remember that at 1400° F silver appears cherry red. The quenching can be done in cold water, which must be located in a container directly at the source of heat to make instant quenching possible. If facilities for *instant* quenching are not available when annealing, do not heat the silver over 1200° F. At this temperature (dull red), silver can be left to cool in air and will be found sufficiently soft for most purposes. When sterling silver is heated above 1250° F and cooled in air, it will be found that there has occurred a definite hardening effect rather than annealing.

If speed of production is an important element, the heated, annealed metal, with the exception of gold less than 14-karat, can be quickly cooled by immersion in cold water or an acid pickle. In such a case, immerse the work quickly—gradual immersion tends to increase warping or distortion of the metal.

If, when annealing, it is important for some reason to prevent oxidation, a thin coat of boric acid in water solution can be applied to the work before heating. After annealing, any traces of the solution can be washed off in hot water.

Always remember that a piece of work with small, delicate parts requires careful annealing to prevent melting these parts. Such small work can be annealed most conveniently by the use of an annealing "nest," in or on which the work may be placed.

The Annealing Nest

A nest, using *iron* binding wire, can be made from a tangle of such wire formed into a roughly circular pad, about 4" in diameter and 1" thick at the center, tapering to a thinner edge all around the circumference. A mass of tangled binding wire (about 20–22 gauge) can be gently shaped on the workbench using one's hands or a mallet. The bottom should be fairly flat and the top either slightly domed or concave, as needed. Such a pad should rest on a square piece of transite or asbestos during use. Because its relatively small mass absorbs little heat and the many air spaces provide access for the heat of the flame, such a nest does its job efficiently and avoids the use of the more expensive charcoal block, which deteriorates substantially with this kind of use.

Some soldering jobs can also be done on this nest—experience will help determine if the nest would be appropriate.

In all cases of annealing one must remember to avoid overheating the metal, heating it for an excessive length of time, and unduly oxidizing the metal. Use a properly adjusted blue flame.

Annealing Wire

When it is necessary to anneal lengths of wire, which is frequently the case to make it workable, the wire can be coiled in a circle to form a tight 3" or 4" ring. If the wire is No. 18 to No. 14 gauge, it can then be heated with the torch. If lighter than No. 18 gauge, it is wise to enclose the coil, sandwichlike, between two sheets of No. 24 or No. 26 black iron sheeting cut into 4" squares. The "sandwich" is then tied crosswise with No. 22 binding wire. Both sides are heated in turn to a red glow. Cut the binding wire, remove the annealed wire, and cool or immerse in pickle.

When annealing, remember to adjust the torch to a blue flame, but avoid the bright blue cone at the center of the torch tip. This would show the presence of too much air and would cool the work rather than bring it rapidly to red heat. Also avoid annealing any metal with soft solder on it. Such solder will melt and the lead present will eat into the surface of the metal being annealed. For this reason, it is wise to clean a piece of metal with emery cloth or steel wool if the metal has been hammered on a lead block.

A worker with limited experience in annealing should slowly move his torch towards and then away from his work, observing carefully the distance at which he gets the most intense heat.

In closing, it might be well to warn against applying this annealing procedure to *all* metals. Steel, for example, when heated to a red heat and immersed in cold water, will become extremely hard and brittle (see *Chasing Tools*).

Heat-Hardening Silver

The most accurate means of hardening silver necessitates the use of a small furnace equipped with a heat measuring device, such as a pyrometer. If this equipment is available, the following procedure will produce an appreciable hardening effect on a soft piece of silver.

Heat the silver to 1400° F and quench it *instantly* in water. (Allow no *gradual* drop in temperature.) The work is next heated to about 600° F and "soaked," or held at that heat for 15 minutes. When next cooled in *air,* it will be found to be in a hardened state. The importance of a furnace will be noted particularly during the 600° F "soaking" period, this being a procedure difficult to attempt with a torch.

The hardening process is useful when a piece of work is found to be annealed due to various soldering operations. If this is the case and the hardening procedure is used, it may be well to protect soldered joints with loam before subjecting the work to the first part of the hardening process—heating to 1400° F.

7

Buffing, Polishing, and Lacquering

The Machine

In order to give an article of jewelry a completely finished appearance, it is generally necessary to polish it on a polishing lathe or buffing machine. For good results, a machine utilizing an electric motor of ¼ to ⅓ horsepower will suffice. A larger motor is unnecessary for jewelry; a smaller one does not do very well. The motor speed may be in the neighborhood of 1750 r.p.m. For a high polish with a muslin wheel, speeds of 3000 and 3500 r.p.m. may be used. If the motor is not a variable-speed, or two-speed, machine, speeds can be changed by using the motor to drive a polishing head. A 2- or 3-step pulley on the motor shaft belted to the polishing head will suffice. The polishing head or the buffing machine should be equipped with two tapered, threaded arbors to hold buffing wheels. The wheels used vary, but the bristle, muslin, leather, and wire wheels may be 3″ or 4″ in diameter for most work.

Lathe splashers or metal shields mounted over the arbors will protect surrounding objects from being spattered with materials from the wheels. Do not rely on them as safety guards. That is not their purpose. The height of the motor arbor from the floor should be about 12″ to 14″ below the eye level of the operator.

The Abrasive Compounds

An article is buffed and polished by applying it with a firm pressure against a wheel charged with an abrasive, which rotates in the direction of the operator. The wheels are ''charged'' by holding the stick of abrasive compound against the whirling wheel for a few seconds. Do not overcharge a wheel, as dirty work will result.

Jeweler's rouge is used for the final high polish or ''color'' on gold and silver. It is generally red in color, although white rouge is also available. Some claim white rouge leaves a less noticeable residue. However, a careful worker removes *all* residue.

Tripoli, a tan-colored, claylike compound, is the most generally used cutting compound. It will remove slight scratches and leaves some luster. It is actually a finely granulated siliceous rock called soft silica. Tripoli is quarried in Missouri, Tennessee, Georgia, and Illinois. For "buffing" compositions, O.G., or "once ground," tripoli is used. "Air Float" is the finest grind and will make a polishing compound. D.G., or "double grind," grade is frequently used without its binder as a parting powder in casting operations. Some workers prefer the less brilliant finish of tripoli to that left by rouge. Remember that tripoli is a *cutting* compound, and if a wheel charged with it is used carelessly, part of the work or detail will be quickly worn away.

White diamond compound is used for both cutting down and polishing operations, though the two separate operations are preferable.

Crocus composition is a fast-cutting compound. It can be used on steel as well as the nonferrous metals.

Emery paste composition is also a fast-cutting compound for the common metals.

Pewter coloring compound is used on pewter and lead-bearing metals.

It is safe to say that the use of tripoli, after the noticeable scratches have been removed by hand methods, is a good preliminary polishing operation. This is followed by the rouge polishing operation for a final high color.

The Wheels

A great variety of wheels is available for a variety of commercial uses. Most of them will be mentioned here, though only a few will be found necessary for the average craftsman. Most common is the *muslin buff,* for final rouge polishing. This is a wheel made up of loose circles of fine muslin held at the center by a lead piece with a hole through it. The muslin buff is also commonly used without a lead center, the circles of muslin being stitched through and through in two or three rows of stitching of different diameter. This gives a slightly stiffer wheel. It is used with either cutting or polishing compounds.

Cotton polishing wheels, made of cotton yarn radiating in several rows from a wood center, are also used for final rouge polishing.

Cotton flannel buffs, stitched as described previously, are used for final polishing.

Woolen buffs, made of stitched wool cloth, are used with various cutting compounds.

Solid felt wheels are used with either cutting or polishing compounds. These wheels come in a variety of shapes and diameters. The common flat type presents a straight edge to a surface and is used when the operator wishes to avoid the spreading and consequent overlapping encountered when using cotton and muslin wheels. The felt wheel is particularly useful for polishing around bezels and "stepped" surfaces. The felt wheel is also available in a knife-edge style for polishing in narrow crevices.

Stitched leather wheels are used for rough cutting operations, as are *walrus hide wheels.*

Felt cones, both pointed and round, are used for polishing inside cupped depressions.

Felt ring buffs are used to polish inside finger rings. A ring buff made of wood, over which special abrasive-paper shells fit, is also used for finger rings.

Solid grit lathe cones are similar to the ring buff but are made of solid corundum with a lead center for mounting. These cones are used for grinding inside rings.

Wood laps are wheels of varied profiles that are charged with different abrasive powders in conjunction with oil or water.

Brightboy wheels are a patented product that can be described as a form of rubber-and-grit compound. This compound is furnished in wheel form and in block or tablet form. The wheel is mounted and run at moderate speed for fast-cutting jobs, never for polishing. The tablet is useful for hand work in removing blemishes from a metal surface.

Bristle brush wheels come in many forms. The most common for the jewelry worker is the ordinary bristle wheel, shaped like any other polishing buff but consisting of stiff bristles set in rows, radiating from a wooden hub. Other shapes are made for working inside goblets, around handles, inside rings, etc.

The bristle brush is useful for working on articles with many recessed portions. The wheel is charged with tripoli. When used with various compounds, it can also provide a variety of textures or finishes on smooth metal objects.

Scratch brushes are available in either brass or steel. These brushes, as far as the jeweler is concerned, will provide a variety of textures or finishes on metal surfaces, such as satin finish, dull finish, or mat finish.

It is inadvisable to use a brass brush on a silver metal, as a slight brass coloration remains on the silver surface. Wire brushes are made with straight and crimped wire. In general, the crimped wire brushes give a somewhat softer finish, although the many different effects which can be obtained will also depend on the size of the wire used in the brush, the pressure of the brush on the work, and the speed of the polishing lathe.

Using the Machine

When using the buffing machine, one must first take certain precautions so as to avoid injury as well as discomfort. First, no flowing clothing, loose ties, or long hair must be near the machine. Wear an apron high up, close under the chin. Wear goggles, or preferably, a clear plastic face mask or shield. The polishing compound will be present in minute particles in the air around the machine, and a mask will keep these particles out of eyes and nose and off the face. Sleeves should be rolled above the elbow.

The work and wheel should be well illuminated. If much work is to be done, thorough ventilation should be provided for.

The portion of the wheel used for buffing is shown in Figure 28. The wheel is shown as a clock dial. The work is held against that segment of the wheel marked off by the numerals 4 and 6. Using any part past 6 is not practical. Using any portion before 4 is extremely dangerous. Note the direction of rotation. If the work is held above 4, it will be thrust violently toward the operator. Below 4 it may possibly be snatched away, but if precautions are taken, it will merely be thrown into the dust collector or against the splasher.

The polishing lathe can be a dangerous machine—particularly because of its seemingly innocuous soft wheels. The wheels, however, do not make the injuries; they cause them.

Because of the occasional snatching action of a wheel, work should be held so that if it were to be suddenly and powerfully torn from the grasp, no injury would result to the operator. This means avoiding the edges of the work as a means of holding. It means avoiding hooking a finger through a ring or bracelet when polishing. Fragile work can be rested on a small flat stick to avoid bending and to make holding easier (see Fig. 29).

A typical job of polishing can be described as follows: if the work has been soldered, it should be pickled before buffing is attempted. All scratches should be removed by use of files, Scotch stone, and abrasive papers. A stitched muslin buff is then charged with tripoli, and the work is given a careful buffing to remove any slight imperfections. It is at this stage that the novice is amazed

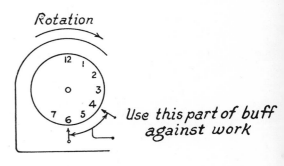

Fig. 28.

Fig. 29. The work being buffed is supported here on a flat stick.

by the emergence of the real beauty of his work. If the character of the article requires it, a bristle brush charged with tripoli is used for cleaning recessed areas. If hard felt wheels are necessary for inaccessible areas, they are employed now. At this point, the particular worker will wash his work in a strong, hot solution of detergent with a slight amount of ammonia added. Use rubber gloves here. This step will remove all traces of tripoli and other foreign matter. If these impurities remain, they will be transferred to the rouge buffing wheel and will not only defile that wheel but will prevent a really fine finish from resulting. If the work has recessed areas, a hand bristle brush or an old toothbrush can be used, together with detergent and hot water, to completely clean the article. Now rinse and dry. If compressed air is available at the soldering bench, it can be used to blow all moisture out of the recessed areas, as well as to hasten drying. An electric hair dryer is useful for drying.

Rouge is now applied to a cotton flannel buff or a loose-type muslin buff, and the work is brought to the required degree of luster. The work can now be washed as previously and dried before lacquering.

At this point it should be emphasized that different compounds should not be used on the same wheel. Using rouge and tripoli on one wheel will make it unfit for fine polishing.

A rouge wheel accidentally defiled by tripoli can be used from then on for some cutting compound other than rouge, but when that cutting compound is used, the wheel should be reserved for that compound alone. A means must be used to identify each wheel according to the compound used, either by storage or by markings.

Buffing by Hand

In some instances, power is not available, or the craftsman works on so small a scale that power equipment is not included among his paraphernalia. Such a worker can get good results by the use of hand buffing equipment. It requires merely more time and more energy.

The preparatory steps, utilizing files, Scotch stones, brightboy tablet, abrasive cloths, etc., take the usual order. Improved results in the use of crocus cloth and rouge paper can be obtained by purchasing prepared flat sticks coated with crocus paper or by making these. Secure sticks from 10" to 12" long, 1" wide or less—depending on the type of work—and about ³⁄₁₆" thick. Thinly coat one surface with a good grade of glue for a distance of about 6" and apply crocus paper or rouge paper. Keep it flat. Prepare a good supply of these, as it is more economical than purchasing such equipment. These sticks are used prior to buffing.

Sticks for buffing and polishing are available commercially or can be made by using the same sticks and gluing a strip of soft leather—unfinished side out—to the wood. Buckskin and chamois are frequently used for this. Other sticks can be covered with a strip of white felt. These sticks are used by rubbing them against the needed buffing compound and then applying them vigorously to the work. Use like a toothbrush but with a longer stroke and emphasis on the forward stroke. The writer has found such sticks useful when covered on two sides—each for a different compound, or one side crocus paper and one side felt or leather for polishing.

Orange sticks of various diameters and about 6″ long are useful for getting into hollows where no wheel can reach. The ends of such sticks are charged with abrasive and then rotated by the fingers or rubbed against otherwise inaccessible areas (see *Flexible Shaft Machine*). Jeweler's rouge in paste form is useful for polishing by this means. Emery paste compound makes a good cutting abrasive for these sticks. Final overall polishing of hand-finished work can be done with a good chamois skin or commercially available prepared polishing cloth.

Use of Lacquer

When it is desired to preserve the finish on a piece of jewelry, regardless of whether that finish is highly polished, chemically colored, satin dipped or brushed, a coat of thin transparent lacquer is applied. Explained simply, this finishing process coats the article with a thin, clear, tough layer of plastic in liquid form. When the solvent evaporates, a layer of the plastic remains, separating the metal surface from further contact with air, thus maintaining the finish imparted by the craftsman.

Some craftsmen rub a thin layer of wax over their work. As a preservative measure, this is not particularly useful. Its only merit is that its surface luster is not as high as that of lacquer. And as the degree of luster is a matter of personal taste, the wax method may seem to some to have no merit. Work that is to be on display for any length of time needs a lacquer finish for practical reasons, since an article not being worn will tarnish more rapidly than one exposed to the rubbing of clothes. Some do not use any coating or preservative and rely on constant use to keep the article of jewelry properly burnished. This results in the proper oxidizing and highlighting of a metal ornament by natural means. When such an article is out of use for a while, it may be brought back to desired finish by simple use of a prepared polishing cloth.

A good lacquer should be purchased from a reliable dealer in metal finishes since good, tough lacquers are carefully compounded. The thinner for this lacquer should be purchased from the same source. Lacquer thickens after a period of time in the bottle. The lacquer may appear slightly amber in color. This does not show up on the finished article if properly thinned and applied. When lacquer is purchased in quantity, a small amount—3 or 4 ounces—can be kept aside for use, properly thinned. If this mixture is kept in a well-stoppered, clear jar, it can be observed for thickness and cleanliness. If, for any reason, the mixture becomes polluted with any foreign matter, the jar can be rinsed with thinner and a new supply added from the large, original store. In the small shop, a setup similar to the one in Figure 30 can be used. This

Fig. 30. A convenient rack for lacquering equipment.

will mean that brushes are always soft and clean, the necessary items are always on hand, and the jars will not tip easily. The surface of the wooden base is recessed for jar and brush vials. The vials are stoppered with a unit consisting of a rubber stopper and brush. To make this unit, heat a nail, slightly less in diameter than the brush handle, to a dull red. Then pierce the stopper through the center. Soft rubber will appear melted around the nail, which may have to be reheated a few times. When the nail comes through, push the pointed top of the brush handle through the hole in the stopper from the bottom, until only enough brush extends from the stopper to reach about one-third to halfway into the vial. The soft rubber will solidify, sealing the brush into the stopper permanently. If enough thinner is kept in a vial to partially cover the hairs of the brush, it will always be in good condition. Change the liquid when it thickens to any extent.

Lacquer is applied in slow, smooth strokes, like nail polish. Do not go over a stroke. Do not work where dust has been agitated into motion. If a beginner has no luck with the first few attempts, the lacquer can be removed by rinsing with thinner. If the lacquer turns a cloudy white, water is present on the article being lacquered, or the air is unusually moist. If a dirty, cloudy appearance results from lacquering, then a residue from the polishing wheel has remained on the article. Remedy this by properly washing the finished work, and then allow it to dry. The grease content of an abrasive compound will occasionally cause a slight rainbowlike effect on the lacquered work. If this happens, remove the lacquer with thinner, wash the piece in detergent and ammonia, and rinse. It may be necessary to rinse the brush thoroughly with thinner and use fresh lacquer to relacquer the piece.

Lacquer can be sprayed if made very thin. This is done in quantity production. Avoid the presence of flame or moisture and make certain of good ventilation for health reasons.

Articles like finger rings and silverware, which receive abuse by much contact with hard objects, should not be lacquered. Even a good, tough lacquer will chip in spots when subjected to rough usage. These spots will tarnish, making unsightly blemishes. It is impossible to clean individual spots for relacquering; therefore, constant cleaning and lacquering of the entire object is the only remedy. Avoid the use of lacquer on silver tableware and clean by prepared polishes or immersion in special baths. A ring never needs lacquer if worn constantly. Any silver can be kept in a tarnish-proof case when not in use.

In closing this chapter, it is interesting to note that transparent lacquers may be tinted to various colors by the addition of soluble dyes.

Dips and Oxidizing or Coloring Solutions

8

Oxidizing, the combination of the elements in the air with the metal, takes place when the silver, copper, or brass used in jewelry is exposed to air. The process takes place more rapidly during heating operations such as annealing and soldering. Gold does not oxidize so readily, although it can be oxidized. This natural process may be desirable or undesirable. If the latter, the work is protected by lacquer. If the former, it is permitted but usually under conditions whereby it may be controlled.

When oxidizing, or antiquing, a piece of jewelry, the following should be borne in mind: to give apparent depth to a relatively flat design or to cause a contrast between the different elements of a design, certain portions of the design can be darkened while others are brightly polished. Done properly, the recessed portions are left dark while the raised portions are polished.

When the proper oxidizing solution has been decided upon, the article, if small, is either dipped into the solution or swabbed with it. When dry, the article being antiqued is polished in the following way: the fingertip is moistened and touched to a dish containing some whiting, which in this case acts as an exceedingly fine abrasive. The finger is then rubbed over the raised portion of the work, where it removes the unwanted oxide. When this is done to the proper degree or to the taste of the craftsman, the work is rinsed and dried by a current of warm air. Do not heat, because an oxide will rapidly re-form.

A small, soft hand buff with a very light application of rouge is then buffed over the raised surfaces, bringing up full luster if this is what is wanted. The work can then be wiped clean with a polishing cloth and lacquered if so desired. If the work is not lacquered, the oxidized portions will not be affected, but the bright portions may dull if the article is not worn sufficiently. This is easily remedied by the occasional use of a polishing cloth.

Interesting effects can be obtained by oxidizing an entire flat surface and following this with steel wool applied in long strokes across the work in one direction. Other effects based on similar action will suggest themselves.

An important point to bear in mind before any oxidizing is undertaken is that the work should previously be finished and buffed to perfection and then most thoroughly cleaned by either caustic bath, detergent and water, or a "bright dip." Oxidizing is sometimes used on cheap commercial work to cover poor finishing. However, this process used on work meticulously done is a very important factor in accomplishing an aesthetically pleasing result.

Dips

Sometimes, before oxidizing is done, an article is rendered completely free of all foreign matter by the use of a "bright dip." This is usually done before metal plating and enameling as well. In either case, it assures a smooth, even process. The "bright dip" can be made up in several ways. Any or all of the following may be tried:

> Sulphuric acid—1 part
> Nitric acid—1 part
>
> > or
>
> Sulphuric acid—2 parts
> Nitric acid—1 part
>
> > or
>
> Hydrofluoric acid—1 quart
> Nitric acid—1½ pints
> Sodium chloride (common table salt)—2 tablespoons

Work should be suspended in the solution up to about 30 seconds at the longest. Watch carefully and use the shortest time necessary. Do not suspend the work by iron wire; use copper or brass. Rinse work in cold running water immediately upon removing work from any of the dips mentioned in this section, then dry. Use rubber gloves and avoid any contact with the acids. Have good ventilation. Do not keep such dips where children may be present. When any dip using hydrofluoric acid is made, the container should be of glass or crockery that has been *well coated with black asphaltum varnish,* obtainable at paint stores. Glass or crockery is attacked by hydrofluoric acid.

Satin Finish

To secure a satin finish similar to a wire-brush finish, a satin finish dip may be used in the same manner as previously described but using any one of the following solutions:

> Hydrofluoric acid—1 pint
> Water—3 pints
>
>   or
>
> Hydrofluoric acid—1 pint
> Nitric acid—½ pint
> Water—5 pints
>
>   or
>
> Hydrofluoric acid—2 pints
> Nitric acid—1 pint
> Muriatic acid—½ pint
> Water—5 pints

When dips using acid and water are prepared, always add the *acid to the water* to avoid possible violent reaction.

Satin dips can be used either to secure a straight satin finish or in conjunction with an oxidizing process.

Gold Finish

To secure a finish on brass similar to gold, suspend work as previously described, until desired color is obtained, in this solution:

> Nitric acid—2 pints
> Hydrofluoric acid—2 pints
> Clean zinc scrap—2 ounces

Rinse and dry.

Oxidizing or Coloring Solutions

Probably the most common oxidizing agent in use on silver and copper is potassium sulphide, or as it is often called, "liver of sulphur." This will give silver or copper a blue-black to black finish. Dissolve 1 ounce of potassium sulphide in 1 quart of hot water. About ¼ of an ounce of ammonia may be added, although this is not essential. Dip or swab the article to be oxidized in this solution. If the article is preheated by previous immersion in hot water, better results are usually obtained. Should a "scaly" black result, the mixture is too strong, and more hot water can be added to weaken it. Potassium sulphide comes in lump form and should be kept in a tightly closed *dark* jar.

Dry the article, preferably by blown air, and treat as described earlier in this chapter. Another solution that will work in similar fashion can be made by adding ammonium sulphide (a liquid) to water until a light straw-colored solution results. This solution can be used after being heated.

Butter of antimony can be applied to brass and allowed to dry. This will oxidize brass very well.

To secure a brown finish on copper, about ⅔ of an ounce of potassium oxalate and 2 ounces of sal ammoniac are dissolved in 1 pint of white vinegar. The article to be colored may be immersed or swabbed with a cloth.

For a red finish on copper, to 1 pint of water add 1 ounce of potassium carbonate and 2 drams of sulphide of arsenic.

To secure a steely gray coloring solution for copper, dissolve 2 ounces of chloride of arsenic in 1 quart of water. The article to be colored may be immersed in the hot solution.

An interesting range of colors in succession can be produced on copper by dissolving 300 grains of lead acetate and 600 grains of hyposulphate of soda into 1 quart of water. The solution can *then* be heated to the boiling point for use. By continued immersion, steel gray, purple, maroon, red, and gunmetal blue can be produced in succession. To stop at any color, quickly remove from bath and immerse in warm water. Dry and lacquer.

For a reddish-bronze finish on copper, dissolve 3 ounces of ferric nitrate and 1 ounce sulphocyanide of potassium in 2 quarts of water. Since a precipitate forms, shake well before using. Immerse the work or swab with cotton swab.

For copper, brass, and bronze, an antique green patina similar to that seen on bronze statues or copper roofing exposed to weather can be secured by any of the following solutions:

On brass or copper: to 1½ quarts of water, add 1 ounce of sal ammoniac and 3 ounces of ammonia carbonate. Use rubber stopper.

Or, add to 1 pint of water

    1 ounce iron chloride crystals
    3 ounces verdigris (basic copper acetate)
    5 ounces sal ammoniac
    2 ounces cream of tartar
    4 ounces sodium chloride (common salt)
Dip the article and allow it to dry naturally.

Or, to 24 ounces of boiling water add

    6 ounces cream of tartar
    2 ounces sal ammoniac
    16 ounces cupric nitrate
    6 ounces sodium chloride (common salt)

On brass, copper, or bronze: to 20 ounces acetic acid add

2 ounces water
10 ounces sal ammoniac
2 ounces cream of tartar   Apply with stiff brush.
2 ounces copper acetate
2 ounces sodium chloride
(common salt)

To give brass a golden bronze color, 1½ pounds of potassium nitrate are dissolved in 1 quart of sulphuric acid. To this are added 1 gill nitric acid and 1 gill hydrochloric acid. Immerse work.

Brass may be given a greenish hue by dissolving ½ pound sal ammoniac and ½ pound copper sulphate in 2 quarts of boiling water. This solution is applied with a stiff brush and permitted to dry naturally.

To color brass steel gray, 2 ounces of arsenic chloride are dissolved in 1 quart of water. The work is immersed.

Colors ranging from brown to red can be applied to brass by dissolving in 1 quart of water 4 ounces of iron nitrate and 4 ounces of sodium hyposulphite.

Although aluminum is not frequently used for jewelry, its occasional use can necessitate the mixing of an oxidizing solution. To 1 quart of hot water add ½ pound zinc chloride and ½ to 1 ounce of copper sulphate, the amount depending on the speed of action wanted. Articles are immersed. The aluminum can be cleaned again by immersion in a weak solution of caustic soda (lye).

Gold can be oxidized by a commercial fluid called "Hil-Ox," obtainable at a jewelers' supply house. Gold can also be oxidized or colored by first heating it, and then with a soft brush, such as camel's hair or fitch hair, applying a warm ammonium sulphide solution, such as used for silver oxidizing. The article is then rinsed and polished. No lacquering is necessary.

Before leaving the subject of oxidizing metals, it should be known that copper can be given beautiful coloring by heat. The results here are not too predictable, although they are varied and often quite brilliant. Such a coloring method is excellent on copper simulations of leaves and flowers.

To use this method, the copper should be polished, washed thoroughly, and dried. It is then heated slowly over a clean, blue gas flame. If first results are not satisfactory, merely clean off the resulting oxide and try again until an effect sufficiently satisfying is obtained. Dip in cold water when this effect is obtained, dry in air stream, and lacquer.

Substitutes for Metal Plating

The craftsman who is producing work on a small scale may not have plating equipment at his disposal, although the cost of a small plating outfit is not prohibitive. If such is the case, he may wish to try substitute methods for gold and silver plating. It is well to remember, however, that although nice effects can be obtained by these methods of gilding and silvering, they are not comparable to electroplating for lasting results.

Gilding

For gilding, it is first necessary to make chloride of gold. This is done by dissolving gold in a solution composed of equal parts of nitric acid and muriatic acid. Dissolve about 6 pennyweight of gold to 1 pint of the acid mixture. The resulting liquid is chloride of gold. The chloride of gold is then used in either of the following two formulas:

5 ounces cyanide of potassium
2 pints chloride of gold
6 ounces washing soda crystals (sodium carbonate)
2 quarts of water

The clean work is immersed in the boiling solution for a few moments or until desired color appears.

Or, to 1 quart of distilled water, add 1 pint chloride of gold. Then add 16 ounces of potassium bicarbonate. Heat over flame for about 1 hour, keeping the solution just short of actual boiling state. Immerse work in warm solution as above.

Commercially prepared gold dips, easily used, are now available.

Silvering

For silvering on copper, various interesting effects other than the allover silver coat will suggest themselves. For example, an article with an etched design can be silvered. The silver can then be partially removed, allowing it to remain only in the recessed portions. To remove the silver on the higher surfaces, make a buff by wrapping three or four layers of cloth tightly around a wooden block small enough to fit the palm of the hand. Evenly charge the surface of the dampened cloth with a very fine abrasive powder and rub in even strokes. Wash and lacquer.

Silvering formulas in paste form are:

7 drams cream of tartar
80 grains silver nitrate
40 grains sodium chloride (common salt—fine grain)

This mixture is light-sensitive and must be kept in a dark glass bottle.

Mix with water to a paste and apply to clean copper with a pad or daub. Rub with pad until satisfactory coating is obtained.

Another method is to set a small jar containing 1 ounce nitric acid and 1 ounce silver scrap in a warm place. When the silver is entirely dissolved, mix with sufficient cream of tartar to form a thin paste. Both copper and brass can be silvered with this paste. Apply with pad, rubbing until a satisfactory coating appears.

Silver dips, easily used, are now commercially available.

Remember, in dealing with chemicals, that many are poisonous. Observe the labels. Keep chemicals in containers similar to the ones in which they were obtained from the supplier. Good ventilation is advisable when mixing formulas. The use of rubber gloves is recommended in general. Good results are most often dependent upon the use of fresh chemicals, provided, of course, that proper preparation has been made.

Domes and Shot

Domes, or hemispheres of metal, and shot, or balls of metal, are frequently used to give depth and richness to pieces of metal jewelry. Sometimes such ornamentation is used in conjunction with stones; at other times, domes or shot are used in lieu of stones—either singly or in groups forming a pattern (Figs. 31, 32, and 33).

Shot

Shot is so called because of the similarity of the process used to that used in the making of shot or ball for firearm use. In Boston, a shot tower still stands, a relic of Revolutionary days. At that time, quantities of molten lead were dropped from the tower into a trough of water below. The molten lead became spherical in shape and, during its fall, solidified before hitting the water, in which the shot was chilled as well as protected from injury.

The craftsman makes shot by melting a predetermined amount of metal dipped in flux on a charcoal block. It is made in sizes ranging in diameter from a pinpoint to about 3/16″. To obtain as nearly spherical a shape as possible without resorting to a shot tower, a small depression can be made in the charcoal block with a dapping punch of small size. This will allow the base of the ball to maintain its curvature in the solid as well as in the molten state. The metal, usually wire or scrap bent or compressed to occupy a small space, is heated in a blue flame until it is molten and appears to "spin." It is then allowed to cool, and when redness disappears, it can be dropped into pickling solution or suspended in a copper sieve, as described under *Pickling*.

Some difficulties arise when an oversupply of borax flux is used. The flux itself forms a molten liquid and adheres to the shot, distorting its form. The remedy for this is to use a thin flux, not too abundantly. Sometimes the small shot is blown away from the surface of the charcoal block by the flame. When this occurs, it is evidence of too intense a flame, and the torch should be adjusted to a quiet, blue flame.

Frequently the use of fine silver is advised in the making of shot because of its slight advantage in luster. The author does not advise this usage for two reasons. First, the fine silver does not wear well, and shot, being particularly exposed in its usual application, must withstand much wear. Second, when fine silver is melted, it absorbs considerable oxygen. This will occur even though a borax flux is used. To use a deoxidizing substance with the silver would mean the formation of slag, permissible in melting silver for a casting but annoying when forming shot. This absorbed oxygen is expelled on cooling. The result, in technical circles, is called "crabbing" or "spitting." Evidence of this phenomenon will be seen on the resulting fine silver shot in the form of tiny spines or extrusions extending outward in all directions. Pure gold does not behave in this manner. Sterling and gold alloys containing a large amount of silver show this tendency only to a slight extent. These extrusions on the surface of fine-silver shot are hard to remove because of the difficulty in handling such small objects. The unevenness and irregularity of these extrusions make such shot unusable for decorative purposes.

Shot formed on a block does not result in perfect spheres, so it is inadvisable to continually remelt in the hopes of obtaining such. However, the slightly flattened base makes it easy to set down each ball in place for soldering. Should the ball refuse to stay in position, it can be flattened on its base without harming its general shape. Place the ball on the end grain of a piece of hardwood, such as maple or birch, and tap once lightly with a flat hammer. The underside of the ball will remain unchanged, while a flat is formed on top. This is reversed and used as a base when soldering.

One of the problems in forming shot concerns the duplication of one already formed. To insure matching shot to one already formed, the latter must be weighed on a balance scale. Enough metal to equal the weight of the finished shot will produce another one of equal size.

However, when a quantity of equal-sized shot is to be made up, the silver can be measured out in two ways. The first method is to measure off equal spaces on a piece of silver wire. These spaces can be marked off with a three-cornered jeweler's file. Cut these equal pieces, curl each up with a pliers, and melt each one of them. Equal-sized shot will result. It will be necessary to determine experimentally the proper length of wire necessary to make a ball of the required size. The craftsman who has frequent need of shot should make a table of shot sizes, listing the length and weight of wire necessary for shot of a particular size. He may do this after deciding the gauge of wire he will use at all times for the shot. Listing the weight is valuable when scrap metal is to be used for making shot. The necessary weight of scrap metal will be in the table.

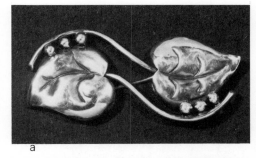

Fig. 31. (a) Simple repoussé leaves with shot ornamentation; (b) use of dome and shot with repoussé work.

Fig. 32. Earrings. Cluster of shot around onyx.

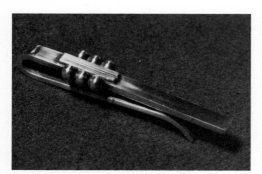

Fig. 33. Tie clip. Ornamentation consists of 14-gauge square wire and shot. (Seven-gauge beaded wire may be used.)

The second method is similar to the method used for making links. The wire is closely wound around a metal rod. The coil is slit along its length with a jeweler's saw (see Fig. 93). It will then fall into separate rings. Each ring, when melted, will form a shot, and all will be equal in size. Here, too, it is necessary to determine wire and link size to obtain shot of a particular diameter.

If it is necessary to polish shot *before* it is applied as ornamentation, a shellac stick, or dop, can be used. For this purpose, a piece of ⅜" diameter dowel about 5" or 6" long is secured. On one end of this rod, melt some stick shellac, obtainable in large paint shops. Another suitable cement is made by melting together equal parts of flake shellac and sealing wax. A candle can be used for melting the shellac as well as for heating prior to attaching the ball. With the ball partially imbedded in the shellac, the end of the shellac stick is then brought in contact with the polishing wheel. Commercially, quantities of shot are polished by tumbling them in a barrel, or mill, together with pebbles and fine abrasive. The mill is slowly rotated on a horizontal axis by a motor.

To conclude, an additional use for shot is its use as a basis for small discs. The finished shot is placed upon a polished steel plate and struck with a similarly polished flat hammer. Very few blows may be struck before it is necessary to anneal the flattened pellet. If the disc is not annealed, it will begin to crack around its edges. When this occurs, the disc will have to be discarded or remelted. This method of making small discs with slightly rounded edges makes available another means of decorating a surface by appliqué.

Domes

Domes of metal are another form of ornamentation used by the jeweler. These domes are generally from ¼" to 1" in size when used for jewelry purposes. Smaller domes can be made, although for such purposes shot is often substituted. Domes can be formed on the surface of the metal jewelry itself, but a dome made separately and then applied to the work makes a finer appearance. Such domes are often the basis of a ring or other piece of jewelry.

Domes can be made in several ways. A heavy nail rounded on one end may be used. The metal is rested on a lead block or the end grain of a close-grained hardwood, such as birch or maple. A blow of a hammer on the nail, which rests on the proper location on the jewelry, will form a dome on the reverse side. A more permanent tool can be made of a piece of cylindrical tool steel, or drill rod, appropriately shaped, hardened, and tempered (see *Chasing Tools*). A dapping punch can be used for the same purpose. These are available in various sizes and can be bought in sets.

When a more perfect dome is desired on a piece of flat jewelry without resorting to an applied dome, the dapping die is useful. This is a steel cube, having its six faces covered with a variety of circular hollows of varying sizes. This die is used in conjunction with dapping punches and dapping cutters or hollow punches. For self-doming jewelry, the cutters are not used. The piece of jewelry

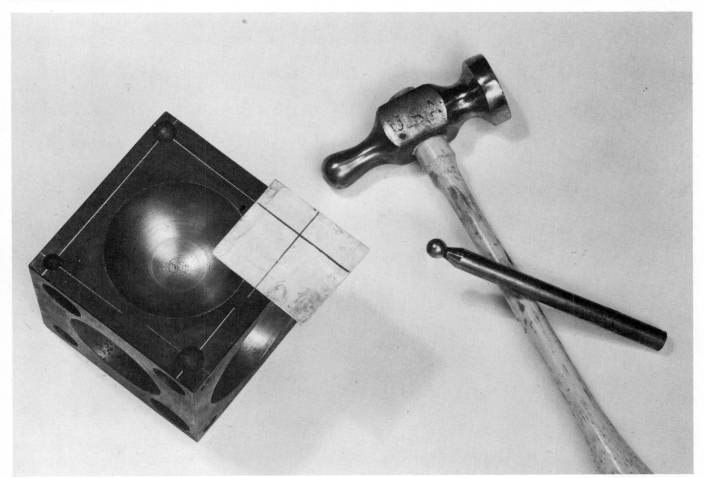

Fig. 34. Setup of work for doming at a precise location.

is placed over the desired hollow, properly located, and a punch of the required size is placed over the metal. The punch is then given a few careful blows of a hammer until the dome is formed on the reverse side. Then, keeping the dome in the hollow, a moderate blow with a flat hammer over the back of the domed area will insure a dome in sharp relief. When this work is done there is danger of cutting through the work at the edges of the hollow. This is avoided by several means. First, a punch should be selected slightly smaller than the hollow in the die. Thus, allowance is made for the thickness of the metal. If possible, the metal is annealed before forming the dome. Last, the beginner should attempt a few practice domes.

There is often difficulty in placing the area to be domed on its proper hollow so that the dapping punch can be properly centered and the dome properly located. When the jewelry is smaller than the die itself, the author's method can be used, which is shown in Figure 34. The lines on the die shown in the photograph are drawn by using a scriber on the face of the die, making permanent center lines across the hollows at right angles to each other. The pencil lines on the jewelry are at right angles and through the center of the area to be domed. The pencil lines and scribed lines are brought into alignment. Place a properly sized dapping tool over the center lines and hammer to form a properly aligned dome.

Dapping punches are usually numbered on the shank. If a set of steel numeral dies are available, the hollows on the dapping die can be identified by stamping a numeral alongside the hollow to correspond with the punch size. Allow for the thickness of the metal before fitting the punch.

To make separate domes for application to the jewelry by soldering, a metal disc of the proper size must first be made. Metal discs can be made, of course, by scribing the proper circle with a pair of dividers and then sawing. However, a much more satisfactory method employs the hollow punch or dapping cutter. Good dapping cutters are made of tool steel rod, with one end hollowed out. The edge around this concave portion is sharpened. Such cutters are used on thin metal, up to No. 24 gauge, and come in sizes from about 3/16" to about 5/8". To use the cutter, place the metal, preferably annealed, over a lead block. Hold the cutter in position, perfectly upright, and strike the solid end a strong blow with the flat of a ball-peen hammer. One or two blows should dislodge a disc. The resulting discs are slightly cupped because the greatest pressure exists at the cutting edge or circumference of the disc. The cupped disc is placed on an appropriate hollow in the dapping die, the proper punch is centered over the disc, and the disc is domed out. To make the dome somewhat deeper, it can be placed in the next smaller hollow and hammered further. (Disc cutting jigs are available. Their use is detailed in Chapter 12.)

The hollow punch consists of a collar of steel mounted on a steel shank. The collar of steel is sharpened at its cutting edge. Such punches are made in small sizes and also in large sizes, over 2" in diameter. They are used in the same fashion as the dapping cutter. In both cases, the end grain of a block of hardwood may substitute for a lead block, although the lead is preferable.

Hollow punches also are obtainable in squares, oblongs, and special shapes from die makers or large hardware dealers. These are quite expensive, however, and their purchase is justified only when frequent production of an item is contemplated.

When discs 1/4" in diameter and smaller are wanted, they can be punched out of No. 26- or 28-gauge silver sheet, using a solid punch of proper diameter. The punch is used in conjunction with a lead plate about 1/2" thick. The punch is placed over the sheet, which in turn rests on the lead plate. A heavy hammer blow will punch out a small flat disc. The blow may push the disc into the lead. To dislodge it, turn over the lead plate, holding it in the cupped hand, and strike the reverse side of the lead a few sharp blows with the ball end of the hammer. If this is done directly opposite the imbedded disc, the disc will drop free into the hand.

When large domes are to be made—1" and over—a suitable hammer can be used for doming out the disc. The largest available hollow on the dapping die can be selected, and a hammer chosen with its striking surface of suitable curvature, so as to fit the curve of the hollow. A disc of the proper size is cut by punch or saw and carefully hammered to shape in the dapping die. It may be necessary to anneal the metal during this process. A substitute for the dapping die is the pitch bowl. The circular metal piece is imbedded in pitch (see *Repoussé*), and a silversmith's hammer or an embossing hammer of proper size is used to dome out the disc.

Small domes can be formed by laying the cut disc over the lead plate and driving a properly sized dapping punch into it. If the dome is to be driven to any great depth, the metal being used for a dome may require annealing at some stage of the forming. Should the dome become firmly imbedded in the lead, it can be freed as explained above.

Domes are generally made from metal ranging in thickness from No. 22 to No. 28 gauge. The lighter weight metal is used for domes as small as ³⁄₁₆". The No. 22 gauge will do for domes about ½" to ⅝" in diameter. For intermediate dome sizes, use the No. 24 or No. 26 gauge. Domes larger than ¾" may be made of metal from No. 22 to No. 18 gauge in thickness.

Leveling Domes

Domes can be leveled at the base by placing a sheet of abrasive cloth with the abrasive side up on a piece of plate glass or a surface plate. The dome is drawn across it in long, level strokes. Domes can be made to fit a curved surface by placing abrasive cloth over a suitable curve or on the jewelry itself and rubbing the base of the dome on this surface until a good fit is obtained.

For instructions on soldering domes, either as appliqué or to form spheres, see *Hard Soldering—Specific Hard-Soldering Jobs.*

10 Chasing and Repoussé, with a Note on Tool Making

Chasing and repoussé are almost synonymous terms. They are methods of decoration similar in some respects to shallow sculpture in metal. They are the means of bringing a design out of a metal surface into bas-relief. They are the means of producing from a flat sheet of metal a three-dimensional result (Figs. 31 and 47).

Actually, repoussé is the French term for chasing, but although the two words are used synonymously, there is a technical distinction between them: chasing, while covering the field of repoussé, or modeling in metal, also includes the technique of enriching a metal surface by the cutting of lines to form a surface decoration. Thus, a chased ornament is frequently one that has *no modeling or raising of the surface* but only intricate design cut into the surface. The term "repoussé" would not apply to such ornamentation, yet an article decorated in repoussé might correctly be described as "chased." The term "chasing," then, is really the *all-inclusive* title, and when *specific* reference *to modeled or bas-relief effects it to be made,* the term "repoussé" will be employed in this book.

The Tools

The tools used for chasing are the chaser's pitch bowl, the chasing hammer, and a set of small, polished, punchlike tools or chisels called, simply, chasing tools (Fig. 35).

The chasing tools are many and various in shape. They are sometimes classified into groups, which help describe their function. Such groups are the *liners or tracers,* the *raising tools, planishing tools, matting tools,* and so on. The beginner needs only a few tools to start. In the actual description of the technique, reference will be made to the individual tools and their functions.

The chasing hammer with its characteristically shaped head is available in various weights, from about 1 ounce to 6 ounces. The

Fig. 35. A group of chasing tools, including a matting tool (center, left-hand container).

4- and 6-ounce sizes are most commonly used. The handle of this hammer is generally oval- or pear-shaped at the grip and tapers to a rather narrow diameter along the major portion of the shaft. This allows for a comfortable grip in the palm of the hand and a "springiness," or resiliency, in the blow of the hammer.

The pitch bowl, or pitch pan, is a container large enough in surface area to permit the work to be comfortably anchored in the pitch. It is also helpful if the area is large enough to permit the side of the hand to rest close to the work. The pitch bowl, which is a hemisphere of iron filled with chaser's pitch, is useful, as it can be tilted at various angles on certain occasions. The bowl is supported on a leather ring or a leather collar which permits the tilting (Fig. 38). The leather collar can be made of leather belting 2" in width, formed to a circle, or collar, with the ends riveted together. The pitch pan may very well be a baking tin at least 1½" in depth. This tin is filled with chaser's pitch and is used in conjunction with a flat sandbag upon which the tin should be rested for best results.

The chaser's pitch is an amalgam formulated so that when its surface is warmed, it will hold a piece of metal securely and yet allow the metal to be worked into its surface at whatever points desirable. A heavy sheet of lead is sometimes substituted for the pitch bowl when the shaping or modeling to be done is minor in character. Formulas for chaser's pitch amalgams are discussed at the end of this chapter.

The Process

A brief, simple explanation of the process of chasing will now be given, followed by an elaboration of each step in detail.

The metal bearing the design to be chased is imbedded in chaser's pitch. The liner or tracer is then worked over the outline. The metal is now removed from the chaser's pitch. On the reverse side should be seen a raised line indicating the outlines of the design. The metal is again imbedded in the pitch, this time with the raised outline up. The proper, rounded raising tools are now used to work out the inside portion of the design, so that it will appear in relief on the other side of the metal. When this is done, the metal is again reversed in the pitch, and the design, which is now in repoussé, is given the finishing touches with the proper chasing tools (see Fig. 40).

And now for the details: a design may be placed upon the metal using a suitable technique, as discussed in the chapter on the transfer of designs. The metal can be imbedded in the pitch by gently warming the top surface of the pitch with a gentle blue flame from the torch. A yellow flame will deposit carbon over the pitch and make it messy to work with. An intense flame will burn the pitch, rendering it useless. The pitch should be heated so that the metal can be pressed into its surface, but not to an extent where the metal tends to sink *under* the surface. The metal should be placed somewhat toward the upper right for a right-handed craftsman. Some pitch may be pushed so as to slightly overlap the edges of the metal. Sometimes a worker rests the metal on the pitch and heats the two together. This is permissible if the method of transfer used will not suffer by the application of the flame. Do not "cook" the pitch bowl *over a flame* in preparing for repoussé work. The pitch should be soft enough at the time chasing is done for it to take the impression of a finger pushed *firmly* into its surface.

Sometimes a worker will coat the back of his work with a thin coating of oil or petroleum jelly. This makes the removal of the work somewhat easier. Remember, however, that the continual use of oily substances will result in a fouled pitch bowl, which will not only be unpleasant to work with, but will not properly hold the metal after a period. To remove work without the use of oil, the pitch bowl and work can be left to cool or can be chilled with cold water either directly or with a wet cloth. The work can then be pried off the pitch with a tracing tool. It will usually part cleanly.

Should pitch adhere to the surface of the work, it can be removed by soaking a piece of steel wool in turpentine and using it to rub off the pitch. To prevent a soiled work table cover the table with a few thicknesses of newspaper.

The liner, or tracer, is now selected. This is a somewhat chisel-shaped tool (see Fig. 36). The width at *A* may vary from about ⅛″ to ¼″, depending on the intricacy of the design. Note the curvature at *B*. This enables the chisel to progress along a curved path without leaving a jagged line. Very sharp curves require a narrow-width tracer.

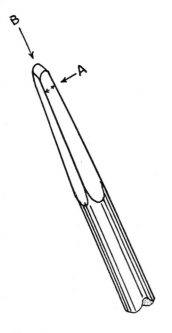

Fig. 36.   Liner or tracer.

Fig. 37. Holding the chasing tool—its position in the hand.

The right-handed worker holds this tool in the left hand as shown in Figures 37 and 38. The first three fingers of the hand are spaced along the length of the shank, with the third finger in contact with the end of the tool as well as the work. The thumb clamps the tracer against the three fingers and also rolls the tool as it maneuvers around a curve. The little finger rests, together with the side of the hand, on the space left on the pitch alongside the work. It will be found that the portion of the hand holding the tracer can move about an inch without actually moving the side of the hand. This is done largely by utilizing the side of the little finger as the pivotal point. Thus, about an inch of work can be traced without shifting the position of the hand.

The tracer travels in a direction *toward* the worker. The chisel is carefully tilted back a few degrees so that the top of the tool is farther from the worker than the point. This makes it possible for the tool to travel along its path (toward the worker) in a very gradual manner, leaving a smoothly indented line. If the angle is *too great,* the tool will skitter over the surface without cutting a proper line. When a sharp curve is encountered, the slight angle at which the tracer is being held is increased, and the tool works its way around a curve almost "on its heel."

The chasing hammer is held so that the pear-shaped portion of the handle is in the palm of the right hand. It is important that, when the face of the hammer contacts the top of the tool, the hammer handle should be at right angles to the shank of the tool.

Fig. 38.   Holding the chasing tool—its position on the work.

The hammer is used in a succession of rapid blows, *from the wrist,* with just enough force to leave an indented line. The progress of the tracer should be almost unnoticeable to get a clean line. If the tracer does not seem to move at all, the cause lies either in a dirty work surface, which retards the sliding, or a vertically held tracer. Either will result in eventually cutting a hole through the metal. It must be remembered that, during all chasing, the surface of the metal being worked upon *must be perfectly clean.*

This chasing operation is not only the first step in a repoussé job, but is also a process used to cut lines on a piece of work that is to have no further chasing operations. In other words, when it is necessary to cut a line on a job to fulfill some part of the design, this "tracing" is the method used.

The importance of perfecting this technique cannot be overestimated. It requires practice. Some require only a short session to master most of its difficulties. Others require hours. Chasing on a piece of jewelry should not be attempted until good results can be obtained in practice. When this first tracing technique has been perfected, the craftsman is ready to continue with the next step in repoussé.

Raising

Work that is designed to be done in repoussé is that in which a portion or portions of the design are raised. To what extent this raising is done depends on the design itself. For example, an ivy leaf can be done. An example of a leaf in repoussé is shown in the photograph in various stages of completion (Figs. 39 and 40).

Work of this nature is relatively simple in contrast to a job requiring the working out of a human face in full detail in repoussé. The leaf, when tracing has been completed, is removed from the pitch and reversed in the pitch bowl. It will be necessary to clean this "reverse" side thoroughly with turpentine and steel wool. The raised lines, outlining the leaf with a central vein, are visible. It now remains to hammer *in* the portions of the leaf between the raised lines. Thus, when the leaf is again reversed to its original position, it will be convex in its general surface appearance.

This "raising" will require the use of chasing tools having rounded ends in various degrees of convexity.

A leaf as large as 2″ might even be raised by the careful use of one or more of the many polished silversmith's hammers ordinarily used for forming bowls and other hollow objects (Fig. 53). The convex-ended tool, whatever it may be, must be chosen not only for its size, but—perhaps even more important—for the arc of its convexity. The shape of the tool must approximate the desired curve of the raised object as nearly as possible.

Fig. 39. Full-size pattern for veined leaf.

Fig. 40. A veined leaf in various stages of construction, and the chasing tools involved in this job.

Fig. 42. Repoussé work in various
stages of completion. Despite the
relative intricacy, these pieces are
successfully managed by young pupils
with only little prior training.

Fig. 41.

When chasing tools are used, they can be held and used in the same manner as the tracer, with this one difference: the tool should be held at right angles to the point on the curve at which it makes contact during raising. This means the angle at which it appears in the worker's hand will vary at different places on the work. Also, the blow of the hammer can vary in weight at different points to produce a gradual curvature or varied depth. The important thing to remember, as far as end result is concerned, is that a curved section in repoussé should give the appearance of a perfect, smooth curve, unmarred by small protuberances or bumps caused by using tools with sharply curved faces.

The work is next removed from the pitch as previously described and freed of any adhering pitch. If the raised surface is now cleaned with fine steel wool, any imperfections on the surface will be easily seen. These imperfections can usually be corrected by returning the object to the pitch bowl and working over the concave surface at the proper points until a smooth surface results.

When it is desirable to correct any errors in shaping by working over the raised, or convex, surface, the work is imbedded in the pitch with this surface up. The hollow portion on the underside must be filled with pitch to avoid collapsing the curve. Test for hollowness by tapping lightly with the tool at different points. Gently heating the work as it lies in the pitch will frequently cause small hollows on the underside to fill in with pitch.

With the raised surface now facing the worker, any necessary work that is required for shaping can be done. Tools must be carefully selected. In the case of intricate jobs, the many odd-shaped tools available for repoussé work may be called into use. This final shaping is necessary in complex work to give sharpness and detail to a finished ornament. *Remember to anneal the work occasionally to make it more workable.*

The finished ornament, at this point, can be cut out with the jeweler's saw. This is done whether the ornament is to be applied or is a single ornamental piece in itself. (Sometimes, on the other hand, an ornamental area in repoussé is worked out of the metal comprising the actual piece of jewelry, as in a series of repoussé designs along the surface of a bracelet.) There is good reason to saw out the ornament *after* it has been worked in repoussé. As an example, the cherub in Figures 41–42 might have been cut out with a saw and *then* worked in repoussé, saving the tracing of the outline. This is inadvisable, however, as the metal around the outline is of inestimable aid in keeping the work properly positioned in the pitch bowl during repoussé work. The result of leaving this metal until the work is completely formed will be a much better repoussé job, more easily obtained.

A chasing tool frequently used in chasing or repoussé is that pictured in Figure 43 (No. 2 in Fig. 40). This tool is available or can be made to the following dimension: width at *B* from ³⁄₆₄″ to ⅛″; width at *C* from ⅛″ to ³⁄₁₆″; surface *A* slopes at an angle of 4 or 5 degrees. Its curvature is slight, similar to a tracer or liner.

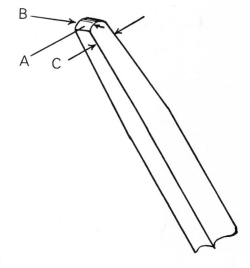

Fig. 43.

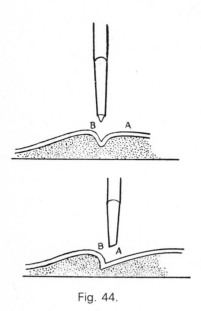

Fig. 44.

This tool is frequently used after the tracer. Properly used, it does away with the appearance of an indented line and gives a sloping surface at the line when this is desirable. Its effect is shown in Figure 40 on the last leaf, where a line is made first with the liner, or tracer, and then followed with the tool just described. Compare the effect with the previous chased lines.

Figure 44 shows the change at surface A when this tool (which might best be referred to as a "beveled chasing tool") follows the use of the tracer. Surface A slopes away smoothly, leaving surface B in sharp relief. The tool should be on hand in a few sizes, and the size chosen for use should be in proportion to the size of the work being done. The tool is handled in the same manner as a tracer, and it is positioned on the indented lines as shown in the accompanying diagram.

Other chasing tools that may be found useful are:

1. A narrow rounded tool, in appearance almost a rounded tracer. This is available in a few thicknesses and is useful to raise a band between two traced lines.

2. A rounded, pear-shaped tool useful for working in oval hollows that end rather pointedly.

Stamping and Matting Tools

Stamping tools are somewhat similar to chasing tools except that their ends are decorated with a small design or unit of a design. The design may be flat, in which case the tool is used in conjunction with a small hammer in order to leave its flat imprint in a metal surface. When the design is rounded or three-dimensional it leaves a small unit *en repoussé*. Figure 45 shows the result of employing such a tool having a heart as a unit for a design. Such tools can be made by the craftsman by using small files to form the shape and polishing the finished punch. They are tempered as described below.

Matting tools are utilized to decorate recessed portions of a design in repoussé and, frequently, the recessed portions of an etched design. Unfortunately, they are sometimes used to cover poor workmanship, particularly in flat-chased work and etched designs.

Fig. 45. Such earrings require only 15 minutes of work. A punch was used for the embossed hearts.

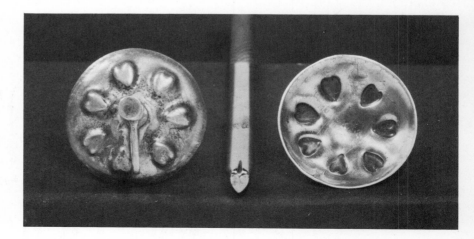

Fig. 46.   A linked necklace showing veining resulting from the use of a tracer on the reverse side of the metal. (Anna Halasi)

Fig. 47. Some articles of jewelry in repoussé. (Anna Halasi).

Forming, Hardening, and Tempering Chasing Tools

It is not difficult for the craftsman to make his own chasing tools. The material used is tool steel, a steel with a suitable carbon content to form good tools capable of being hardened and tempered. Drill rod may be used, although for chasing tools hexagonal steel lengths are most suitable. This material makes up into an easily manipulated tool. Square stock may also be used. Old fencing foils yield sufficient material for six or seven tools of varying cross-sectional areas. Thus, a relatively heavy raising tool can be made of the material near the hilt, while a fine tracer can be made from the material nearer the button end of the foil.

The first step in making a tool is the annealing of the steel. If tool steel is purchased already annealed, or soft, this process may be eliminated, but if the craftsman is using pieces of foil or other discarded tool steel, it is best to anneal the metal to make certain it is soft and can be properly hardened later. Tool steel is annealed by heating in a blue flame until it glows red. Do not overheat to orange—this damages some steels. The steel must then be set aside to cool in air or may be laid in sand to cool. The object is to allow the steel to cool slowly. When cool enough to handle, it may be ground or filed to required shape. A tracer is ground as shown in Figure 36. Dimensions vary according to the size tool wanted. When the tracing edge has been made, it can be touched up with an oilstone to make sure its surface is smooth. The edge can then be polished on its working edge to avoid an actual sharp edge. Hold the edge against a hard felt wheel charged with tripoli. The edge should be held so that its broad surfaces are parallel to the sides of the wheel. Polish lightly, rocking to polish the full curved edge. The two slanting surfaces that form the edge should be polished, being held so that the surfaces are flat against the polishing surface of the wheel. Finish with rouge. Be careful not to use great pressure and pay attention to the safety precautions mentioned in the chapter on polishing.

Raising tools, as well as specially shaped stamping tools, can be filed to shape and polished. Small needle files were used to make the heart-shaped punch used in making the earrings shown in Figure 45.

Fine emery cloth used in conjunction with lubricating oil is excellent for finishing off tools that have been ground or filed to shape. If such tools are polished without the use of emery cloth and oil, the marks formed by the grinding wheel or file will be very obvious.

Making Matting Tools

To make matting tools, select an old file of the 6″ or 8″ flat variety. Lay it flat on a work bench. Heat the end of an annealed piece of tool steel to a red heat. Have a large can or pail of cold water close at hand. When the *end* of the steel is red hot, grasp the steel near the center with a sturdy pliers and place the red hot end of the tool steel against the teeth of the file. The end of the steel, of course, should have previously been filed perfectly flat. Strike the top of the steel piece sharply with the flat of a 1-pound ball-peen hammer. Now heat the end red again and plunge it into the water, stirring while it is kept immersed. The steel, which will have a reverse imprint of the file teeth, will now be hardened. Stirring in the water keeps the steel constantly in contact with cold water. The sudden change in temperature is necessary for proper hardening. Test for hardness by lightly pushing a small, sharp file across the end of the tool. When properly hardened, the steel will resist the cutting action of the file, which will seem to slide over the tool smoothly without "biting" into metal. If, for any reason, the file "bites," anneal the tool and then harden again by heating red hot and plunging it into cold water. This same hardening process is used for the other chasing tools, and it is always preceded by the annealing process. It is not necessary, however, to do it immediately after the annealing process—no time element is involved. At this point, it is well to note the different effect such a heating process has on carbon steel in contrast to the effects on silver, brass, or copper.

When a piece of steel is hardened in the manner described, it is in its hardest but most brittle state. To keep it hard and yet eliminate the brittle quality, the tool must be tempered. This is the third and final heating process used in making all chasing tools and will be detailed later in this chapter.

Fig. 48. Gold lion's head brooch. Cast, pierced, and chased finish. (L.W.)

Tempering Steel Tools

Before tempering, the otherwise *completed* tool is cleaned at its working end. This is easily done with very fine emery and oil or a piece of worn emery cloth and oil. This will restore the original silvery steel color on the front or working end of the tool. Tempering is done to remove the brittle quality of hardened steel and to remove inner strains and tensions. In addition, tempering imparts a particular degree of hardness to a piece of steel. To obtain the degree of hardness wanted, the steel must be heated to a specific temperature and then plunged again into cold water. Inasmuch as the small shop rarely has a pyrometer on hand to measure the heat of the furnace or flame used in tempering, another method of measuring can be employed. This method makes use of the oxides formed on the surface of the heated steel to ascertain the degree of heating and thus the hardness. The oxides appear in various colors in a definite order. First to appear is a pale yellow, then a deep straw, then brown, purple, blue, and black. The ranges from yellow to blue are useful in tempering. The yellow indicates the extreme hard end of the scale; the blue indicates the relatively softer, springier, and tougher tempering. The color needed for chasing tools is deep straw. To obtain this color, the *upper half* of the tool shank is moved about in a hot, blue flame. The flame will obscure the colors, but the portion of the steel not actually in the flame—the *lower half*—will show the entire scale of colors. The deepest will appear close to the

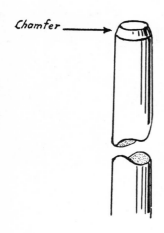

Fig. 49.

flame, merging with the rest of the colors in the scale, with the yellow nearest the end of the tool. When this yellow color slowly creeps down to the tip of the tool, it is plunged into cold water. The upper half of the tool will not be very hard, but this is not necessary and will eliminate the chance of the tool's snapping in two. If the entire tool were tempered an even yellow, the upper end of the tool would probably injure some hammers, and the shank of the tool would be likely to snap.

Another and somewhat better method of tempering requires a small gas burner or stove. A plate of iron or steel at least ⅛" thick and large enough to accommodate a chasing tool is heated over the gas burner. The chasing tool is then placed on the hot plate, with the lower working end or point extending over and off the edge of the plate for a distance of about 1 inch. Keep the plate heated and watch for colors. Allow the major portion of the shank to go through the colors until purple is reached. Then push the tool point back so that the entire tool rests on the heated plate. Concentrate attention on the tool's *point,* and when a deep straw color is reached, plunge it into cold water. This results in a properly tempered point and an evenly tempered, softer shank.

To finish the tool, it can be cleaned of all color with fine emery and oil or left as is. The only work really necessary involves grinding or filing a chamfer around the upper end of the tool (Fig. 49). This is done so that the constant hammering on this end does not form a "mushroom." Such a formation frequently results in cut fingers and should be avoided by the aforementioned grinding of a chamfer.

Chasing Pitch Formulas

It is best to purchase prepared chasing pitch. It is not expensive, will last for a long period of time, and will save the craftsman a great deal of the bother necessary in preparing such pitch. Yet should such pitch be difficult to obtain in a particular locale, a formula will prove of value if the ingredients are obtainable. Also, it is to the interest of the worker to understand the nature of his materials as well as his tools.

An old and tried formula for chaser's pitch consists of Burgundy pitch and plaster of Paris in equal parts. The pitch is melted in a tin over a moderate flame. When melted, the plaster is added slowly, stirred into the pitch until a homogeneous mixture is obtained. Five pounds of this mixture will suffice for ordinary use. About an ounce of tallow is melted and stirred into the mixture of pitch and plaster. During the winter, when pitch tends to become harder and less adhesive, the amount of tallow used in the pitch may be increased somewhat.

Another formula uses shoemaker's pitch, plaster of Paris, and rosin. These are combined by melting the pitch and rosin and stirring in the plaster slowly. The proportions for a 5-pound batch are 2 pounds pitch, 2½ pounds plaster of Paris, ½ pound rosin. Sometimes an ounce of tallow is added.

Chamfer

A common and reliable formula is the following:

  2 pounds green pitch
  3 pounds plaster of Paris
  ¼ pint lard oil

The ingredients are combined in a manner similar to previous formulas. Here the lard oil takes the place of tallow; for decreasing the hardness of a mixture, lard oil may be added to the melted mixture.

A consideration of the foregoing formulas will show that they are all somewhat similar. Different workmen prefer slightly different mixtures. Sometimes lard oil is used, sometimes tallow. The pitch is always somewhat similar regardless of name. Plaster of Paris has been successfully replaced by finely powdered brick, as well as by fine white sand. Plaster of Paris is generally the agent used *to increase* the hardness of a mixture, whereas tallow or lard oil *decreases* the hardness. Venetian turpentine may also be added to the melted pitch to make a softer mixture. Some craftsmen keep a separate winter and summer pitch mixture. The major precautions for mixing are the avoidance of lumps by thorough melting and stirring and the avoidance of igniting the mixture by careful heating over a moderate flame.

11

Using Miscellaneous Small Tools

The Drawplate

When it is desired to reduce the diameter of a length of wire or to change its cross-sectional shape, a drawplate is used. The drawplate is also used, as will be explained a little later, to form small-diameter tubing. The plate consists of a series of holes graded in size. These holes are tapered; on one face of the plate a hole appears larger than it does on the reverse side. Wire is fed through a hole on the large-diameter side and is drawn through, thus assuming the diameter of the hole at its smallest size.

Drawplates are made of hard, tempered steel and are available with hole-series covering different ranges. They are also available with holes having various shapes, such as half-round, oval, square, rectangular, etc. Plates are also made in combination types. These have a row of round-hole and usually two other rows of holes of different shapes, such as square and half-round.

To use a drawplate, first remove any kinks in the wire. It is not necessary to straighten the wire very much, as the drawplate will have the effect of forming a coil anyway. File a long taper on the wire about 1" long, so that the wire will protrude through a hole just less than the wire diameter for the distance of at least ¼". If the wire is not annealed, coil and anneal as described in the chapter on annealing. The wire should be frequently lubricated. Beeswax is an excellent lubricant, and the coiled wire may be dipped into a container of melted beeswax. Otherwise, one end of the wire can be held in a vise and, with the wire held stretched, a piece of beeswax rubbed its length.

The plate is then mounted in a vise so that wire can be drawn in a plane parallel to the floor. The plate's surface should be protected by placing ''cheeks'' of copper or other soft metal in the jaws of the vise. The wire is then fed into a hole not quite the diameter of the wire, and by gripping the tapered, protruding point with a draw-tongs, it is drawn through toward the worker in a straight line. The wire is drawn through a series of holes, skipping none, until its final diameter or shape is obtained. It is usually necessary to anneal it after four or five drawings. Lubricate for each hole. Anneal the wire before it is put to use in jewelry work, unless its hard state is particularly wanted for some purpose. No silver is removed during the drawing process; the wire is merely lengthened as its diameter decreases.

Forming Tubing

To make narrow tubing, annealed metal is cut from the sheet. Nos. 24, 26, and 28 are commonly used gauges of metal, depending on the diameter of the tubing. The lighter weight is used on the narrowest tubing.

The width of the strip of metal to be used for tubing is determined by multiplying the diameter of the desired tubing by 3.1416 ($\pi \times D$). This is roughly three times the tubing diameter. The strip is then tapered on one end by use of the shears for a distance of 1". Inasmuch as the tubing used in jewelry work is generally of small diameter, a narrow-edged chasing tool can be used to start shaping the strip to a **U**-shape (see Fig. 50). The strip may rest on a block of hardwood or on a lead block. In either, a narrow groove is previously made, over which the strip is placed and shaped as shown in the figure. The tapered end is then carefully shaped to a point. A hammer, pliers, and file may be employed at different stages to accomplish this. Lubricate the strip with beeswax and draw through the nearest fitting hole. The far end of the strip should be held with a pliers to prevent twisting. Continue through a series of holes until the edges meet and a seam is formed. Anneal and lubricate as necessary. Remove lubrication by a bath in a hot caustic solution and hard-solder the seam. To do this, cover the seam with flux and place small pieces of hard solder about ¼" apart. Heat to dry the flux and then heat tubing until solder flows. Wire solder may also be employed. Cover the seam with flux, heat tubing to red heat, and touch the hard-solder wire (previously dipped in flux) to the seam of the bright-red tube. The solder should run along the seam as the flame is played along the length of the tubing.

If it is desired to eradicate any sign of the seam, the soldered tubing must *first be pickled* then lubricated and drawn again through the drawplate, using a hole just barely smaller in diameter than that of the tubing. A piece of piano wire of the proper diameter can be lubricated and inserted in the tubing before this final drawing to preserve the final diameter. The wire can then be removed.

The Ring Mandrel

The ring mandrel is useful for forming the shank of a ring, for making wire rings, for reshaping distorted rings, and for stretching finished rings.

The mandrel is a piece of tapered steel. One end has the appearance of a handle, and this end can be placed in the jaws of

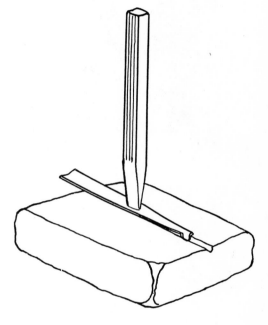

Fig. 50.

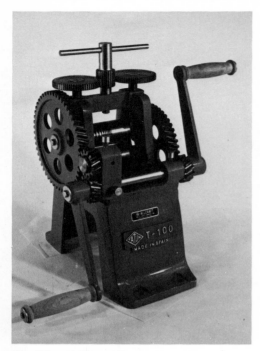

Fig. 51. Rolling mill.

a vise. The mandrel may or may not be marked in a series of graduations indicating ring size. Some mandrels are cut with a groove running along the length to permit a ring with a stone extending through the setting to be placed and worked on the mandrel. Mandrels are obtainable in hardened state as well as nonhardened.

When forming a ring shank from a strip of flat stock, the shank should be frequently reversed on the mandrel to compensate for the taper. A rawhide or fiber mallet is used to beat the strip to form. If a shank having the shape of a complete circle is to be formed, it can be roughly shaped, hard-soldered, and then trued on the mandrel. Wire rings are also shaped approximately, soldered, and then trued on the mandrel by use of a soft mallet. When a ring that has been partially crushed is to be repaired, it can be similarly worked on the mandrel. If necessary, the grooved mandrel is used, although, if too much work is not involved, it is preferable to remove the stone first. To stretch a finished ring, place on a graduated mandrel and carefully beat around its circumference with a flat polished hammer. This stretches the metal. Do not beat a decorated shank, as the hammer will mar the decoration. A ring can be stretched only about one-half a size, unless it is made of unusually thick material. If it is necessary to make a ring considerably larger in size, saw through the back of the shank, beat to required size with a rawhide mallet, and insert a piece of metal where the sawed ends of the shank have separated. Hard-solder, reshape on mandrel, file, and polish.

Mandrels are also available for bezel making in round, oval, square, hexagonal, and octagonal shapes. For shaping bracelets, large mandrels of round and oval shapes are made, but pieces of iron pipe of various diameters may be trued on a lathe and serve as well or better.

The Rolling Mill

A useful piece of equipment in the jeweler's shop is the rolling mill (Fig. 51). By means of two hardened and polished rollers, which are parallel to each other, metal can be rolled flat to a desired thickness. The metal is compressed and, because of this, hardened. After two or three successive rollings, the metal should be annealed. The rollers should be so adjusted, by a geared wheel, as to make the reduction in thickness a gradual one. In feeding metal into a mill, the same end of the sheet should be fed through every time. Twisted and braided wire are sometimes fed to the rolling mill. The flattening effect is quite decorative. Special rollers are made to produce half-round and square wire (see Fig. 89 and *Wire Working—Further Processing the Wire*).

Pliers

Among the most useful tools in the jeweler's shop are the pliers, which are available in a great variety of styles. Pliers should be of good quality tool steel. On hand should be round-nose and flat-

Fig. 52. An original flat-nose pliers and two remodeled examples.

nose pliers of at least two sizes. Pliers are used for bending and forming operations mainly. A pair or two of gripping pliers should be kept available, but others would be improved by the careful removal of the serrations, or teeth, on the inside of the jaw. This can be done by filing or grinding and should be followed by the use of emery and oil. A half-round-nose pliers has one flat jaw and one round or convex jaw. This is among the most useful pliers for bending curves. An excellent one can be made using a Pexto No. 200 flat-nose pliers as the basis. Anneal the "head" of the pliers. Remove the serrations from one jaw and hone it smooth and square with a fine oilstone. Round off the inside of the other jaw so as to get the effect shown in Figure 52. Hone smooth, harden, and temper, as described in the chapter on chasing tools. Another pair of this same pliers can be reshaped so as to have both jaws perfectly flat and smooth on the inside. Such a pliers can be used to good effect to obtain sharp, square corners when bending bezels, for example.

The Utica needle-nose assembly pliers No. 82 is unusual in having a long pair of handles and small but powerful jaws. When a very powerful grip is needed and little gripping area is available, this pliers will be found invaluable. A similar excellent pliers is the Utica duck-bill wiring pliers, in No. 31. A series of unusual pliers having a patent feature are the Bernard parallel jaw pliers. Of particular value is the flat-nose type. The jaws of these pliers remain parallel to each other regardless of the extent to which they are opened.

A pair of long, flat-nose pliers of a cheaper make should be set aside for handling hot work or for soldering. Such pliers should be used instead of spoiling more expensive tempered and polished pliers.

When it is desirable to grip or bend a portion of a job without leaving any marks, a strip of sheet tin-foil or lead-foil can be wound three or four times around each jaw of a pair of pliers. This procedure will safeguard work against possible injury.

A pair of side-cutting or end-cutting nippers should be used to clip the various types of wires used by the jeweler. Never use a shears or scissors of any sort to clip wire. The blade edge will be impaired.

The Drill

A sensitive drill of the electric type is really a miniature drill press. These drills are useful for drilling operations and, in conjunction with burrs, for working on stone settings or cutting recessed areas. When purchasing twist drills for use in jewelry work, high-speed steel drills should be obtained in preference to carbon steel drills. The drills used are small in size and much breakage will be avoided by the use of high-speed steel drills.

When a drill is to be used, whether of the hand or electric type, a small indentation must be made exactly at the point at which the hole is desired. This is made by resting the work on a flat steel surface and placing the point of a center punch on the mark. Strike the top of the punch a light blow with a small ball-peen hammer. The indented mark should be visible on only one side; do not try to drive the point through the metal. This tiny dent will prevent the drill point from "walking" over the surface of the metal and giving an inaccurate result.

When using the electric drill, place the work on the drill table, set the drill in motion, and bring the drill down close to the surface of the metal. Then adjust the position of the work so that the center punch mark is directly under the point. Use a moderate pressure on the drill to avoid vibration or bending the drill shank. The worker should keep his eyes well above the level of the top of the drill table so that any metal thrown out radially from the drill table will not strike the eyes or face of the operator.

Pin Vises and Broaches

The pin vise is essentially a tiny split chuck on a hollow length of metal comprising the handle. Thus, it is possible to insert a length of wire into the chuck, as the wire extends through the hollow handle. The end of the wire protruding from the chuck may be sharpened with a file for use as a pin. The end of the wire may also be "turned over" as a rivet head while it is held in the pin vise and tapped with a small ball-peen hammer or the ball end of a small chasing hammer.

When a small hole is to be cleaned out or reamed slightly larger as is sometimes necessary in the case of joint-and-catch combinations, a small twist drill or a broach is mounted in the pin vise. The handle of the pin vise can then be twirled backwards and forwards between thumb and forefinger, making of this tool setup a miniature drill.

The Silversmith's Raising and Planishing Hammers

A large variety of silversmith's hammers are available, and some of these can be of great value to the jewelry worker. The heads of these hammers are usually cast of a good grade of steel. Some are hand forged. All have polished striking surfaces. These surfaces vary in their areas, shapes, and curvatures. Such hammers should be kept in perfect condition and should never be used for striking other tools such as center punches or chasing tools. The hammers are designed to do their work on metals softer than steel.

The raising hammers are essentially for raising bowls and large hollowware of metals such as silver and copper. They are valuable to the jeweler as a means of giving shallow smooth curves to objects of jewelry. For example, if a design is chosen consisting of the stylized outlines of an animal, the cutout silhouette is given added depth by slight raising. To do this, the worker must first contemplate the area he wishes to raise. He then selects a polished raising hammer with a curvature related to that area. By doing this, his hammer blows will not leave a series of small, raised bumps on his work. Rather, the work will gradually become concave on its reverse side, while the surface of the metal remains virtually unmarred. When this raising is done, the work should rest on a lead block. It sometimes helps to pound a slight gradual depression into the lead block with the raising hammer. The work can then be placed over this depression and pounded from the reverse side to the desired outcome (Fig. 53). The curvature of such hammers is more important than the area, although when both curvature and area are somewhat similar to the shape desired with regard to the work, the process of shaping is much easier. The work may be set in a pitch pan as described in the chapter on chasing and the section on doming, instead of utilizing a lead block.

Fig. 53. Using a raising hammer and a lead block for shaping the leaf shown in Figure 40.

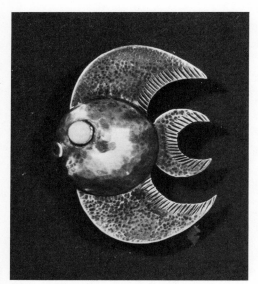

Fig. 54. A pin showing reasonable use of "peening" on a surface.

Planishing has become a treatment of a metal surface to give it a texture. Originally, objects raised from metal retained the slight irregularities of surface caused when the object was beaten to shape with steel hammers. These marks disappeared when objects in modern times were stamped or spun to shape without the use of hammers. However, the modern technique was evolved for mass production and hence created a cheaper product. Manufacturers then evolved the idea of creating "false" hammer marks to liken the product to the old handmade work. Handmade products were more expensive and thus were aped by the modern makers. Actually, the texture resulting from the skillful blows of the early artisan with his well-polished hammers was quite decorative in itself. Today, silverware and jewelry frequently display the "hammered" finish.

This surface treatment should be employed with good taste, not haphazardly. It should not be used to decorate a surface that would seem to be smooth by nature. The area of each hammer mark—which depends on the curve of a hammer surface—should bear a relationship to the area of the work in its entirety. The hammering itself is not done until the planishing hammer selected is inspected and found to possess an unblemished striking surface. Laziness and carelessness, as well as poor taste, are behind the use of damaged hammers. Blemishes of a minor character may be removed by the judicious use of fine files, fine emery cloth, crocus cloth, and the polishing wheel.

When a perfect hammer is selected, the metal surface to be planished should be brought to a state of equal perfection. Dirt should be removed with fine steel wool, and the blemishes thus revealed removed by careful work with emery cloth. When every scratch has been removed, the metal can be polished at the wheel, providing a final polished result is wanted. If polishing is done after hammering, the crispness of the hammer marks is deadened decidedly. Assuming the metal to be ready, place it, if flat, on a flat steel plate at least ¼" thick. The hammer mark will depend on the weight of the blow, so determine by practice, if a novice, the blow necessary. Then, using the *wrist* for the blow, instead of the arm, strike the hammer blows on the metal surface. Avoid hitting the steel plate. Each blow should produce a bright concave "mirror." The handle of the hammer should be *parallel* to the bench top when the hammer face contacts the work. Remember when hammering a surface that two results are concomitants of this process: (1) the metal is hardened, and (2) a delicate outline may be somewhat distorted at the edges. If desired, the work may be annealed (not generally desirable) and the edges filed smooth and polished (generally desirable).

If a piece of metal is to be domed as well as planished (Fig. 54), it is well to dome first and planish later. This is because of the stretching involved in doming. When a hammered surface is stretched, the hammer marks lose much of their character. Therefore, domed pieces of metal to be planished are placed over "stakes" and hammered on the outside, or convex, side. A smooth, polished stake should be used, and care must be taken to see that the work is in contact with the stake when a hammer blow is struck. Otherwise the domed piece will collapse slightly at each blow. A study of the tool catalogs issued by the large jewelers' supply houses will afford a clear understanding of the types of hammers available.

The Circle Cutter

Cutting a small disc of metal to a perfect circle can be a time-consuming task involving both sawing and filing. If such discs are required in quantity or with some degree of frequency, acquiring a circle cutter (Fig. 55) will be very worthwhile. Such a device will cut metals commonly used in jewelry—up to 16 gauge. Buttons, earrings, and enameled pieces are just a few items that often make use of circular discs.

Fig. 55.   A circle cutter. (Allcraft)

To use the circle cutter, the rodlike punches must be removed from their holes in the upper plate. The metal to be punched can then be slid into position between the plates and the proper size punch selected and inserted into its proper opening. The device itself should rest on a firm, solid support. The punch, which is of very hard steel precisely cut and fitted, must then be struck firmly with a ball-peen hammer, using the flat face. Hammer weight should be from 16 to 24 ounces, depending on the gauge of the metal. The disc should be punched out with a single blow to avoid its disfigurement. Properly used, a circle cutter can produce in 5 seconds what otherwise might take 15 minutes or more. The author suggests, for an initial attempt, using a piece of scrap metal such as copper to "get the feel" of the tool. Two sizes of the device itself are currently available, each cutting several holes of differing sizes. No. 1 will cut ⅛", 3/16", ¼", 5/16", ⅜", 7/16", and ½". No. 2 will cut ½", ⅝", ¾", ⅞", and 1".

If the cutter is to be used simply for cutting a hole of a specific size in a precise location on a piece of metal, the metal should first be thinly coated with white tempera color. The circle can then be marked with a compass or other means exactly where the hole is wanted. The metal then can be inserted below the plate, with the circle moved into position so that it can be seen through the punch hole, and punched in the usual manner.

The Flexible Shaft Machine

Figure 83 illustrates the flexible shaft machine being used with a burr. The handpiece—that part comprising the major part of the illustration—is the basic operational part of the machine. It is connected by a long cable to a more or less stationary small electric motor. The flexible connecting cable, or shaft, makes it possible to hold the handpiece in an infinite number of positions as the tool set into the handpiece does its work. The speed of rotation is controlled by a small foot-operated device called a rheostat, which varies the amount of voltage supplied to the motor.

Not only are there many small rotatable implements that can

Fig. 56. Some accessories for the handpiece.

be fitted into the handpiece to a great many jobs, but the handpiece itself is available in several different models. Basically, however, the purpose is the same: to provide a hand-held device that can be fitted with some form of cutting, polishing, or hammering tool, and used in a considerable variety of positions to do its work.

The small implements that are fitted into the handpiece are mounted on short steel shanks usually 3/32" in diameter. On the working end may be a burr, a hard steel cutting tool available in over a hundred different shapes. Burrs cut away metal. Small rotary saws are available, from approximately 5 mm to 1½" in diameter. Shaped emery wheels—miniature grindstones, actually, mounted on the always necessary shank—are available. Mandrels, which are shanks terminating in screwlike forms, may be used with tiny polishing wheels of muslin and felt. Shaped "bobs" of felt or abrasive-bearing rubber can be purchased. Bristle brushes of wire or fiber are available for cleaning work. Some of these are illustrated in Figure 56. Catalogs from the major supply houses show the vast variety of such accessories available.

When a cutting tool such as a saw, burr, or grindstone is used, the direction of rotation must be kept in mind so that the tool can be kept in control. The handpiece must move "away" from the direction of rotation. If this is not done, the tool may run wildly across a piece of metal, ruining the job. With the rotary saw blade, clamping the work is strongly advised!

Polishing with the Flexible Shaft

Pieces of jewelry may be polished by using the small, shank-mounted cloth wheels mentioned above. The rotating wheels are held against a block of rouge or tripoli, as required, until charged with the abrasive. The handpiece with its buffing wheel, held in penlike fashion, is then used against the jewelry where it can reach otherwise inaccessible areas. Separate wheels are used for tripoli and rouge compounds.

Scratchy, rough surfaces, when not smoothed with Scotch stone and water, can be smoothed by using the several grades of Bright-boy rubber abrasive wheels available. Be careful not to remove too much metal or make grooves in the work. Cloth polishing wheels are used for final polishing.

A useful polishing technique used by many trade craftsmen makes use of a wooden match-stick for polishing. The Foredom No. 8D handpiece, furnished with a ³⁄₃₂″ collet, will do for this work. Snip off the match-head and use the wooden match-stick as the shank. The best length is about 1⅝″. About ½″ of the match is stripped of its corners (the matches are usually square in cross section) by using a sharp knife scraper-wise. This end is pushed into the collet of the handpiece, leaving about 1″ protruding. Cotton balls are used for the polishing. A very small puff of cotton is held in the fingers and the rotating match end is allowed to catch in the cotton, which is guided to shape by the fingers (Figs. 57A and B). The resulting swablike end can be held against a bar of the desired polishing compound until it holds a usable quantity. The rotating, charged cotton may then be used as a polishing device, simply and cheaply renewed as needed. This is particularly useful for polishing stone settings and carved work.

Fig. 57A. Applying cotton to a wooden match-stick for polishing.

Fig. 57B. Shaping the cotton.

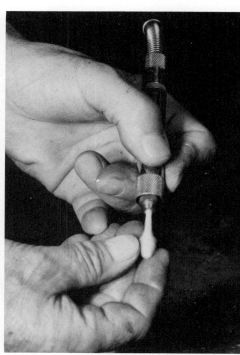

The wooden match shank, being of soft wood, may itself be used for cleaning and polishing small, difficult-to-reach areas. To do this, the working end of the match-stick should be cut off squarely or rounded with a file and held against an abrasive bar until the wood itself holds some of the abrasive material. It is then used against the work. The match shank provides a firm surface when pressure against a recessed metal area is necessary.

Using the Handpiece as a Miniature Lathe

A need for immobilizing the handpiece while shaping a decorative element (see Figs. 112A, B, and C) required a device at the present writing unavailable from any commercial source. The author devised the following accessory, which in essence provides a means for using a handpiece as a miniature lathe.

A pair of wooden blocks was cut from common ¾" pine to the dimensions shown in Figure 58. Two pieces of styrofoam were cut and cemented to the faces of the two blocks. (Access to a power tablesaw made it possible to cut the styrofoam from discarded pieces used for packaging electrical appliances. Sheet styrofoam, however, is available in various thicknesses.) Elmer's glue served as an effective cement.

The handpiece intended for use in this case was the Foredom No. 8D. The barrel of this unit has a diameter of ⅝". It is designed so that the barrel slides back and forth to expose or cover the chuck. The sliding portion measures 2" in length. This dimension determined the *width* of the wooden blocks. A channel was cut 1⅛" down along the styrofoam "facing" (measuring from top to the *center* of the channel). To lay this out, the two prepared blocks were placed face to face and the center of a ½" circle marked, 1⅛" from the top. The ½" circle was made across the *edge* surfaces of the stryofoam. From the upper and lower edges of the circle a line was squared across the two faces to the *opposite* edge, where the opposite circle was drawn. Using a ball-shaped steel burr in the handpiece, the material within the channel marking was carefully removed. An additional small groove was cut above the circle on each face. This allows space for a small screw-head on the handpiece barrel that acts as a slide stop. The discrepancy between the ⅝" barrel and the ½" channel was planned so that, when the barrel of the handpiece is positioned and the completed accessory placed snugly in a vise, the compressibility of the styrofoam accommodates the handpiece firmly without excessive pressure on the sliding action (Fig. 59).

Note the hinged bottom. The writer used a cut-down 3½" × 3½" loose-pin door hinge. A hacksaw cut the hinge, leaving two outer knuckles on one-half of the hinge, with a single center knuckle on the other. The "pin" was cut down in length, and the necessary new screw holes drilled. Two screws were inserted into each wooden block. A square of thick leather or heavy rubber might be used in place of the hinge if less work is desired.

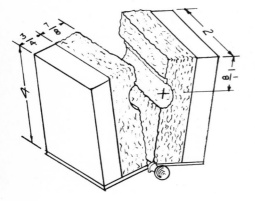

Fig. 58.

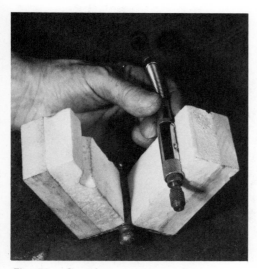

Fig. 59. Styrofoam accommodates handpiece in this miniature lathe.

The completed accessory is shown in use (Fig. 60). The hand-piece can be moved easily back and forth for access to the chuck without loosening the vise. Hands are left free to use any files needed to shape the job under way. Rotation direction is *towards* the user, as with a buffing machine.

With suitable chucks and/or handpiece, work up to ¼" in diameter can be "turned." Heavy wire can be shaped as it turns, or work soldered to an *end* of a short length of wire can be shaped. The budlike end of the buckle-pin (Fig. 112) was finished by such means. Small files used for shaping should be moved across the work so that a full stroke, using most of the file's teeth, accomplishes the work cleanly, without undue clogging.

When using the flexible shaft machine, freely or secured, at least goggles should be used. A clear plastic face shield is desirable for optimum protection.

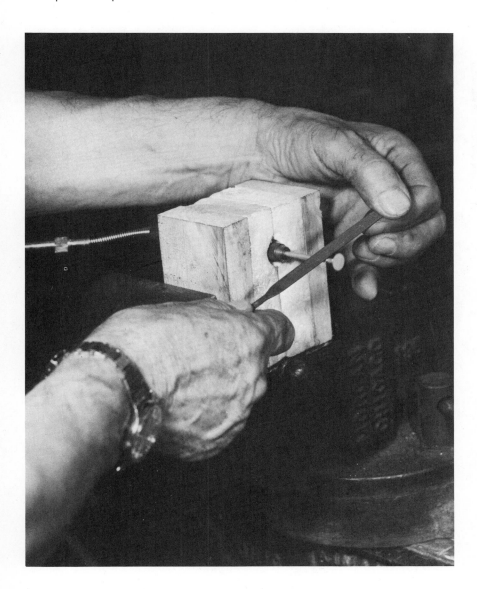

Fig. 60.   Holder for handpiece in use.

12 Casting Jewelry

Fig. 61. Earrings: miniature lion's head, sand cast. (Mouth rings are free-fitted heavy wire.) (L.W.)

The craftsman who is engaged in the small-scale production of handmade jewelry has two simple methods of casting available for his use. One method involves the use of cuttlefish bone as a medium for creating a mold. A second method utilizes fine casting sand and a flask consisting basically of a cope and a drag.

The cuttlebone method is a simple, effective method of casting a basic ring. The ring can then be carefully finished and engraved, or it can serve as a basis for a more complex piece of jewelry involving a setting for a stone and applied ornamental pieces.

The sand-casting procedure is slightly more complicated and involves equipment necessitating the initial outlay of more money than required for cuttlebone casting. This is compensated for by the fact that the sand can be used very many times, whereas a new pair of cuttlefish bones is required for every casting made using the cuttlebone-casting technique. Sand casting is also capable of greater detail, as well as greater variety, in the type of work that can be done (Figs. 48 and 61).

A third method will be mentioned here merely as related information. That method is the casting of jewelry by centrifugal force. The centrifugal method is not considered in this book for several reasons. The great advantage of centrifugal casting is that a jeweler can make up a wax pattern of a delicate, involved piece of jewelry of considerable complexity and reproduce this piece of jewelry in metal many times by a simple set of operations involving the centrifugal casting machine. This takes the hand craftsman into the realm of mass production and renders secondary the many skills that place a hand craftsman on the level of an artist. These castings are quite accurate, hence the great use of this method of casting in the field of dentistry. The method cannot duplicate exactly *any* piece of jewelry made by a skilled craftsman, but it does have great flexibility in application. The machine and its accessories are rather expensive, and their successful application to jewelry manufacture requires skilled handling.

CUTTLEFISH BONE CASTING

Cuttlefish bones are available in three sizes. The intermediate or medium is most frequently used for making small jewelry such as finger rings. Note that of the two broad surfaces of the bone, one is soft and spongy, the other hard and brittle. Both surfaces are somewhat domed. Because the ring pattern is to be sunk to half its depth in each of the flat surfaces of two bones, compare the thickness of the two bones to the widest portion of the rings, remembering that the soft, domed surface *must* be sanded flat before use.

When two suitable bones have been selected, they are trimmed with a hacksaw (Fig. 62, whole series) by cutting from the soft side until the bonelike shell is reached and then breaking off the unnecessary edges. The two rectangular pieces produced should be fairly equal in size. The soft surfaces of each must be rubbed flat and true. This is done by using a piece of plate glass about 10" × 12" or a surface plate of similar size, covered with a piece of No. 6/0 sandpaper placed abrasive side up. The soft side of the bone is rubbed with an oval motion on the sandpaper, making certain that the hand moves in an accurate plane *parallel* to the plate's surface. It is best to rub until an area that will allow a flat margin around the ring pattern about ½" wide is created.

The two flat, soft surfaces can then be sprinkled with extremely fine, pure, graphite powder, which is gently rubbed into the surface. The ring pattern is then pressed very carefully into one of the bones until it has reached a depth equal to half its width. Note the position of the ring model in the bone (Fig. 62), which permits the cutting of a fairly long funnel, or gate, into which the molten metal is poured.

Now prepare three pegs about ⅝" long and pointed on each end. These pegs are made of common wooden matches and are pressed for half their length into the cuttlebone containing the half-sunken ring. Note the position for each peg in the photograph. Observe the space left clear for the gate.

Now press the second cuttlebone over the first one, keeping the edges of each in good alignment. Hold the cuttlebones in the palms of the hands, keeping the pressure equally distributed over the outer surfaces of the cuttlebones, and apply pressure. Clasping the hands containing these bones and placing them between the knees (Fig. 63) will aid in applying sufficient pressure. One-half of the ring and each peg will now be pressed into the second bone.

The gate must be cut next. Notice that it meets the back of the ring. This is always done so that the decorative front portion of the cast ring is unharmed by the metal remaining in the gate. Mark off the width of the top of the gate on the proper end of the mold. This width should be about ⅝". Use a sharp scriber for marking. Now carefully separate the two halves of the mold. The pegs make it possible to align these halves properly when necessary. Remove the ring. Take care to leave a clean, sharp impression.

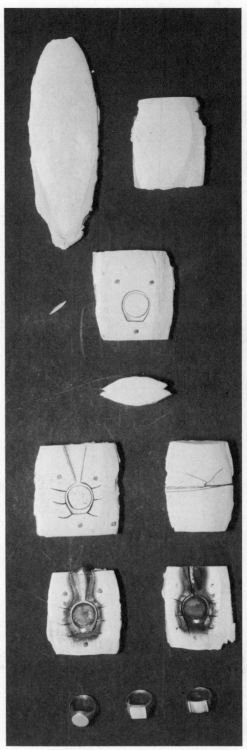

Fig. 62. Various stages in casting in cuttlebone, and some resulting semifinished rings.

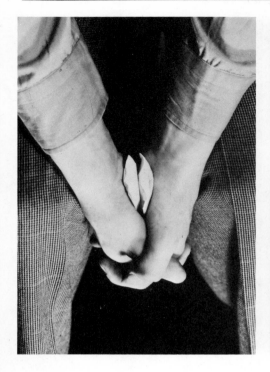

Fig. 63. Method of obtaining final pressure for a cuttlebone impression.

Fig. 64. Pouring the molten metal into a cuttlebone mold.

With a narrow-bladed sharp knife, pare out a gate extending from the top end of the mold to the ring. The width of the gate at the ring should be about 3/16". The gate is cut in *each* half, so that the two halves together form a mold with a funnel cut into one end.

Sprinkle a little graphite into the two halves of the *impression.* A small cardboard container of graphite with a nozzle can be used for this. Such an item is usually available in automobile supply stores as well as in hardware stores. A similar but empty container can be kept and used to blow clear the impressions made in cuttlefish bone. Replace the ring and press the two halves together again. Now, when the ring is again removed, a clean, heat-resisting impression will be seen.

In order to prevent the trapping of air and gases in the mold, the impression must be vented. To do this, scratch a series of fine lines extending upward from the impression to the outer edge of the bones. Make sure these lines are clear at the impression (see Fig. 62). These lines, which are cut with a scriber, are particularly important near the bottom of the impression. They should not be so large as to permit the molten metal to run through them.

Blow clear and assemble the mold with pegs in place but with the ring pattern removed. Tie the two halves firmly with fine binding wire. The two flat surfaces should fit snugly without any sign of rocking. The mold may be held in a specially bent long tongs, or it may be set upright in a pan of clean, *dry* sand. If a tongs is used, hold the mold over a can of sand in case any molten metal escapes (see Fig. 64).

Melting the Metal

The metal to be melted can be brought to its molten state in a crucible either held by a tongs and heated with a large torch or placed inside a gas-air furnace such as the "Little Giant No. 1." This furnace uses gas and a supply of compressed air. If the crucible-torch method is used, a blowpipe crucible (see Fig. 65) should be secured. The metal scrap or cuttings should be placed in the crucible, and prepared reducing flux should be sprinkled over it. The crucible is held in a crucible tongs. The flame from a large gas-and-air torch is played into the crucible until the metal melts down and beings to "spin." Add a little more reducing flux, keep the flame on the metal, and then agitate the metal slightly by a gentle rotary motion of the arm. This causes any slag that may form to move aside, permitting free pouring of the metal. If any slag pours along with the metal, it will result in an imperfect casting. The metal is poured when in a "spinning" state. The flame is kept on the metal in the crucible during pouring to keep it fluid. Pour until the gate fills to the top. When the button—the metal remaining in the gate—loses its redness, clip the wires holding the two halves together. Knock the mold apart with a tongs and carefully place the finished casting into an acid pickle. The casting should next be rinsed clean and the button removed. This is done by clamping the button in a vise and sawing off the ring, leaving a slight amount of excess metal on the shank to be filed off in the finishing operations. The cuttlebone mold, of course, is used only once.

Fig. 65. Heating the metal in a blowpipe crucible using a gas-air torch.

The appearance of tiny holes or pits in a casting is due to the absorption of gases. This can be prevented by using a reducing flux, avoiding overheating, and rapidly melting the metal being cast.

The ring is filed to its final shape, at which point it may be polished and engraved or embellished with stones or added ornament and then polished. It is not necessary to lacquer a silver ring unless it is to be placed on display for an extended period of time.

Using a Single Bone

It is frequently possible when using the larger size cuttlebones or in the case of a small casting to use a single cuttlebone, cut in half, for a complete mold. When this is done, there is very little change in procedure. The bone is cut across its length. It is generally left untrimmed, and the gate is cut from the flat edge left by the sawing. The pegs are inserted as described previously. Other operations are the same. Make certain at the start that it is possible to fit the model ring into the bone, inasmuch as the heaviest portion of the ring will come out at the narrow tail-ends of the bone.

Ring Models

In selecting models or patterns for casting in cuttlebone, many common commercial rings can be used, providing there is no overhang or any undercut portion. The model selected should be shaped so that it is possible to press it halfway into a cuttlebone with smooth results. Upon removal, it should leave a true imprint of its actual shape.

A slight alteration in the width of a ring is possible. To make a model narrower than the original, press it somewhat less than halfway into each half of the mold. To make a model wider than the original, first press up a mold in the orthodox manner. Open the mold again. Now insert the model in one half of the mold and press it deeper than half its width. Remove it from the bone and do the same to the other half of the cuttlebone mold. When the mold is reassembled with the pattern removed, it will accommodate a ring wider than the original.

To alter the *size* of a finished casting, saw a small section out of the back to make the ring smaller. To enlarge the ring size, saw through the back, carefully spread open, and add a piece of metal. Hard-solder the seams in either case and file smooth to shape. Only small alterations are possible.

Using Silicate and Borax Solution

Some jewelers substitute for graphite a silicate and borax solution which gives finer detail on castings where this fine detail is necessary. Mix borax and water in a fairly strong yet fluid solution. Mix separately a solution containing equal parts of silicate of soda and water. Make the impression in the bone and gently blow it clear of any tiny bone particles. With a good camel's hair brush coat the impression carefully with the borax solution. The silicate of soda solution is now coated over the *wet* borax solution. Allow the water to seep into the bone for a short while, and then, with the mixture *still damp,* return the model or pattern to the mold and press the two parts tightly together again. When the pattern is removed, the impression should appear very smooth and sharp. The mold should *not* be used until every vestige of moisture has dried out of the bone. Keep the mold open and bake it slowly until certain no moisture remains. Do not apply a flame to the face of the mold. When all moisture has completely evaporated, the mold can be retied with binding wire and the pouring operation can go ahead as previously described. Remember *never* to pour molten metal into a moist or damp mold. The resulting steam will violently drive the molten metal up out of the mold, scattering it around with possible injury to the worker.

A Second Silicate-Borax Method

Mix equal parts of silicate of soda and borax with enough water to make the mixture fluid. This mixture is applied to the impression as previously mentioned, but in a single operation. When the mixture begins to dry, dust the impression with a fine parting powder, such as used in sand casting, and reset the pattern in the mold. Press the two cuttlebones firmly together again, separate, and remove the pattern. A sharp impression should result. Bake dry, retie, and pour as previously described. Before retying, care should be taken to clear the air vents previously cut in the faces of the mold halves with the scriber.

SAND CASTING

Sand casting can be used instead of cuttlebone casting for the production of rings or any small cast parts needed in jewelry work. Models used can be commercial rings or patterns fabricated from fairly hard, close-grained wood, such as cherry or maple. Plastic wood can be used. In making a model, the hole needed for a finger is bored to suitable size, and the shape of the ring is jigsawed around it. Files and a knife are used for shaping. The wooden model should be given several light coats of shellac. Each coat should be rubbed down with fine steel wool when dry before the next coat is applied. The final coat is rubbed perfectly smooth to make easy withdrawal from the mold possible. As in the case of cuttlebone casting, avoid undercut models, for these cannot be removed from the sand without destroying the mold.

The Flask

The major part of the molding equipment consists of the molding flask. This is in two parts—a cope and a drag (Fig. 66). Such equipment can be bought commercially but is easily made in the shop. Both cope and drag consist of portions of brass tubing about 4" in diameter and 2" in length. For best results the tubing should be accurately faced in a lathe to assure a close union when cope and drag are assembled prior to pouring. Draw a circle equal to the outside diameter of the tubing on a sheet of paper, and draw a diameter line through the circle. Place the tubing in position on the circle. The ends of the diameter line indicate the positions for the "ears" on the drag. The two ears are made of flat brass stock about 3/16" thick sawed to shape and soldered to the tubing. The holes, either 1/8" or 3/16" in diameter, are drilled in line with the diameter of the tubing. The drilled hole should be close enough to the tubing wall to make contact with it.

The cope half of the tubing should be clamped in alignment with the drag half and two short rods of proper diameter inserted into the ear holes, so that part of each rod rests against the side of the cope (Fig. 67). The portion of the rod resting on the cope is soldered permanently to the cope, and the flask is complete.

Fig. 66.   A commercial sand-casting outfit.

The Mandrels

Two types of mandrels are used for the casting outfit. The round mandrel bears the ring model. Therefore, a size must be available to fit the ring used as a pattern or model. This mandrel can be of wood dowel or metal, turned in the lathe. Its *length* should be about 1" less than the inside diameter of the flask. A line can be drawn or scribed across the diameter of each end and along the sides of the mandrel to indicate the halfway mark when it is sunk into sand. Two lines can be drawn or scribed around the circumference of the round mandrel, about ¾" in from each end. These lines indicate the position for the ring model or models used. This position will insure alignment with the sprue holes.

The split mandrel is used in conjunction with the sprue pins in preparing the drag half of the mold (Fig. 68). A round mandrel split in two along its length will form two split mandrels. A saw can be used for this. The flat portion of the split mandrel must be perfectly level. It should be made of the same diameter stock as the round mandrel used for the particular ring model selected. The length of the round mandrel and the split mandrel should be exactly the same.

Rest the split mandrel flat on the work table and measure in from each end exactly ¾". Bore holes about halfway through the split mandrel at these points. These holes should be bored to receive the narrow ends of the sprue pins, which should stand vertically when inserted.

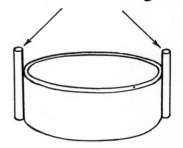

Pins soldered in place to engage with "ear" on Drag

Fig. 67.

A - Sprue Pins
B - Half-Mandrel (or Split-Mandrel)
C - Molding Board
D - Drag (half of the molding flask)
E - "Ear" on Drag

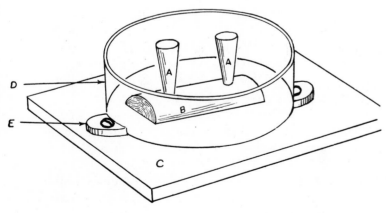

Fig. 68.

The Sprue Pin

The sprue pin forms the gate into which metal is poured for the casting. It can be turned of wood or metal, and its length should be such that it *protrudes above the upper edge of the drag by about ½"* when placed in position as in Figure 68. The diameter at the large end should be about ½"; at the small end, ³⁄₁₆".

The Molding Board

The molding board is merely for working convenience. It is about 8" square and about ½" thick. It can be a piece of plate glass, marble, or smooth hardwood.

The Sieve or Riddle

Casting sand is always sifted into the flask. This insures proper packing around the model and eliminates possible foreign matter such as bits of metal from previous pourings. The riddle can be a shallow, wooden, boxlike frame, somewhat larger in area than the flask opening and covered with ordinary metal window screening.

The Core Tube

The core tube can be a length of brass tubing. Its inside diameter is equal to the round mandrel in use and also equal to the mandrel in length. It must be smooth inside, with no sign of a burr on either end. It is used with a wooden dowel equal to its inside diameter and about double its length.

The Parting Powder

The parting powder insures easy parting of the cope from the drag or the mandrels from the sand. It is put into a small "pounce," or bag, made of cotton or an old flour bag. Shaking the bag over the area to be dusted will release sufficient parting powder to do the job.

The first step in preparing the mold is called "tempering" the sand. Very fine casting sand is used, such as Albany #00. Some craftsmen have had excellent results with the substitution of fine powdered pumice for the sand. The tempering is done by mixing the sand with enough water so that when a handful of sand is grasped and squeezed, a lump is formed showing clearly the impression of the inside of the closed hand. No water should be visible when squeezing is done. Break the lump with the fingers and watch for a clean, sharp break. Remember to avoid using too much water; this is dangerous because of the steam that may be formed when molten metal is poured into the mold. Naturally, after repeated use, the heat will dry out some of the water, so that retempering may be necessary. Sometimes glycerin is used in sand or pumice casting as a substitute for water. If glycerin is used, the test for properly tempered sand is the same as that for water-tempered sand. A commercially prepared sand is available which requires no tempering even after repeated use.

A split mandrel B of the required ring size (see Fig. 68) is now placed on the molding board C. If one ring is to be cast, place a sprue pin A in a hole on the split mandrel. If two rings are to be cast, which is economical as far as time is concerned, place a sprue pin in each hole on the split mandrel. Next, place the drag D in position on the molding board and dust a fine layer of parting powder over the parts inside the drag.

The drag is now to be filled with tempered sand. The sand is sifted down into the drag through a sieve or "riddle," pausing when the drag is about half full to pack the sand firmly but very carefully around the sprue pins. Continue to fill the drag to overflowing and pack the sand firmly when this is done. With a flat stick, such as a ruler, strike off the top of the drag so that the sand is level. Avoid jarring the protruding tops of the sprue pins.

Remove the sprue pins by turning them upward. Invert the flask gently on the clean molding board, and the flat bottom of the split mandrel will be seen. This can be removed by carefully sticking a sharp scriber into it and rapping the side of the scriber lightly to free the mandrel from the sand. Lift upward with the scriber and the mandrel will come with it. In place of this procedure, a little hole in the center of the split mandrel can be made to receive the end of a long screw, which may be substituted for the scriber. Any sand grains which have fallen in should be gently blown out.

The models of the rings to be cast are now placed on a round mandrel in proper position so as to be aligned with the sprue holes. Dust the impression in the drag lightly with parting powder, and press the round mandrel, bearing the rings, into the impression in the drag. The mandrel should fit into the impression, and the rings, with their fronts up, should add a further impression to that left by the split mandrel. This ring impression should be directly over the sprue holes. The round mandrel should, at this point, be sunken into the sand to its halfway point.

The cope is now aligned over the drag so that the pins at the sides of the cope enter the holes in the ears of the drag. The sand remaining exposed at this point, together with the mandrel bearing the rings, is dusted with a fine layer of parting powder. Complete the filling of the flask with sand by sifting sand into the cope, over the mandrel and rings. Pack the sand in firmly but carefully with the fingers. With a ruler strike the top off level, and lift the cope up off the drag, exposing the rings again. Remove the mandrel bearing the rings and gently blow out any sand particles that may remain in the impression. The cope and drag will each contain one-half of the impression of mold for the rings. A core must now be made to take the place of an empty mandrel in the mold, so that the only spaces left to receive molten metal will be those spaces left by the impressed rings.

A piece of tubing having an inside diameter equal to the diameter of the round mandrel is packed with the tempered sand. The length of this tubing is also equal to the length of the round mandrel. When the tubing is packed, a length of wooden dowel rod of the proper diameter is used to push out the sand core. This is done in such a way as to leave the core standing end-up on the work table. If the tubing is smooth and has no burr inside the two ends or openings, no difficulty should be encountered.

This core is carefully lifted and placed in the *cope* half of the flask, which should now be resting, impression upward, on the molding board. The *drag* half of the flask is now very carefully aligned over the cope and slipped into place. The mold is now complete, with the sprue holes, or gates, ready for the molten metal. Enough metal should be melted to fill the gates to the top. The melting and pouring procedure is identical to that used in cuttlebone casting. The worker should be careful to avoid having his face over the mold when pouring. When the red glow completely disappears from the metal in the sprue holes, the flask can be pulled apart, and the castings removed with a tongs. The procedure from here on is again similar to the procedure followed in cuttlebone casting.

DETERMINING AMOUNT OF METAL NEEDED FOR A CASTING

To determine the amount of metal needed in casting a ring, either of two methods may be used, depending on the circumstances. The first method is universal in that it covers practically all circumstances. This method involves the use of a glass graduate, such as used by chemists. This is a glass cylinder with a wide base that permits the cylinder to stand upright firmly. The cylinder is marked or graduated along its length. Measurements indicated are usually based on the metric system.

To use the graduate, partly fill it with water. Tie a piece of fine binding wire around the shank of the ring to be used as a model and lower it into the graduate. Note the level of the water as indicated on the scale of the graduate. Now remove the selected ring model and drop an amount of the metal to be used in casting into the cylinder. When the water level reaches the same point reached when the model was immersed, it is an indication that the amount of metal is sufficient to make a ring equal to the model. It must be remembered, however, that metal is melted in sufficient quantity to fill the sprue as well as the impression in the mold. This additional weight of metal in the sprue hole helps in securing a complete and perfect casting. Therefore, after it has been determined how much metal is necessary for the actual ring, additional metal may be measured out to raise the water level two or three times the height to which it was raised by the model. The amount is not critical and depends upon the size of the sprue hole or gate.

An example of measuring is given as follows: the graduate is filled to 30 cc. The ring model raises the level to 35 cc. The volume of the model is 5 cc. The model is removed and metal is substituted until the water again rises from 30 cc to 35 cc. To double this amount of metal, in allowing for the sprue, additional metal is added until the reading is 40 cc. If triple the amount is needed, the reading is raised to 45 cc.

If casting is frequently done, it may be found convenient to determine the actual amount of metal involved in filling the sprue or gate. Assuming that these gates are fairly constant in their size, all that is necessary is to keep the button formed during the first casting. This button, which is the metal attached to the ring and which extends to the top of the gate, can be measured for volume by immersion in the graduate. Then all that is necessary is to make a note of the amount of displacement in the graduate and add this to the displacement caused by any individual casting pattern or model.

The second method in determining the amount of metal needed is useful when an original ring or model is to be duplicated in the *same* metal as the model. For example, if a gold ring is being copied in a casting, the ring is placed on one pan of a balance scale, and sufficient gold is put into the other pan to equal the weight of the original model. The sprue metal, of course, is additional.

Some Notes on Melting Metal

The need for some knowledge concerning melting metals is readily comprehensible. Forms from sheet metal are sawed by the jeweler. The metals may be copper, nickel, bronze, silver, or gold. In the case of the nonprecious metals, the small shop rarely attempts to salvage any scrap other than pieces of sheet metals large enough to be useful in making small forms. When the precious metals, such as silver and gold, are involved, there is good reason to utilize filings as well as scraps from sawed forms and castings. These scraps should be collected and kept separately. They may be melted down and utilized in bulk pieces for castings, or they may be poured into lengths in preparation for rolling into sheet or flat strip form, as well as wire form. It is not the purpose of this book to give detailed data on metal refining. This work is not generally done by individual craftsmen, who are content to sell their scrap to refiners. However, scrap known to be all sterling or fine silver or all gold of equal karat can be readily melted without complicated equipment and reused with resulting savings that make the effort worthwhile.

Filings are known to the refining industry as "lemel." The word is a corruption of the French word for filings, *limaille*. Filings most frequently contain foreign matter—bits of steel from files and saw blades, scraps of copper, lead, brass, or other metals used in the shop. Filings often also contain abrasives from the polishing equipment. Grease from mechanical equipment is sometimes present. To prepare filings for the melting crucible, the filings can be boiled in a caustic solution and then rinsed. Iron filings can be removed from the cool lemel by use of a magnet. Presence of any quantity of other metals requires refining processes and need not be attempted by the small-scale craftsman. Abrasive materials will be taken care of in the slag that forms during melting.

Scrap strip silver or sheet silver should be clipped into small enough pieces to fit a crucible. Such scrap can be cleaned in the same manner as used for the filings. Care should be exercised to avoid including bits of old binding wire in the melt.

The crucibles used are generally sand crucibles. Graphite crucibles are frequently used in silver melting. These can withstand more heatings than sand crucibles. They are thicker, however, and require more heating.

When silver or gold scrap is to be melted, a gas-air furnace is generally used by the small-scale shop. A large gas-air torch may do, as described in the section on casting. At any rate, there must be melted, together with the scrap, a flux, such as borax or boric acid. Sometimes some powdered charcoal is added as well. The fluxes, added in powedered form. are helpful in purifying the molten metal.

Borax and boric acid fluxes tend to exclude oxygen from the metal. Fine silver and platinum absorb oxygen when in molten state. The oxygen is expelled as the metal cools. This will sometimes prevent a good casting: hence, the addition of borax and boric acid flux. Such fluxes also dissolve and separate oxides of base metals that may be present. Powdered glass has the same effect.

Another type of flux removes oxides already present in the melt. Such fluxes are powdered charcoal, pearl ash, and sugar. Dealers in equipment for jewelry casting generally stock a "reducer" flux which will work effectively to keep the molten metal in as clean a state as possible without chemical refining. These reducing agents are used with either gold or silver.

Platinum requires a very high temperature for melting—3191° F. Palladium also requires a high temperature. In order to melt these metals, oxygen or hydrogen from a tank must be used in conjunction with city gas. The torch must be able to withstand such heat, as should the crucible, which is usually of lime. It is not practical for the hand craftsman to concern himself with this type of work unless he utilizes these metals extensively. This is rarely the case, and further discussion is left for books on the subject of refining precious metals.

Stone Setting

13

The use of precious and semiprecious stones in handmade jewelry adds greatly to the color, interest, and beauty of one's work. Large, important-appearing stones are usually the basis of the design of a piece of jewelry (Fig. 69). Small stones frequently point up a design based primarily on the manipulation of the metal (Fig. 70). The various elements of a design should not vie with one another for interest; hence, stones are used only after considerable thought has gone into the design as a whole.

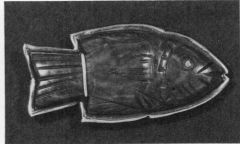

Fig. 69.   (a) A native-cut Mexican stone set with a rivet and tie-wire by the author; (b) linked bracelet containing square cabochon stones set in bezels. (L.W.)

Fig. 70. Mounted moonstones. (Anna Halasi)

Fig. 71. *Top*: 1. Carved and pierced; 2. Scarab; 3. Head; 4. Cameo. *Second Row*: 1. Flat, decorated; 2. Mosaic (Italian); 3. Cameo; 4. Chevee. *Large Center*: Scarab (Ivory). *Third Row*: 1. Oval cabochon; 2. Flat top (square); 3. Cabochon (oval); 4. Cushion (faceted). *Fourth Row*: 1. Flat top; 2. Cabochon (round); 3. Cushion (faceted); 4. Oval (faceted).

The most popular type of stone used for hand jewelry is the cabochon-cut type. Such a stone is cut to present a domed surface with a flat base. It is a popular type of cut for colorful semiprecious stones and is available in stones cut with square, round, and oval bases (Fig. 69b).

Flat, polished stones are also used, as well as the well-known, antique "scarab" style. Faceted stones are those cut with a multitude of geometrically arranged surfaces, accurately cut and polished on different planes. This type of cut is reserved for transparent stones and is responsible for the brilliance and "fire" in many otherwise less sensational stones. The faceted stone is not as frequently used in hand jewelry. One reason is that it looks its best in a delicate, pronged setting not too often used by craftsmen for hand jewelry. Another reason is that a faceted stone often requires only a setting; the stone itself comprises the actual jewelry. A group of various cut stones appears in Figure 71.

THE BEZEL

The bezel can be thought of as a low fence or rim around a stone with the upper edge turned in to prevent the loss of the stone. Bezels are made round, oval, square, or rectangular. A bezel setting is most popular for cabochon-cut stones, although it is used occasionally for multifaceted stones set very low in a ring. The bezel may be merely a low rim soldered to a flat surface to receive a stone. Frequently, however, the bezel contains an "inner bezel," or bearing surface, usually made of square or round wire, shaped, sized, and soldered so as to fit just inside the outer "holding" bezel. The purpose of this inner bearing is to provide a level, even base for the stone when the bezel itself has been altered to fit over a curved surface. At other times, a bezel is made high, either to raise the stone on a piece of jewelry or to allow for decorative treatment around the base of the bezel. A high bezel, however, requires the use of an inner bearing in order to prevent the stone from dropping deep into the setting.

The bezel is best made of fine silver, although sterling may be used. The advantage of the fine silver is its softness, making it easy to turn the bezel edge over the stone with a burnisher. Once burnished, the fine-silver bezel is sufficiently hard to withstand use. The fine silver is also less likely to melt when being soldered, a point important to the novice at hard soldering. Fine-silver sheet of No. 26 gauge can be used for the bezel. This can be cut with a small, sharp shears to the width required for the stone. The bearing can be No. 20 or No. 18 square or round sterling wire. Sometimes the bearing is cut from sheet sterling. No. 22 gauge can be used and, naturally, the width of the strip should be less than that of the bezel material. To determine the width of the bezel, consider a cabochon stone used in two ways. Figure 72*A* shows a stone set flat upon a surface with a low rim. No bearing is used. Figure 72*B* shows the stone set high, resting on an inner bearing. The bezel, of course, is much wider in this case. In either case just enough width should be given the bezel to permit the upper edge to be turned in over the curve of the stone, holding it firmly in place. The curve of the domed surface must be considered carefully and *only enough* bezel allowed to hold the stone. *Too much* metal will not turn in without puckering and will also tend to obscure the stone.

To measure the circumference of a stone, turn a piece of No. 24 or 26 binding wire around the stone at its girdle or widest diameter. Twist the ends tightly and remove the loop. Cut this loop and spread out as shown in Figure 73. This will give the length of the bezel. A rectangular stone can be measured for its bezel by ruling a line on a piece of paper. On this line, lay off, with a pair of dividers, the length of each side of the stone. If these lengths are laid off end to end, the total length will equal the length needed for a rectangular bezel. Solder the joint at the middle of any one side. Do not solder at a corner.

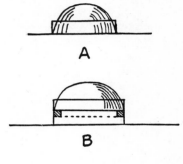

A

B

Fig. 72.

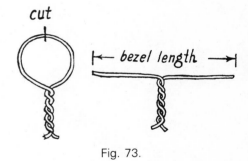

cut

bezel length

Fig. 73.

To solder a round or oval bezel, follow the soldering directions given in the section on bezel soldering. All that is necessary is to have the ends meet. The bezel may be shaped on a round mandrel after soldering has been done. Avoid using a greater length than necessary. The bezel diameter cannot be reduced without resoldering, but a bezel that is *slightly* undersize can be stretched by hammering it carefully over a mandrel using a rawhide mallet. Also, when only shaping is necessary, hammer the bezel on a mandrel with a rawhide mallet. A square bezel can be bent with flat, accurate pliers (see *Miscellaneous Small Tools*) or by carefully hammering the square corners over a square steel mandrel. The stone must be able to fit into the bezel from either side. A tapered mandrel will tend to form a tapering bezel. To avoid this, reverse the position of the bezel frequently on the mandrel while hammering or use a cylindrical mandrel such as round steel rod.

The Inner Bearing

The round inner bearing for a bezel can be made after determining the length needed to fit the inner circumference of the bezel. Square or round wire of No. 20 or 18 gauge can be used. The bearing is shaped to fit the inside of the bezel, and the ends are then soldered, employing a technique similar to that used in soldering the bezel. The two "rings" are then assembled, and if the fit is correct, the inner bearing is set at an appropriate level inside the bezel, with the soldered joint opposite that of the bezel. A loop of fine binding wire can be run once around the bezel and its ends twisted. This will prevent the bezel from opening. The two "rings" can then be bound together with light binding wire twisted in place at three different points. Cover the two joints with flux, run additional flux around the bearing inside the bezel, and space a few tiny squares of hard solder inside the bezel. Place the unit on a charcoal block, apply a gentle blue flame to dry the flux, and continue until the solder flows. Remove binding wire, and pickle. If too much solder has been used, the top of the

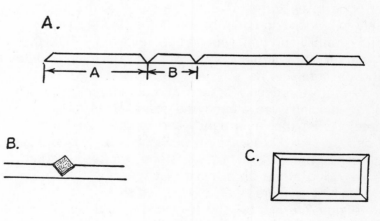

Fig. 74.

bearing surface may not present a clean right angle at the junction of bearing surface and bezel wall. The stone, therefore, may not rest evenly on the bearing. Remove any excess solder with a three-cornered hand scraper or a cylindrical, flat-bottomed burr, mounted in a sensitive drill. The use of round wire as an inner bearing will eliminate the aforementioned difficulty.

The square inner bearing can be made of square wire. In order to achieve a clean right angle, bend at each corner. The corners are mitered as shown in Figure 74. Before filing the miters, the proper length of each side must be marked off with a scriber. Figure 74 shows a rectangular inner bearing. Side *A* equals the inside length of the long side of the rectangle. Side *B* is the inside length of the short side of the rectangle. At each mark, on the opposite surface, a **V** is cut for the miter. A needle file having a square cross section is used, since the corner of the file will cut a 90-degree **V**. Note in the diagram, at *B,* how the file lies in the cut. The depth of the cut should be about three-quarters of the way through. The bearing can then be bent to fit inside the completed bezel. If the corner seems to pucker slightly and leaves a bump on the bearing surface, file the bump down flat. Loop a piece of binding wire around the *bezel* to secure the joint or touch it over with loam, and apply flux at each corner of the mitered *bearing*. Put a piece of solder at each corner of the bezel and apply the torch. Heat each corner so that the solder seals the miter and also unites the bezel to the inner bearing. Remove wire, pickle, and clean up bearing surface if necessary.

An Alternate Bezel and Bearing Method

A bezel of any form—rounded or angular—can be made together with the inner bearing if reasonable care is taken. Refer to Figure 75. The strip for the bezel is measured and cut in the usual way. A strip of sterling can then be cut (No. 22 gauge will do) and placed over the bezel strip as shown. Both pieces should lie perfectly flat. A rawhide mallet used *gently* will help flatten the metal. Flux and clipped solder are now applied. The two pieces are hard-soldered and then pickled. The narrow strip provides the inner bearing surface. Bend the bezel to shape, remembering not to judge the inside diameter from the *bearing wall* but from the inner *bezel wall.* The two ends should meet, showing no light. Solder as described in the section on bezel soldering. If a square or rectangular bezel is being made, lay off the sides with a scriber and file through the piece comprising the *bearing.* Use a square needle file, as previously described. Bend the notched strip to form the complete bezel and bearing. Tie with binding wire. Apply flux and a piece of solder inside each corner and heat until solder flows. Remove wire, and pickle. Clean the bearing surface with scraper or burr, if necessary. A prepared "stepped" bezel strip is available commercially.

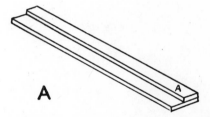

A

The narrow edge of strip A will become the bearing surface for the stone

Cut-away view of bezel formed of strip

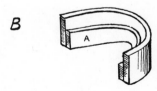

B

Fig. 75.

SETTING THE STONE

The stone is never set until *all* heating and chemical treatments have been completed. Sometimes the polishing may be completed before the stone is set, but if the setting is of a delicate type, avoid polishing it until the stone is set.

The Burnisher

The burnisher is held as shown in Figure 76. The jewelry may be held in the fingers. A ring may be held in a ring clamp. The bezel edge is turned in lightly at first. Pressure is then increased until the bezel hugs the stone tightly. If the burnisher does not seem to move smoothly over the bezel, the surface of one or the other may need to be cleaned. If cleaning does not solve the problem, moisten the burnisher with soapy water before using. It is *imperative* that the burnisher be wiped thoroughly dry when its work is completed in order to prevent the highly polished surface from rusting.

The Setting Tool

Sometimes a stubborn bezel or prong will not turn in under pressure of the burnisher. A stone-setting tool is then used. This tool is similar to a chasing tool of square cross section, with the end ground off flat. Mount the ring in a ring clamp, which can be set in a vise. Hold the flat end of the setting tool against the bezel or prong. Tap the top of the tool *lightly* with the flat face of a

Fig. 76. Burnishing a bezel.

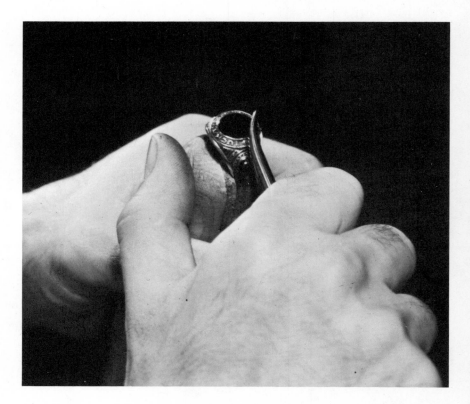

chasing hammer. Do this at four opposing points and then completely around the bezel. Follow this with the burnisher. If the setting tool has left any marks, remove them with a very fine file or a Scotch stone before burnishing. If the stone is being set in a piece of flat jewelry, the piece may be temporarily held on a shellac stick or in a pitch pan until the use of the setting tool is no longer necessary. A shellac stick can be made by joining a piece of ¼" plywood, measuring about 1½ × 2", to a piece of ¾" or 1" dowel (see Fig. 77). Use two long brads to fasten the two pieces together. Melt a mixture composed of flake shellac and sealing wax in equal parts over the top of the plywood to a depth of about ⅛". Warm the shellac compound to mount a piece of flat work as well as to remove it. When necessary, any small bits of shellac that may adhere to work are removable by washing with alcohol.

A small-diameter dowel tipped with the shellac or pitch compound can be used to lift a small stone out of a bezel. This is sometimes necessary when a stone is placed in a bezel to check its fit, since the smooth surface of the stone makes grasping with the fingers difficult.

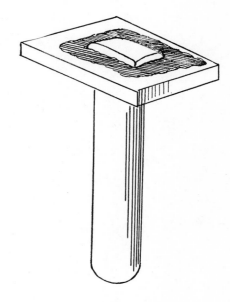

Fig. 77.

The Bezel Backing

When transparent or translucent stones are used in a piece of jewelry, a portion of metal behind the stone and inside the bezel area is usually removed. This piercing, the purpose of which is to allow the passage of light through the stone, is done with the jeweler's saw, except in the case of tiny settings on which a small drill can be used. The metal is removed, when possible, after the bezel has been soldered in place. If the design of the piece makes this impossible, the area to be removed under the setting must be carefully figured out beforehand and then cut.

On many pieces of jewelry using opaque stones, metal is removed in back of the stone to reduce the weight of the piece. A brooch that is too heavy will hang awkwardly. Also, in the case of precious metals, material may be saved by removing unnecessary metal.

Fitting a Bezel to a Curved Surface

When it is necessary to fit a bezel to a curved surface, as in a bracelet or a ring, assemble the bezel in the usual way but make allowance for the contour of the curved backing when calculating the width of the bezel band. Refer to Figure 78. View *A* shows the position of the stone on its bearing surface. The back of the stone must clear the curve of the ring below. The appearance of the fitted bezel is shown in a side view at *B*. To fit the completed bezel to the curved object, a half-round file can be used. Check the progress of the curve frequently. No light will show when a job is properly fitted.

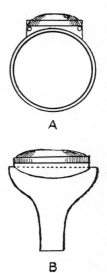

Fig. 78.

A simple way to secure a well-fitted bezel on a ring involves the use of a mandrel. Place a piece of No. 0 emery cloth over the mandrel at the portion equalling the ring curve. The abrasive side of the cloth faces upward. Rub the bezel carefully over this, along the proper axis if the bezel is not a perfect square or circle, until the curve is made to fit the ring. To save time, start the curve with a small half-round file and finish by rubbing on the emery-faced mandrel. Reverse the position of the bezel regularly during the rubbing process to compensate for the taper of the ring mandrel. Rub until a perfect fit is obtained but be careful not to go past the inner bearing.

Dome Setting

An unusual type of setting utilizing a hemisphere of fine silver is particularly effective in some applications. Figure 79 shows a pin in which star sapphires are set in tiny domes, reversed to receive the stones. This setting is recommended for cabochon-cut stones. Punch the required size disc out of 26-gauge fine silver.

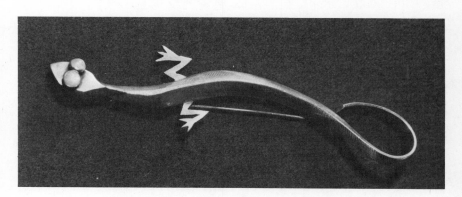

Fig. 79. A cup burnisher was used to set these stones. (L.W.)

Using a dapping die or lead plate with the proper dapping punch, make a small dome or hemisphere. Clean this for hard soldering and put a small jump-ring inside the cup of the dome, choosing a size which leaves a small rim of metal showing above the ring. This rim becomes the bezel (see Fig. 80). Flux the ring, place a square of solder where the ring touches the side of the dome, and solder, using a small blue flame. The dome will also be annealed during this operation, as red heat is reached.

Annealing is necessary as the metal hardens during the "punch and dome" operation. After the dome is soldered (point x) to its position on the work and all other heating has been completed, the stone, seated on the jump-ring, can be burnished in place. A cup burnisher (Fig. 81A) of proper size is worked over the rim, and the stone is set.

Claw, or Prong, Settings

A type of setting usually reserved for faceted stones utilizes small projections of metal spaced at intervals around the circumference to hold the stone in place. Such settings are known as

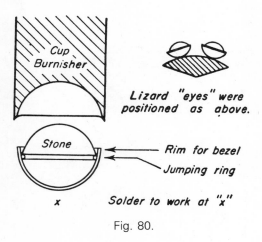

Fig. 80.

claw, or prong, settings. They are very commonly seen on commerical rings, where they frequently hold diamonds. Obviously, then, such a setting, properly made, is quite serviceable. The advantage of such a setting is that it exposes as much of the gem as is possible. This exposure is not so much ostentation as it is intelligent workmanship. Such a setting permits light to strike the many facets that are cut on the *bottom* of the stone as well as on the top, resulting in a brilliance unattainable by walled-in settings.

Figure 82 shows a cast ring in several stages of preparation for receiving a faceted stone. The ring is filed to shape as in *A*. The top surface follows the general shape of the stone and is equal in size to the stone at its girdle. At exact center a hole is bored through the ring. The drill should be somewhat smaller than the stone. At this point the grooves are cut that form the separate claws. It is wise to paint the top portion of the ring with a machinist's blue layout stain in order to carefully scribe the outline of the prongs before filing. Use needle files to form the prongs. The tiny rattail or round file cuts the grooves or channels. Be careful to avoid cutting away the tops of the prongs, thus making the setting too wide for the stone.

When the prongs are fairly well formed, a burr of the proper size is inserted in a hand drill or flexible shaft (Fig. 83). The ring is held in a vise, protected by copper or wood cheeks. If a sensitive drill is used, a small drill press vise can hold the ring. Bore into the hole in the ring with the burr to form a seat for the stone. Note that the burr will cut a straight-walled section on the upper part of the prongs. The rest of the seating will follow the angle of the bottom of the stone. Test for fit. When the stone fits the setting with the girdle or widest rim *very slightly* below the tops of the prongs, the seat is of correct size. Finish off the prongs carefully, filing them thin on top without removing any length. Check again with the stone. If satisfactory, clean up the prongs with a very fine abrasive paper or cloth and *carefully* polish them.

Fig. 81. (A) cup burnishers; (B) stone setting burrs.

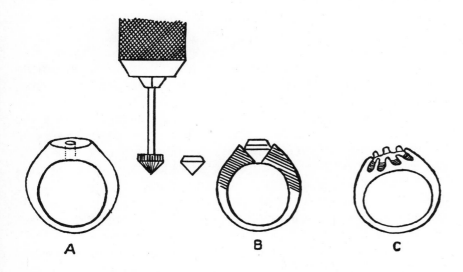

A   B   C

Fig. 82.

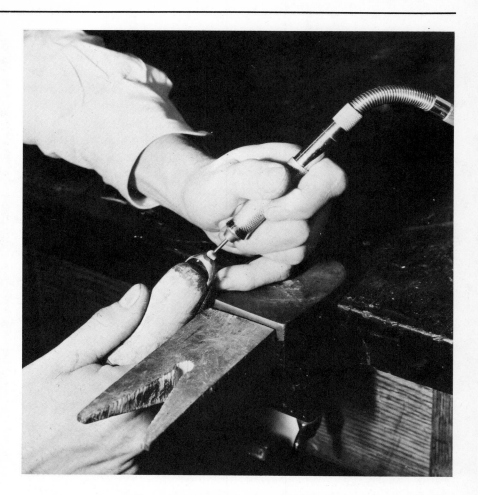

Fig. 83. Using the burr in a flexible shaft machine.

Fig. 84.

Now set the stone, turning the thin-filed prong tops down over the stone with a burnisher. Turn down one prong, then the prong directly *opposite.* Carefully finish polishing the entire ring, wash with soapy water, blow dry, and use polishing chamois skin.

NOTE: The stone must *not* be set in such a way as to permit the point at the stone's base to extend through the ring, touching the wearer's finger.

Claw Settings of Sheet Metal

When rings are built up of sheet metal and wire, decorative claw settings that form an integral part of the design can be used. Such settings are well adapted to faceted stone usage.

The diagrams in Figure 84 show such settings in the round and rectangular forms. A small, *tapering* bezel is formed. The slope of the taper is not nearly as extreme, however, as the base of the stone. The height of the bezel should be slightly more than the height of the stone from the point at the base to the girdle. The gauge of the metal used depends upon the size of the stone. Such bezels are of somewhat heavier metal than "ring" or "collar" bezels. Weights up to No. 16 gauge may be used.

When the bezel is shaped and soldered, a series of holes can be laid out around its "waist." Saw piercing may be done but is difficult because of the cramped working space. Whittle a wooden dowel to a taper so as to accommodate the bezel. Slip the bezel over the wooden "mandrel" so formed and lightly center-punch wherever a hole is to be drilled. Place the wooden "mandrel" in a vise with the bezel, extending horizontally, and drill at each center-punched mark.

When drilling has been completed, make an inner bearing out of No. 22 or 24 wire. This will support the stone just under its girdle and prevent it from canting in the setting. Set this inner ring in place. It should leave exposed enough of the upper bezel to allow for the prongs. Test for fit by placing the stone in the setting with the inner bearing in place. If satisfactory, hard-solder the bearing into the bezel.

Cover the exterior of the bezel with layout stain and mark out the claws or prongs. Make them all uniform and evenly spaced. File out the intervening spaces with a three-cornered needle file. File the claws carefully to reduce their thickness at the top, making it easier to burnish each claw over the stone. Continue to make the complete ring and, when all heating and polishing operations are completed, set the stone.

NOTE: Paper and glue may be used to make a model of the tapered bezel.

When a satisfactory size has been made, cut through the seam and use as a pattern for the metal bezel.

The Gypsy Setting

Occasionally, a round stone of the cabochon type is set into the surface of a piece of metal without a bezel. This is done by boring or carving a recessed area in the metal. Such settings are generally found on cast rings. The top of such a ring is shaped so that it is similar to the base of the stone in shape but just barely oversize. The outline of the stone is then scratched on top of the ring and a small hole bored through the center. A burr of the required size with an obtuse point is used to bore out the recess (Fig. 85A). The depth to which the boring is done depends on the curvature of the stone. If a high-domed stone is used, the depth is somewhat greater than would be necessary for a shallow stone. In any case, the stone does not sink very deeply into the recess in this type of setting. The base of the stone is supported at the angle formed by the pointed portion of the burr. The stone is set with the setting tool, which is tapped with a chasing hammer in order to "upset" the rim of the recessed setting over the stone. All marks are then filed away and the metal gone over with a burnisher.

Sometimes a setting similar to the "gypsy" type is used with this difference: the recess is made larger than the girdle of the stone to the extent made necessary by an inserted bezel. The edge of the bezel extends very slightly above the top of the ring after it has been soldered into place. After the stone has been placed into its setting, this protruding rim is burnished over the stone (Fig. 85B).

NOTE: When "gypsy" or similar settings are made on relatively thin gauge metals, the recess may be carved out by engraving

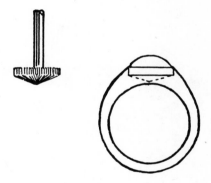

Fig. 85A.

Fig. 85B.

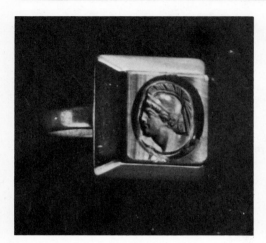

Fig. 86. This stone was set by expansion-fit, a rather precarious method. The opening for the stone is just slightly undersize. The ring is heated, and the expanded opening is pressed over the overturned stone. (L.W.)

tools instead of a burr. The outline of the recess is cut with a small "point" graver. The center of this setting can be removed by piercing if a translucent or transparent stone is used.

Boring Holes in Stones

Sometimes an ornament is to be mounted on the surface of a stone. The use of a cement is not workmanlike nor is it permanent. The best method is to hard-solder a tiny piece of tubing to the ornament. The tubing is then passed through a hole bored in the stone. The end of the tubing is permitted to extend slightly past the underside of the stone. It is then "spread" or burnished over the underside of the stone, making a permanent union between stone and ornament.

Soft stones can be scratched with a file. Such stones may be drilled with a fine, high-speed twist drill or a dentist's diamond drill. The drills should be used at high speeds and lubricated with turpentine or water at the point of drilling.

Hard stones can be drilled with an improvised drill consisting of a piece of hollow tubing and an abrasive. The tubing selected need not be particularly hard, since it merely carries the cutting abrasive.

To use the tubing, "upset" it on its working end by slightly hammering it with a flat hammer squarely on its end. The end will thereby become slightly enlarged, permitting it to rotate freely in the hole it bores. The abrasive, into which the "drill" end is occasionally dipped, may be Norbide (Norton Abrasive Co.) or a silicon carbide grit of fine grain. The abrasive grit is mixed liberally with a bit of petroleum jelly. The resultant compound is applied to the end of the hollow "drill." Occasionally, add a bit of light lubricating oil while drilling. Use a high-speed sensitive drill. The size of the hole bored should equal the diameter of the tubing used for mounting the ornament. The stone can be held in place on a board during the boring operation with a drop of chaser's pitch or melted flake shellac. This method of boring is frequently used to bore holes in glass vessels. Diamond drills, used by jewelers as well as dentists, are very effective for drilling hard stones.

Wire Working

14

A supply of wire of different gauges should be kept in stock, since it provides an almost endless source of decorative or ornamental material. Wire need not be kept in all gauges if the worker wishes to make use of a drawplate. Wire should be kept in various shapes (cross-sectional), such as round, half-round, and square. Drawplates are again useful here, but a supply of the various wires will save much time and labor. Fancy "gallery" wire bears the same relation to jewelry work as wood molding does to the woodworker. Such wires are obtainable at the larger jewelry supply houses and are invaluable as decorative additions around stone settings, pin borders, etc.

Ordinary square and round wire have possibilities for decoration and construction that will be dealt with in the remainder of this chapter.

Twisting Wire

Round wire can be twisted to obtain a variety of effects. The technique of twisting the wire is simple. A piece of wire twice the required length is bent at the center and doubled, yielding a double wire half the original length. Remember in computing the length to allow about an inch for waste. This waste is the somewhat distorted wire remaining at the ends of the finished twist. A hand drill is used as the twisting device for wires up to No. 16 gauge. Beyond this gauge, it may be necessary to use a carpenter's brace or a spool and rod, as explained further on. A hook, such as a common cup hook, is inserted in the drill chuck. The two original wire ends, now side by side, are clamped tightly for a distance of approximately ½" in the side of a vise. The loop formed at the other end by doubling the wire is caught on the cup hook. Hold the handle of the drill so as to keep the wire tautly horizontal, and turn the handle slowly, twisting the wire (Fig. 87). The best twists are fairly close, reaching a point where the re-

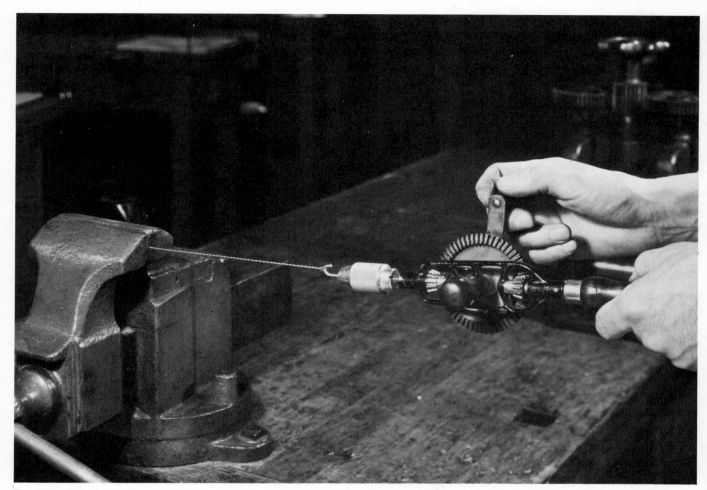

Fig. 87.   Twisting wire with the aid of a hand drill.

Fig. 88.   Twisting heavy wire with rod and spool.

sulting work loses the appearance of two wires and assumes a ropelike decorative effect. Too much twist, which can be felt as the wire resists the twisting, may snap the wire. If more than one twisted length is to be used side by side, remember the direction in which the drill was rotated. By reversing the second twisted length and laying it next to the first, a herringbone effect is obtained. To twist heavy gauge wire, insert a heavier hook in the chuck of a carpenter's brace and work in a manner similar to the hand-drill technique. A spool and rod may be used for twisting light or heavy gauge wires. The wire is looped, as previously, clamped in the vise, and a spool is slipped over the doubled length. A slim rod of steel or iron, such as a long, heavy nail, is put through the loop. One end of the nail is left protruding as a turning handle. The spool is held snugly against the nail, keeping the wire taut (see Fig. 88).

Further Processing the Wire

Twisting the wire is only the first step in a series of decorative effects that can be obtained by further processing of the twist. The twist may be hammered so as to flatten it on two sides. This is done with a polished flat hammer. The wire rests on a smooth steel plate. Excessive hammering will yield a thin, easily broken tracery of wire that is usable only as appliqué. Such work must be carefully annealed if it is to be bent, otherwise many fragments will result. A twist can also be rolled flat in the rolling mill. This yields an effect slightly different than that obtained by hammering. The reason is that the rolling mill squeezes the metal ahead of the roller, resulting in a spiral having a lengthened appearance (Fig. 89).

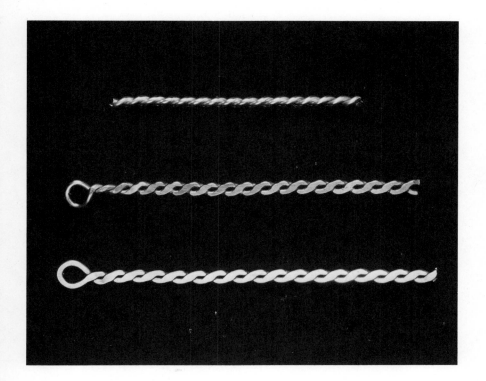

Fig. 89. Twisted wire (top); hammered twist (center); rolled twist (bottom).

When hammering a twist, the flattening effect is to be obtained gradually, working back and forth along the length of the wire. If heavy gauge wire is being worked, anneal occasionally to avoid breakage. Also anneal before forming a circle for a bracelet. The breakage is caused by the twisted wires crossing over each other. When they are hammered, the wires cut into each other, forming many possible points of breakage. Frequent annealing will eliminate the brittleness and consequently the breakage.

Squaring the Wire

When wire from 6 to 10 gauge is used, it can be hammered square after twisting. This is done by hammering on a steel plate to form the two opposite flat sides. Do not hammer very flat at this point, but turn the work as soon as flats appear. The remaining two sides are then hammered. Anneal and work carefully over all four surfaces until a perfectly square cross section results. When this is done, the result is an excellent material for forming bracelets, cuff links, earrings, and brooches (see Fig. 14).

The Drawplate and Twists

Twists can be drawn through various types of drawplates so as to obtain square, oval, or half-round effects. Remember to anneal frequently. A tendency of the wire to separate at the ends can be overcome by hard-soldering the end of the twist to be fed into the drawplate hole. This end is then easily filed to a point and threaded through the plate holes. Twisted wire drawn through the common round-hole drawplate results in a twist of an entirely different character.

Triple Twists

A length of wire can be divided into thirds and folded, making a three-strand piece. Such a length of wire may be clamped in a vise, but if difficulty is encountered in keeping three ends in the drill chuck (no hook is used), solder the chuck end of the wire for a distance of approximately ¼''.

This twist is quite decorative and may be treated by hammering or drawing, yielding a fine material for bracelets and finger rings. Such a twist, bordered on each side with a slightly heavier length of square wire, will produce a lovely finger ring or bar pin.

Single Wire Twists

Wire having a rectangular or square cross section can be twisted to good effect without doubling the length. The method is similar to that used for other twists. The sample in Figure 90, showing alternate twist and plain sections, was made by using a pair of small open-end adjustable wrenches.

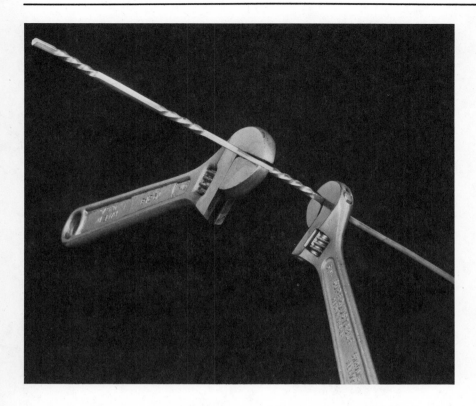

Fig. 90. Twisted sections of square wire.

Joining Ends on Twist Circles

When twists are used to form rings or bracelets, the ends to be joined must be matched so as to hide the location of the joint. To do this, saw off the waste ends as shown in Figure 91, after which the ends can be joined by hard soldering. Wire solder is useful for this type of work (Fig. 14).

Final touching up of the joint with a needle file will result in a joint difficult to detect even upon close examination.

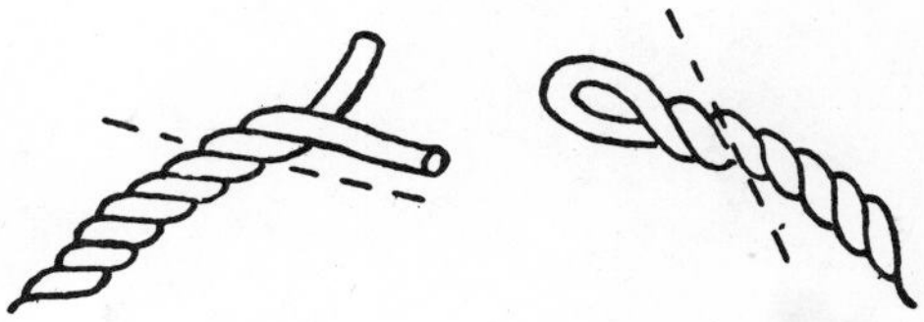

Fig. 91.

Links and Chains

Chains can be made of silver wire for use as bracelets or neck-laces. While chain is available in commercial form for holding pendant jewelry, much more imaginative chain can be fabricated by making a study of the many possible link forms that can be combined to make up a chain.

Simple circular links can be made by winding a close coil of wire around a rodlike mandrel, such as a heavy nail. The diameter of the mandrel will determine the size of the link. The shape of the link may be varied by utilizing mandrels of various cross-sectional shapes.

In order to insure a tightly wound coil, some workers utilize the following method: a narrow slot is made in the end of the mandrel to be used, or a hole may be drilled in its stead. The wire coil is started by inserting the end of the wire in the slot or the hole. A few tight turns are made, and the started coil is then placed, together with the mandrel, between the wood-lined jaws of a vise. Moderate pressure is applied, and the mandrel is then rotated.

The wire is fed on the mandrel from a coil or length hanging below the vise (Fig. 92). To rotate the mandrel, any one of several methods may be used. A carpenter's brace can be used by fitting the free end of the mandrel to the chuck. Another method involves the hard soldering of a cross-piece to the end of the mandrel. The **T**-shaped device is easy to rotate by hand. The same results can be obtained by bending one end of the mandrel at right angles to the portion upon which the wire is being wound.

When the coil is removed from the mandrel, saw through one side of the coil, as shown in Fig. 93. A ring clamp may be used, as in the figure. In sawing, thread the blade through the coil and saw from the inside out. This will yield a quantity of single rings slit at one point. To open the links, use the method shown in Figure 20.

Fig. 92.   A jig for coiling wire for links.

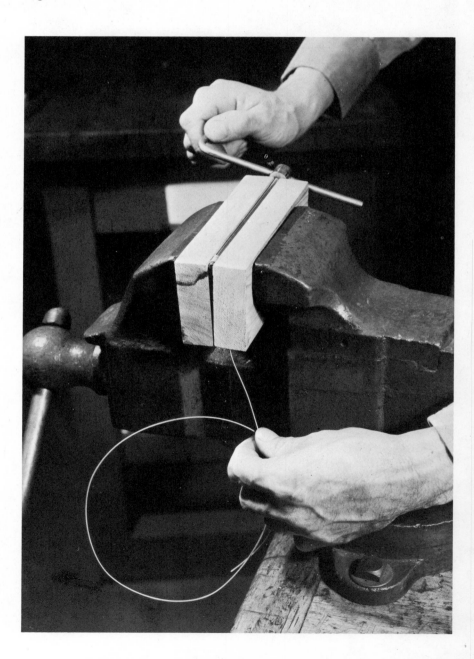

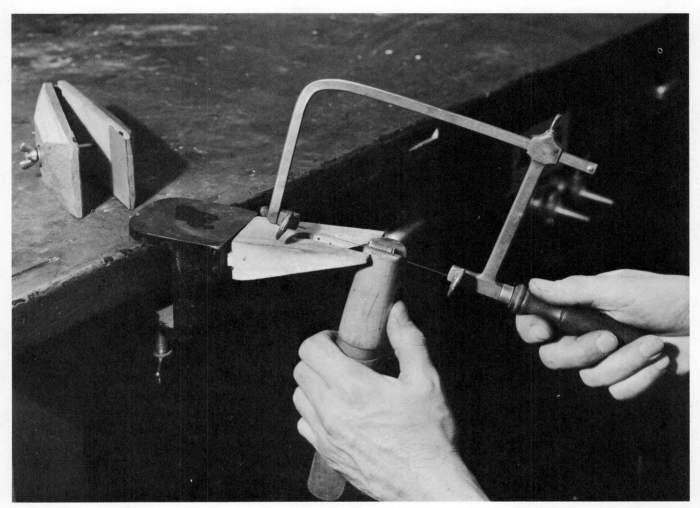

Fig. 93. Sawing open a coil to make individual links. A ring clamp may be used, or hinge clamps like those on the bench can be made.

If method *B* is used, it will be difficult to close the ring. A group of links may be closed and soldered. Wire-form solder may be used. After flux has been applied, heat the link to red heat and touch the joint of the link with the wire when the link glows. The group of closed links can then be consolidated by joining two closed links with a third open link. Solder this link. Such groups of three can be joined with additional open links, etc.

Several forms of chains are shown in Figure 94.

The connecting links shown at *E* (Fig. 94) can be made of round or half-round wire: three lengths are placed side by side on an asbestos block. (The wire pieces must be absolutely straight or considerable difficulty will be encountered during soldering. To make straight lengths of wire, clamp one end of a length in a vise, grip the other end with a draw tongs or heavy pliers, and pull hard.) The straight lengths are placed side by side. A brush dipped in flux is drawn along the length of the wires. The flux will be drawn into the crevices formed by the junction of the wires. Place tiny pieces of solder at ½'' intervals and heat the entire assembly. The wire can be held in place by using a staple having the shape of a **U** with a flattened base at each end. Such a staple form may also be made of stiff binding wire (see Fig. 95).

Fig. 94.

Fig. 95. Hard-soldering parallel sections of wire.

The resulting stock, composed of the three-wire lengths can be cut to proper lengths, and links formed. Do not attempt to make such lengths greater than 5'' or 6''. Longer lengths of wire are difficult to place in parallel groups.

The wire links shown in the necklace in Figure 96 can be made by driving nails, spaced properly in parallel lines, into a block of wood. The heads should be removed from the nails to facilitate the removal of a link. Bend the wire around the shank of each nail to form the links, which are later closed by hard soldering. The links are soldered at the ends and at points where wires cross over. The completed units are connected with ordinary circular links. The alternate solid units may be decorated with stones or applied details.

Fig. 96. Necklace. Such links can be made with a nail jig, as described in the text.

WIRE PROJECTS

Rings

Endless designs will suggest themselves once the craftsman has attempted a few formed principally of wire. Figure 97 shows two popular rings formed entirely of wire. A piece of wire, No. 16 or 14 gauge and about 4'' long, is knotted in the center. One end of the knotted wire is grasped with a heavy pliers or draw tongs. The other end is held in a vise. Pull the wire to partially close the knot. The second wire is inserted through the partially closed knot and then knotted to form the double-knot ring. Both wires should be pulled in turn to make the knots identical in size. The shank portion of the ring is soldered after being squeezed parallel. The ring is then bent on a mandrel to the proper size. The knot is flattened somewhat by hitting lightly with a fiber or rawhide mallet. Saw the ends square and solder. Clean up the joint with a fine needle file if necessary, true up the ring on a mandrel, and polish.

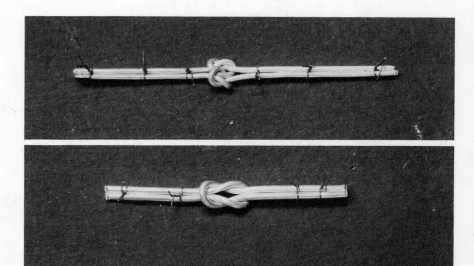

Fig. 97. Two knot rings tied with binding wire in preparation for hard soldering.

Open-End Bracelet

A heavy bracelet consisting principally of twisted wire can be made by referring to Figure 98. The twisted and square wires are soldered to a base consisting of a piece of flat silver, No. 18 gauge, about 6½'' in length including the shaped ends. The wires applied are the following:

1. A length of wire or strip, half-round in cross section, and at least ⅛'' wide
2. A length of No. 18 round wire, doubled and tightly twisted (this length may be slightly flattened by hammering)
3. A length of square No. 16 wire
4. Similar to No. 2 but twisted in opposite direction
5. May be any large unit, elaborate or otherwise (Fig. 98 shows a coil of No. 18 round wire, hammered with rawhide mallet so as to lie fairly flat.)

Following this is a repetition of group 1-2-3-4 reversed. A strip of flat silver, No. 20, covers the ends of the wires, overlapping slightly, to the underside. This piece may be chased or left plain. The whole can be shaped on a bracelet mandrel after all hard soldering has been completed.

An alternative to the coiled center unit can be made by utilizing two strands of twisted No. 18 wire. These two strands are re-twisted into one high, decorative, central unit.

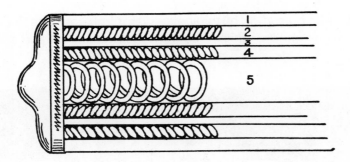

Fig. 98.

Bangle Bracelet

A beautiful bangle bracelet can be made by twisting strands of No. 16 wire to form a herringbone pattern. Two lengths are twisted, remembering to twist each the same number of turns and *reversing* the direction of the twist on the second strand. The two twists are soldered together, side by side, with ⅛" diameter shot mounted as shown in Figure 99. Square **U** staples will aid in keeping the twists flat. When joining the two ends of the formed bracelet, coat the bracelet liberally with yellow ochre, leaving only the ends clean.

Fig. 99.

Clip-on Type Bracelets

Figure 100 shows a group of very decorative clip-on bracelets. An analysis of the procedures used follows.

Left row; top: Three lengths of No. 10 silver wire soldered parallel. Ends cut off square.

Left row; center: Length of No. 14 round, doubled and twisted. A second length of same, doubled and twisted in *opposite* direction. Middle wire is No. 10 square. Three lengths soldered parallel. Ends cut square and slightly rounded.

Left row; bottom: Two lengths of No. 10 square, separated by a single length of No. 10 square twisted with carpenter's brace.

Right row; top: Two lengths of No. 10 square are rolled or hammered, reducing thickness slightly, but resulting in a broader top surface. A length of No. 14 or No. 12 round is doubled and twisted by spool method or brace, then rolled or hammered flat and to same thickness as "square" wires. The ends of this bracelet were treated by a method favored by some Mexican craftsmen.

A powerful flame is concentrated on an end until it melts and the wire ends flow together. (The rest of the bracelet might be protected by laying a magnesium soldering block over it.) The solid end is then filed to a desirable, slightly tapering shape, and a pair of crosslines filed where the solid merges with the wire shape.

Right row; center: A "ribbon" of No. 18 sheet, ⅜" wide, is coiled around a piece of No. 8 copper or silver round wire. A length of No. 18 round is doubled and twisted. The resulting "twist" is then wound into the ribbon spaces. The ends may be soldered or melted as previously described.

Right row; bottom: This bracelet was filed from a solid silver bar ⁵⁄₁₆" wide and ³⁄₁₆" thick. The sections are laid out and wirelike

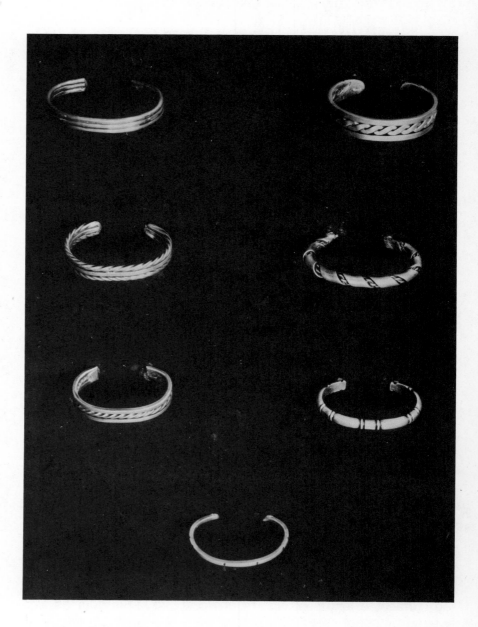

Fig. 100. A group of bangle bracelets. (Frank Frost)

separators filed first. The long ovals are filed next, and then the half-sectioned octagonal form (midpoint).

The last bracelet on the bottom of the plate is simply a piece of No. 10 square wire with a few filed notches.

All bracelets are formed with a rawhide or fiber mallet on a bracelet mandrel, after wire working and end soldering have been completed. Polishing and antiquing complete the bracelet.

Forming Whorls of Wire

Whorls, or flat coils of wire, are useful as decorations to be applied, or they may form in themselves pieces of jewelry such as earrings, cuff links, or bracelets (Fig. 101A and B). These whorls can be formed by various methods but the simplest and most satisfactory involves the use of a small hand vise. First, prepare a surface upon which the wire coil can rest during winding. This can be done easily by securing a small coin, preferably of nickel because of its hardness. Rub one surface on a piece of No. ½ emery cloth placed faceup on a surface plate. This will yield a disc with one smooth working face. Drill a hole through the center of this coin large enough to permit the entry of the size wire to be used for coils. Now, with the jeweler's saw, cut a path to the center hole, reverse, and cut out to the edge of the coin again, leaving a slot wide enough to permit removing the coin from the wire if double coils are to be wound, such as are needed for the whorl bracelet.

To form whorls, use *annealed* wire. Most wire is purchased in this form. Pass one end of the wire through the center of the disc and double that end over for a distance of approximately ¼". This prevents the wire from slipping in the vise jaws. Now tighten this end in the center of the vise jaws and slide the disc against the top of the jaws, smooth side up. Carefully start the center of the whorl. It is at this point that the greatest tendency for the wire to break exists. Hold the hand vise as shown in Figure 102 and wind the coils, rotating the vise in the hands as the work proceeds. To avoid breakage, wind the wire about the coil as the vise is turned rather than relying on the rotation of the vise alone to form the coils. After the required number of turns, the coil can be slightly flattened and stiffened by tapping its surface lightly with a smooth, polished hammer against the nickel disc. The whorl can be removed from the vise, and the under-end cut off. These whorls may be slightly cupped by working them into the hollow of a dapping die or by shaping in a lead block. Shot can be applied at the center of the whorl, if desired, for further decoration.

The whorl bracelet illustrated in Figure 103 consists of links. A length of wire, No. 18 or 20, approximately 8" in length is cut. A coil is wound on each end, consisting of about four or five turns. The slot in the disc used with the vise makes the removal of the disc possible. The coiled wire is then bent as shown in Figure 104A.

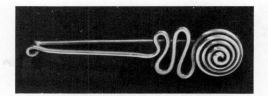
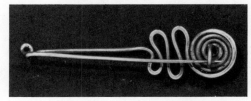

Fig. 101A and B.   An interesting pin made of a single piece of bronze wire.

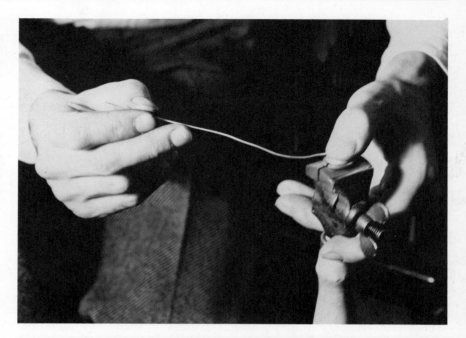

Fig. 102. Forming whorls of wire using a hand vise.

Fig. 103. A whorl, the end-links, and the bracelet.

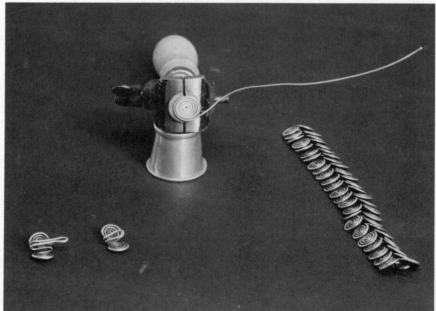

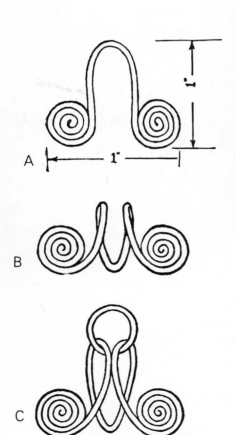

Fig. 104.

The distance across the coils is about 1''. The total height of the loop is the same. Next, bend the loop over in back of the coils (Fig. 104B). Enough of these links are made to provide a necklace or bracelet. The loop on each set of coils is inserted through the previous loop. When a chain of such links is complete, put a link through the top of the first set of coils. The last set of coils is wound from wire 1½'' longer than the previous lengths used. This provides enough material for the double-bent, final set of coils, as shown in the figure. A jump-ring links the two ends of the bracelet (Fig. 104C). The coils of this linkage are bent at a slight angle to each other, forming the sloping sides visible in the photograph of the finished bracelet.

Additional decorative effect can be secured by soldering a shot in the center of each coil. Antique the coils, rub with whiting for highlights, and give shot a high polish.

Figure 105 shows an Etruscan design for a link, originally of bronze wire. This is a combination of the whorl technique and the bending technique described elsewhere in this chapter (refer to the making of links such as shown in the necklace, Fig. 96). Six nails are used for this whorl-type link. Here again, the whorl may be used as is or may be decorated with shot at the center of each whorl.

Figure 106 shows a novel belt buckle devised by the author, which utilizes a length of No. 14 Sterling wire 4' in length. Essentially, the buckle is a rectangular coil consisting of eighteen turns of wire. The starting turn is bent to form a "tongue," as shown in the diagram. The final turn is bent at a right angle to the tubular body of the buckle and is positioned so as to be at the "bottom" of the buckle. The end of the coil is soldered closed at x after the buckle body is finally formed *and* soldered.

Forming is done around a metal mandrel consisting of a length of steel measuring 3/16" by 1" by about 8" in length. The corners must be carefully rounded with a file and smoothed and polished with emery. The length of the mandrel permits a portion of it to be clamped in a vise, leaving sufficient working length protruding on which the buckle can be formed. Sterling wire is normally supplied in an annealed state, so it can be wound firmly around the mandrel, occasionally helped, if necessary, by careful blows with a rawhide mallet. The beginning 1¼" of wire can be clamped in the vise alongside the mandrel. This facilitates winding and can be used later to form the "tongue" of the buckle. It should be protected from damage by the vise jaw by inserting a piece of ¼" plywood between it and the jaw surface.

Fig. 105.

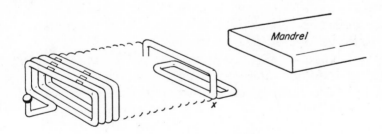

Fig. 106. Silver wire buckle. (L.W.)

When the "body" has been formed, it will be found somewhat 'springy" and imperfect in shape. Slip it off the mandrel and carefully anneal. Then replace it on the mandrel, and with careful use of the rawhide mallet, shape it closely to the mandrel. When satisfactorily formed, it should be pickled clean, rinsed, and prepared for soldering. Solder first one side, and then the other, using "easy" or "medium" flow silver solder. The wire-solder form (No. 26 gauge) is most convenient and is placed as shown in Figure 106. Remember that in order to solder effectively, the coils must touch each other. A turn of binding wire through each side of the buckle will help bring the coils close together.

Fig. 107. Wire buckle with monogram. (L.W.)

Fig. 108. Wire appliqué work. (Anna Halasi)

The final loop is used for attaching the belt. Note a small "shot" soldered atop the tongue. A small stone, such as a star sapphire, might be substituted. To vary the design, a cutout monogram may be applied on the top face of the buckle.

Figure 107 shows such a monogrammed buckle. In this case the basic wire buckle was completely prepared and soldered as above. The design for the monogram was then precisely laid out within a compass-drawn ¾" circle. The individual letters were constructed from 16-gauge silver. A pair of dividers was used to accurately lay out a ¾" circle on the wire buckle. A circular saw-blade about ½" diameter was used in the flexible shaft handpiece to cut out a 5/16" square opening in the middle of this circle. The sequence: two cuts 5/16" apart at *right angles* to the wire, then two cuts, similarly distanced, parallel to the wire. A small square of silver should drop out.

A steel burr, ball-shaped or cylindrical, served to grind out the remaining metal until a perfect circle of proper diameter resulted. Check the fit of the monogram elements for a snug fit.

During these procedures with the flexible shaft—particularly when the small rotary saw blade is being used—great care must be taken to protect the fingers from the blade. Burrs are not particularly dangerous, although they are capable of ruining the work, but when the saw is used, a hand-held small clamp, or a vise is recommended.

Before soldering the monogram in place, a thin wash of loam was brushed over the wire buckle, leaving a margin of about ⅛" *uncovered* around the open circle. The "tongue" of the buckle, standing apart from the heavier bulk, was rather heavily protected with loam to avoid annealing it during heating. The loam was dried with gentle heat. The monogram parts and the edges of the circle were checked to see that they were bright-clean. Flux was carefully applied inside the circle and completely over the monogram. (*If necessary,* a very small square of soft asbestos sheet can be pushed inside the buckle to keep the monogram in place, slightly elevated over the surface of the buckle.)

Tiny squares of silver solder were placed on the buckle surrounding the monogram and actually *in contact* with it. (Silver solder in wire form is also convenient. Clean the wire, cut into 1/16" pieces, and position.) The flux was gently dried, then full heat was applied and the buckle brought up to red heat. With the flame slightly reduced in size and played about the center, the solder was made to flow, and the work was completed. The loam was then brushed off, and the work was pickled and polished. If the buckle is to be given a high polish, the monogram, raised above the surface, may be given a contrasting mat finish by pushing it across a sheet of 400-grit Carborundum (or aluminum oxide) sandpaper lying faceup on a flat surface.

Miscellaneous Constructions

Although silver, gold, and base metal findings are available from many sources—principally manufacturers in Providence, Rhode Island—there are occasions when the craftsman wishes to construct his own bracelet or necklace catches. Joints, catches, and ear-wires do not usually play any conspicuous part in the design of a piece of jewelry, but the clasp or catch may very well be integrated as part of the overall design of a necklace or bracelet.

The basic mechanism of a clasp, when understood, can be incorporated into a link, either plain or highly decorated with some form of overlay.

Essentially, a common clasp is a small box or socket that receives the tongue or catch and holds it fast. In Figure 109 the essentials of such a clasp are shown. The box can fit underneath a link or a link can be so designed as to leave room for such a box. No. 24-gauge metal will suffice for its construction. The tongue can be bent over a knife edge and hammered hard to give "spring" to it.

Construction details show the evolution of the box catch from the flat layout to the completed link (Fig. 109). Note the two possible forms for the spring. *A* is a bent-over piece of metal. Though this is quite common, there is a possibility of breakage at this bend after much use. At *B* is another form in which the spring is cut free from the previously hardened piece of metal. This is pierced free with a jeweler's saw. It is bent upward to allow sufficient spring. The upright projection which takes the knob is soldered on. If necessary, rehammer to harden. The knob projects somewhat over the top of the box catch, so that it can be depressed to release the spring. Study the principle of this mechanism; it is applicable to innumerable forms of links.

Figure 110 shows another type of clasp useful for bracelets and watchbands. Parts *A* and *B* are cut from sheet metal. The gauge of metal used will depend on the weight of the metal used for the remaining links. Two pieces of No. 20 are suggested. They are to be cut and pierced identically except for the slight difference in the pierced pattern. Part *A* is sweat-soldered over *B* to produce *C,* with two little inner ledges at the front.

Parts *D* and *E* are made of similar material. *E* is sweat-soldered over *D,* and a little strip is soldered over the projection on *D.* This strip equals in size one "leg" of the **H**-shaped section cut in part *C.* The resulting piece is shown at *F.*

The assembled clasp is shown at *G.* Note part *X* occupying its proper "closed" position after having been inserted up through the rear leg of the cutout from the underside. It is then slipped forward to rest on the ledges on the front leg of the **H**-shaped cutout. The entire unit may be slightly curved over a properly shaped mandrel so as to conform with a wrist curve.

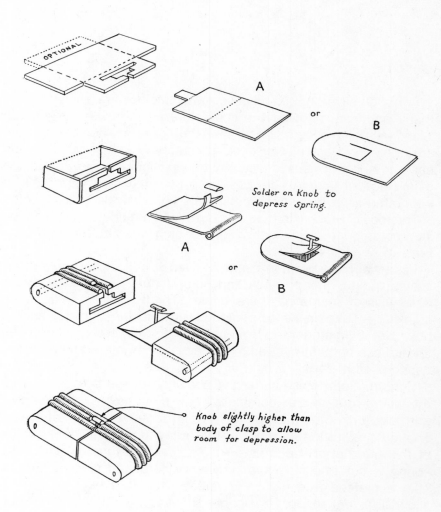

Fig. 109.

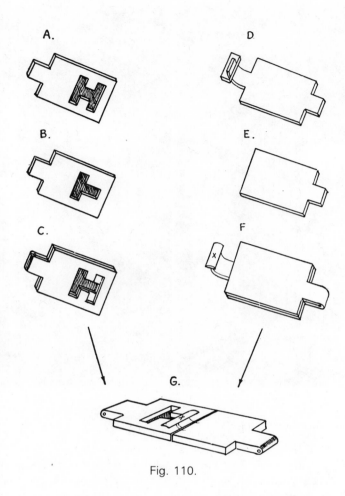

A.

D.

B.

E.

C.

F.

G.

Fig. 110.

Figure 111 shows a type of link construction with a simple clasp. Many forms of this link can be used, and applied ornament possibilities are limitless.

Essentially, the links are slightly curved rectangles of metal. On one end of each link is centered a piece of tubing (see *Using Miscellaneous Small Tools* for tubing construction). On the opposite ends of each link are two shorter pieces of tubing of similar diameter. When the links are properly assembled, they are permanently connected by passing a length of rivet wire or the desired metal wire of proper diameter through the tubing. The ends of the wire pin are then riveted over the tubing by gently hammering with the ball end of a small chasing hammer.

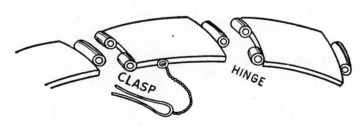

CLASP

HINGE

Fig. 111.

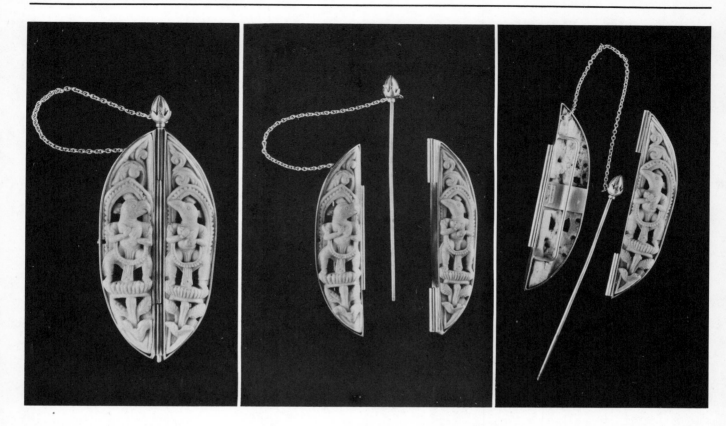

Fig. 112A–C.   Silver buckle using Tibetan bone carvings. Note tube-type hinges and "pinned" clasp. (L.W.)

The clasp for such a bracelet of links is formed by substituting a removable pin for one of the fixed pins. This removable pin takes the form of a piece of hardened wire bent somewhat like a hairpin or cotter pin. This pin is permanently secured to a link by a piece of fine commercial chain. The "legs" of the pin are given an outward spring so that after insertion through the hinge of a pair of links, the pin tends to stay in place. This is quite an ancient form of clasp but is nevertheless effective.

A novel use of the spring portion of a leather snap fastener is shown in Figure 113. The bracelet proper is made in two sections, hinged with a tubing-type hinge.

To the underside of the hinged end of the bracelet is *soft-soldered* the knoblike spring of an ordinary snap fastener. The point on the opposing piece of bracelet at which the knoblike projection rests is marked with a scriber. Center-punch this spot and drill a hole slightly less in diameter than the knob. A good way to estimate the drill size is to fit a drill into the unused cap portion, or opening, of the other half of the snap fastener. The opening and drill diameter should be similar. Press the snap into the hole to close the bracelet. The metal at which point the hole is drilled should be hammered fairly hard before drilling to avoid wear on the drilled hole.

The thickness of the metal at the hole should not be excessive—the snap should be of enough length to protrude *through* the hole, otherwise it will not act as a fastener.

Fig. 112D.   Neckpiece using as hinges tubing sections. Note "pinned" closure. (Lee Kagan)

Fig. 112E.   Neckpiece. Tubular-hinged at rear. (Sydney Scherr)

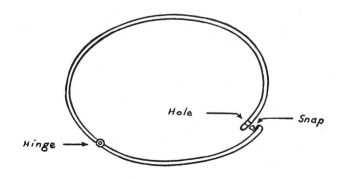

Fig. 113.

Neckpiece Clasp

Woven multistrand (braided) nylon has been in use for some time for lightweight beads such as pearls, but with the growing popularity of larger metal neckpieces that weigh more than the traditional small necklaces, monofilament nylon has been found by the author to be a durable, practical choice. Fishing line (braided or monofilament) is available at sporting goods stores. Line weights from 12 pounds to 40 pounds—and even more—make excellent suspensions for assembling neckpieces.

Monofilament tennis stringing can also be used for such work, but whereas knotting is relatively easy for attaching clasps when lightweight nylon is chosen, a different technique must be used if tennis-weight nylon is decided upon.

Fig. 114.

Tubing should be selected *just short* of admitting the heavy monofilament nylon. Two pieces of such tubing, about ½" long, must be fitted with rings, which are hard-soldered in place (Fig. 114). For one ring a hook will be needed. Either of the two shown can be used. If the hook with the drilled hole is used, it must be put on the ring before soldering. The other type of hook may be attached later unless the end looped around the ring is to be soldered, in which case this should be done and treated as the drilled hook. The construction finished, the tubing must be threaded internally with a suitably sized jeweler's tap. The tap should be selected to cut an internal thread only moderately deep, so that only moderate force should be necessary to turn the tap, as it is very brittle. A silicone lubricant may help in cutting, but if used, a solvent such as benzene or gasoline (flammable!) should be used to wash out any residue after the thread has been cut. After thread cutting and cleaning, the clasp is complete, and one of the two units can be attached to the heavy nylon by forcing the internal thread in the tubing to cut its own track on the end of the nylon string. If all goes well, a tight, secure union will result. If any concern is felt about the security of the clasp, undo it by reversing direction and unscrewing the tube. Mix a bit of two-part epoxy cement, wipe some onto the nylon end—which should show some signs of the thread having cut into it—and immediately rescrew the clasp onto the nylon. If all traces of any lubricant used have been eliminated, the clasp should be secure when the cement has dried. The other end of the clasp should be treated similarly *after* all the neckpiece elements have been strung in proper order.

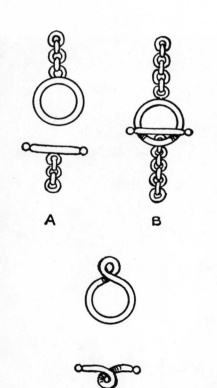

A   B

C

Fig. 115.

Simple Clasp

A simple type of clasp, particularly useful for a necklace, is shown in Figure 115. The large circular link is from ¼" to ⁵⁄₁₆" inside diameter. To it is soldered a smaller link, to which the end of a necklace or chain is connected. The large link may be of No. 18 or No. 16 wire. The bar is made of similar wire. Its length, minus the shot, equals the outside diameter of the large link.

To each end is soldered a small shot. At the center is soldered a small link similar to the one on the large circular link. This connects to the other end of the necklace or chain. Assembled in closed position, they appear as in Figure 115*B*. At *C,* a constructional variation of such a clasp is shown. These clasps are used in the necklaces in Figures 46 and 96.

Mounting Spherical Shapes

The author, having acquired a number of undrilled, $9/16''$ spheres of both onyx and carnelian, had to devise a method for mounting that was both attractive and practical. A twelfth dynasty Egyptian necklace suggested a working solution. Essentially, what was done was to wrap the sphere within a cage consisting of four "arms," or bars. The diagrams in Figure 116A and B show the plan. Twenty-two-gauge sterling was used. The cruciform pattern was wrapped around the sphere, and the arms were extended to form a "stem." One longer arm was carried over a nail of suitable thickness to form a loop and continued down about half the length, where it met the upward-extending arm from the opposite side. The arms were pinched snug at the top of the sphere with a smooth-jawed flat pliers. The stem portion was then tightly wrapped with silver wire (20 or 22 gauge will do). The wire binding started at the top of the *sphere* and was wound upward. At the starting point a short length of the wire was bent up along the stem, between arms, before commencing the winding. The wire was then bound around the stem, securing the short starting piece as well. The top ending of the wire "coil," $1''$ away from the stone, was hard-soldered with a short, intense blue flame after the tip was bent into a crevice between the arms. A length of 20-gauge binding wire helped secure measurements for the arms and stem by trial bending. For the novice attempting this construction, try practicing with a child's ordinary playing marbles.

An alternate treatment can eliminate the coiled wire and give a contemporary effect. This method makes use of square tubing. Such tubing is available in both silver and brass in several sizes. One-eighth silver tubing, having an inside measurement of $3/32''$, is suggested. If two opposite arms are narrowed to this dimension and the remaining two narrowed to fit between them, they can then be fashioned as previously directed. The square tubing can be forced down over the stem to the top of the sphere. If this is done, the suspension loop at the top of the stem must be shaped *after* the tubing is forced over the stem. If there is any problem with stone security caused by a loose assembly, the inside of the tubing may be cleaned, fluxed (soft-solder type), and then soldered with *tin.* (Most jewelry suppliers now carry a special soft solder that stays bright and has a low melting point like tin.) Heat the tubing with a gentle flame and apply the solder at the top of the tubing.

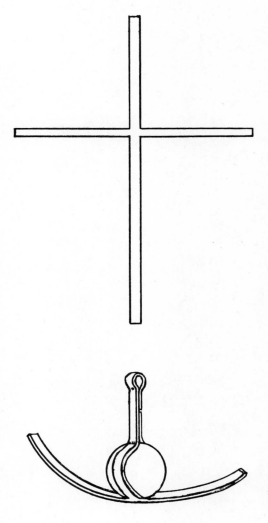

Fig. 116A and B.

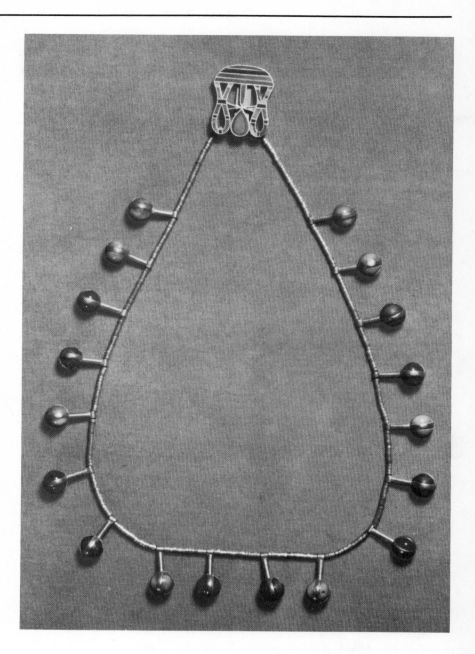

Fig. 116C. Egyptian necklace, Twelfth Dynasty (reconstruction).

If large beads are to be used instead of undrilled spheres, a short length of wire should be hard-soldered in vertical position to the center of the cruciform. The bead, slipped over this wire, will not shift its position, thus keeping the holes hidden from view.

The Bow

A construction that is a usable piece of jewelry in itself is the bow (Figs. 117 and 118). This can be made in a size suitable for earrings, or it can be made larger for use as a brooch. The parts are cut out with the jeweler's saw, following the outlines given in the figures, and then filed smooth. The metal surfaces should be thoroughly smoothed and polished before any bending is done because the final bent form is difficult to work on with abrasive papers. Shaping is done almost entirely with the fingers. Final assembly is achieved by placing the piece pictured on the top in Figure 118 under the "looped" piece. The "tongue" is then brought over the complete assembly from below and bent snugly over the top through the notched portion. It is squeezed tight with a smooth-faced flat pliers. It may be soldered from the reverse side if desired, although if properly assembled, it will remain quite firmly in shape.

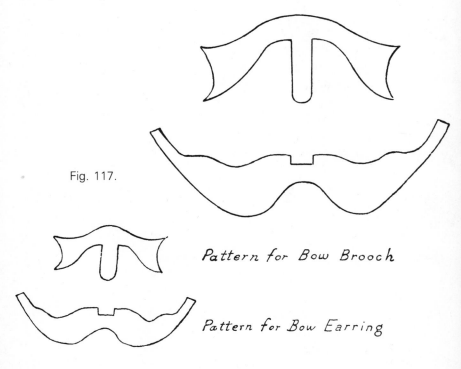

Fig. 117.

Pattern for Bow Brooch

Pattern for Bow Earring

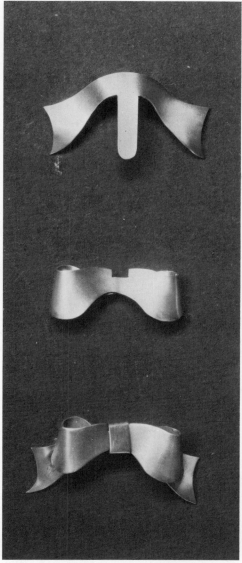

Fig. 118.   The bow in several stages of construction.

Tubular Forms from Wire

In the section describing the use of the drawplate, a method of drawing metal tubing was described. Another means of forming tubing involves the use of wire.

When the inside diameter of the desired tubing is known, wire or rod of that diameter is employed as a mandrel, or form, around which a coil of wire can be closely wound. When a length of such coiled tubing is formed, it can then be made into a rigid tube by soldering the individual turns of the coil together. The easiest way to do this is to employ hard-solder filings mixed with a suitable flux.

The mixture of flux and solder filings is brushed over the coil of wire from which the mandrel has been withdrawn. Heat the coil until the solder flows around the turns of the coil. This will occur in an even, thorough fashion if the coil is made of clean wire, closely coiled.

Such lengths of "corrugated" tubing are useful for forming hinges or for use as hingelike links (Fig. 111). In making such tubing, remember that as the inside diameter of the coil decreases, the diameter of the wire used in making such a coil should also decrease.

Miscellaneous Construction Buckles

Before getting into the construction of buckles attention should be given to a generally overlooked aspect of *design*. A buckle designed with a monogram (see Fig. 107) or one designed to be viewed (and used) "right-side-up" (see Fig. 122A) must be constructed so that the bar, or loop, to which the belt is to be attached, is on the proper end.

A *right-handed* person usually inserts the "starting" end of a belt through trouser loops beginning at the *left* hand side of the trouser, and continues leftward around from that point. When the belt is in position this will leave the buckle on the *center-left* side of the wearer.

A *left-handed* wearer usually starts a belt from the right-hand side, inserting the belt into loops starting at the *right* hand side and working around from that point. This will leave the buckle on the *center-right* side. If the same belt has been used, the buckle will now be upside-down.

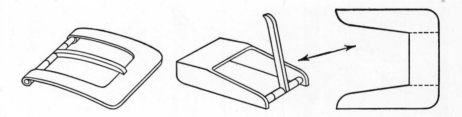

Fig. 119. Two buckles.

Therefore, providing the design requires it, a buckle that should be viewed right-side-up must be designed and constructed with the belt-attaching bar or loop on the proper end. *For custom-designed work it is important to know how the prospective owner "loops" the belt—with the right or the left hand.*

Figure 119 shows belt buckle construction. The emphasis in these sketches is on the movable "tongue." Although commercial practice generally utilizes nothing more than a heavy wire looped over a bar, fine handmade construction requires more refinement.

A bar of wire is placed across the width of the buckle. Before this is soldered into position, a piece of tubing is cut into three pieces to be placed over the bar. The total length of the tubing should equal the inside measurement across the buckle. (Check current styles for width of leather belt to get this dimension.) The end pieces of tubing are *equal* in length. The center piece may be shorter or longer, in whatever proportion the craftsman prefers. The bar, with the tubing in place, is held in position by the pressure of its fit and then soldered. Two squares of solder at each end should suffice to hold both bar and end tubing. The center tube remains free to move, as the tongue is to be shaped and soldered to this part. The end joints are protected with a thin coat of loam during this operation. Many variations are possible utilizing this basic construction. Figure 120 shows a finished model by the author. Another form of buckle can be found in *Wire Working.*

Fig. 120. Buckle. (L.W.)

Fig. 121.   Buckle. (A) front; (B) rear. (L.W.)

Fig. 122.   Buckle. (A) front; (B) rear. (L.W.)

Figures 121 and 122 show two additional buckle designs. Both avoid the use of the movable tongue to secure the belt and use instead a piece of 10-gauge wire hammer-flattened at the base, rounded on its end, and shaped as per Figure 123. This simplifies buckle construction and interferes less with basic design, as the wire "hook" is out of sight. The barrel-shaped portions of two of the buckles shown are constructed from pieces of ½" diameter sterling tubing with sections removed and closed to provide flat bases.

Fig. 123.

Fig. 124. Pendant.

Pendant Pieces

Figure 124 shows an attractive pendant or bracelet charm, possible only where initials can be interlaced as shown. Suitable letters are traced and applied to a heavy gauge metal such as No. 12 or No. 14, depending on the height of the letters. These are interlaced and positioned on a disc of similar gauge metal and hard-soldered. The position of the soldered loop on top will determine which initial will face forward when worn.

Earring Suspension

Figure 125 shows one of the methods used for attaching and suspending an earring from the ear. This method uses a standard wire and friction nut device. The wire and nut may be purchased as a complete unit. If quantities are used, it may be economical to buy only the friction nut. Large supply houses specializing in findings can supply these. The wire, which should have a tiny groove around its end, can be made quite simply using 19- or 20-gauge sterling wire. Before doing this, it would be wise to check the wire size the friction nut was designed for, as this sometimes varies. To make the wire part, cut a piece about 7/16" to 1/2" long. Place the wire on a smooth steel slab, and with the edge of a dull knife blade, make the groove by pressing the knife edge *hard* against the wire end and rolling the wire under it back and forth. The groove should be about 1/16" from the end and need not be very deep. It acts as a "stop" to deter the loss of the friction nut. The earring pictured shows this wire attached to a silver ball or shot. The upper portion of the earring was cut away in a curve so that the lower part of the shot might be fitted into position and soldered as part of the design instead of being "applied" to it. If this procedure is used, drill a hole partway into the back of the shot, place the wire in position, and hard-solder. This makes a secure job and an attractive addition to the design when the shot is polished to reflect a spot of light.

Fig. 125. Earring suspension. (L.W.)

Fig. 126.   Earring suspension. (L.W.)

Fig. 127.

Figure 126 shows another method of suspension. This features a movable joint which assures the wearer that the earring will hang vertically in all head positions. It is also an attractive addition on its own merits. A "tab" of 14-gauge silver should be shaped as in Figure 127. A slot must be cut in the upper part of the earring equal to the gauge of tab. *Across* the slot is placed a short length of silver tubing (14 gauge should do) which is to be soldered in place. After soldering, the portion of the tubing across the opening should be cut away. The remaining pieces will be in perfect alignment. The metal suspension tab must then be positioned and the spot where the hole is to be drilled marked by using a needle or drill bit pushed through the tubing and against the tab. The hole should then be drilled *very slightly* oversize, to allow motion. Remember to use the center-punch before drilling, for accuracy. The ear-wire should be attached to the tab before it is permanently riveted in place. The ear-wire, for a pierced ear, can be 22 gauge, soldered into a saw slot at the upper rear of the tab. Rivet into place, lightly tapping the ends of the rivet wire to "head" them over.

To polish and smooth the cut ends of ear-wires, hold such ends, after filing flat across, against a hard, solid felt wheel charged with tripoli. Move the wire around to shape its end.

Closures

Figures 112A, B, and C show a woman's buckle made by encasing a two-piece Tibetan bone carving in silver. The buckle makes use of the tubular clasp as illustrated. The hingelike closure is shown in detail. One-half of the buckle is connected to each end of a wide belt by means of the bars shown. The buckle is then fitted together and closed with the long pin. The pin is permanently chained to half of the buckle to prevent its loss. This type of closure can be adapted to other large ornamental buckles as well as hinged bracelets.

Links

In Figure 128A, links marked *x* have alternating construction. One utilizes a piece of tubing on each end. The length of the tube equals the link width minus the thickness of the two overhanging pieces on the connecting link. The links have their ends carefully filed (hollowed) with a small round file. These filed portions accommodate the tubing and the rounded portions of the overhang on the alternate links. The overhanging strips on the "alternate" link, which are soldered in place, should be made of fairly heavy-gauge stock, such as No. 16, so that the holes can be countersunk slightly on the outer surfaces. This allows the pin, which holds the two links together, to be riveted in place and filed flat. This assembly, when carefully made, presents a fine appearance.

In Figure 128B, links *x* are heavy stock drilled through the width at each end to receive the pins, which act as hinges. This requires a small, sensitive drill press for accuracy. The connecting device consists of two pieces of 16-gauge metal drilled and countersunk to receive the pins. The assembly is shown. Links can be decorated in any desirable way and either curved slightly or left flat.

Still another means of making movable joints is shown in Figure 130. This construction permits much originality in design and is usable for necklaces as well as bracelets.

A suitably designed link is made of round or square wire, 16 or 14 gauge or even heavier. Part of the unit may be widened, as in the diagram, by striking the proper place using a polished hammer with a face only slightly domed. To each unit is soldered a heavy wire jump-ring, soldering the joint of the jump-ring closed against the wire "link" unit. When enough of these units have been made, saw open at *x*, which is the point at which these units were originally soldered. (It is easier to form and "work" these units when soldered closed.) Position each link in turn through a jump-ring, as shown at *A* in the diagram, and resolder the joint. Loam protection of the nearest jump-rings may be necessary.

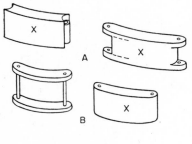

Fig. 128.

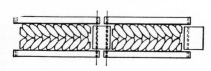

Fig. 129. Another link variation using heavy square wire combined with heavy flattened herringbone twist.

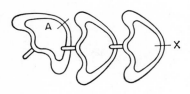

Fig. 130.

Fig. 131.

Probably the simplest "hinge" method of all, yet one capable of much variation in design, is shown in Figure 131. Wire is shaped to a design similar to that shown. A piece of tubing of proper size is soldered to close the ends of this unit and receive the next unit. Note that one unit shows an alternate method. Instead of tubing, a group of jump-rings are soldered together to form a more decorative tube. Also shown, on the plain tubing unit, is a small shot soldered to the tubing. If the tubing is then softly oxidized, the shot can be touched to a high polish with a flat hand buff and a point of light added at each joint. This makes a nice necklace or bracelet.

An excellent, easily made link is illustrated in Figure 132. Square silver wire can be used; recommended gauge is from No. 4 to No. 8. Length can be as desired—assume ⅝″ as an example. Cut lengths of wire with a jeweler's saw. A flat-faced polished hammer is then used to hammer one end thin. The width of this end is increased at the same time. The piece is turned 90 degrees, and the opposite end is similarly hammered. The positions for holes are then carefully marked, center-punched for accurate drilling, and drilled. Finally, the ends are evenly rounded, and the completed link is polished. A hard felt wheel is recommended to keep surfaces flat and edges crisp. Hammering should be done on a thick steel block or anvil with a *smoothly polished* face.

Still another easily made link utilizes either round or square wire and an easily made jig (see Fig. 133). Look at the link. The size of the holes wanted determines the diameter of the nails. The length of the link will be determined by the space between the two nails. Not too great a distance should be used, but enough space should be allowed so that the center of the link can be pinched closed with a small needle-nose or round-nose pliers. The thickness of the wire is a factor to consider. To make the jig, drive two nails of the required size into a block of ¾″ wood, 2″ × 3″ in surface size. Nip or saw off the tops of the nails, allowing about ⅝″ to remain protruding. File the newly exposed nail surfaces smooth. To make a link, wrap the desired type of wire around both nails. Saw a clean joint, file if necessary, and solder closed. Place over the nails again and squeeze closed at the center with the pliers. Remove the link from the jig and solder it at center, which should be in close contact. The links can be used as is (connected by jump-rings), hammered flat over the entire surface, or hammered at the ends only. If necessary, holes can be redrilled for larger openings after hammering is done.

A link construction using pieces of tubing as "hollow rivets" is shown in Figure 134. Basically, the linking element consists of short lengths of tubing (same metal as the jewelry) fitted into somewhat larger openings. Both ends of the tubelike rivets are spread to secure the rivets yet allow link motion (The writer has found two sizes of sterling tubing to be useful: 3/32″ and ⅛″. These are outside diameters. For sufficient clearance, thus allowing link motion, the use of a No. 33 drill for the former and a No. 28 drill for the latter are recommended.)

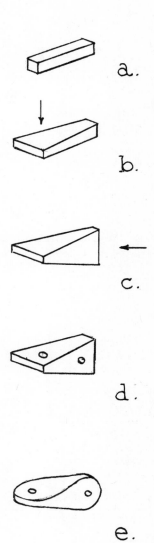

a.

b.

c.

d.

e.

Fig. 132.

Fig. 133.

Fig. 134. Neckpiece. Linking with hollow rivets. (Shirlee Novak)

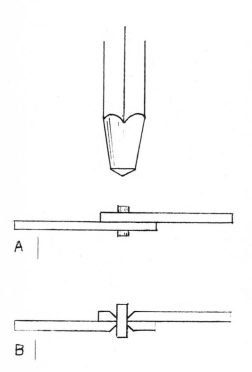

A

B

90°
Burr

Fig. 135.

The length of tubing to be cut (by jeweler's saw) for a rivet is determined by checking the thickness of metal for a *single* link and multiplying it by five. Thus a linked joint, which consists of two drilled pieces of metal, will have an "excess" of rivet on each side just a bit more than the thickness of a single link. The spreading tool for ⅛" tubing may be a ⁵⁄₃₂" dapping punch or a blunt-ended center-punch (Fig. 135). The work should rest on a hardwood surface. Strike the punch carefully until the rivet no longer is able to drop through the drilled hole. Reverse the work and do the opposite end of the rivet. *Be sure to allow link motion.* To finish the job, rest the riveted joint on a polished flat steel plate and tap gently with the flat end of a chasing hammer, again checking to see that the rivet is not made so tight as to stop the easy movement of the links.

At *B* in Figure 135, another version of this linkage is shown. The difference involves "counter-sinking" the drilled hole. This method uses a slightly shorter piece of tubing and, more importantly, results in less protrusion of the rivet. The holes are drilled as above, but additionally, a 90-degree burr is to be used to remove a small amount of metal around the perimeter of each hole on the outward-facing surfaces. The burr, pictured, is used lightly in the flexible shaft handpiece. It may also be inserted in the jaws of one of several small pin vises available and, spun between the fingers, used in "drill" fashion.

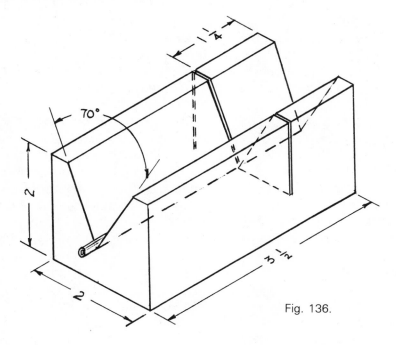

Fig. 136.

Figure 136 shows a device the author uses for cutting short lengths of heavy wire or tubing without the worry of having the short piece roll away and get lost. The device is cut from a block of hardwood. The slot, which accommodates a jeweler's saw used horizontally, is made with a very fine-bladed saw. A woodworker's dovetail saw is ideal. At the apex of the inside inverted **V**, measuring lines can be laid out. A piece of steel rule from an old flexible tape rule is fine for this. (The figure shows a piece of tubing in position).

A linkage system suitable for bracelet or necklace use is shown in Figure 137. The decorative portion of the system can be made of half-round wire of a fairly heavy gauge. These links should be oval in profile, as they are most comfortably worn in this form. The connecting links, shaped as shown, are also oval but made of round wire of a somewhat smaller gauge.

Closure construction is suggested in the sketch: a simple closed ring on one end and a piece of wire shaped to hold an added spring-ring on the other end. This piece of wire should be soldered to the *spread* ends of the last two oval links.

Fig. 137.

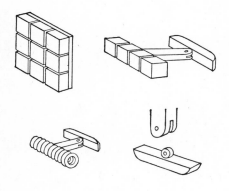

Fig. 138.

Fig. 139. Cuff links with semicylindrical stones. (L.W.)

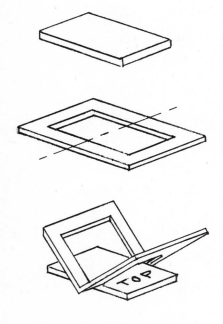

Fig. 140.

Cuff Links

The sketches in Figure 138 show some suggestions for cuff link construction. The first sketch shows a base of metal about ⅝" square with an arrangement of solid squares cut from square bar silver and soldered in place. The bottom of each cut piece can be leveled on a flat file or emery cloth, and when all are flat on *one* side, they can be soldered. Final leveling of all tops is done after soldering. Square tubing is also available and can be used similarly or in other arrangements. If such tubing is used, the individual cloisons formed can be filled with enamel. Similar arrangements can be made with large-diameter round wire or tubing.

The second sketch shows a cuff link made of a single piece of heavy square bar. The grooves are made either with a saw blade or the edge of a flat jeweler's file.

The third sketch shows a cuff link made of a group of jump-rings soldered together. A somewhat similar effect can be achieved with a short coil. Small cabochon stones may be set at each end if desired.

The last sketch shows a breakdown of the cuff-back finding shown. This is made of silver square wire, No. 8 gauge or heavier. The ends of the cross-piece are filed to curve as shown (see Fig. 18). A section of round wire of similar gauge is cut and drilled as shown in the sketch and soldered to the center of the cross-piece. The thickness should equal that of a flat needle file, as this file is used to make the slot in the shank which attaches to the cross-piece. The shank end is rounded as shown and drilled for a suitable rivet wire. The shank may be made slotted and movable at both ends, or it may be solidly soldered to the "face" portion of the cuff link.

A cuff link design requiring the use of semicylindrical pieces of lapis lazuli on silver (Fig. 139) was created in the following fashion. A base was cut to match the bottom of the stone. A second, larger piece was cut as per Figure 140, with the center portion, also equal to the base, removed. This second piece, of 20-gauge silver, was sharply and carefully bent at its center (see Fig. 140). The angle was made with a polished-face hammer over a steel block plus the use of a flat, smooth-jawed pliers for a crisply defined angle. A hard-soldered cuff-back was used, and the "joint" portion was soldered to the base at this stage and then loamed. Next, the bent rectangle was aligned so that it was centered on the base with the inside surface at the bend on the same level as the top of the base. It was then hard-soldered, cleaned, and given a preliminary polish. The V-shaped piece was then carefully bent back with the fingers until the stone could be slipped into position. With the smooth-jawed pliers the retaining piece was returned to a straight-lined, angled position, high enough to hold the stone without unnecessarily obscuring it. The remainder of the cuff-back, a double-swivel type, was riveted on, and a final polish completed the job.

Although fashion will dictate the vogue in cuff link size, it is recommended here that a man's cuff links be conservative in size. A large, cumbersome mass of metal at each wrist will prove annoying when one's arms are resting on a desk or table, regardless of how attractive such links may appear in a box.

Tie Clips

One kind of finding on the market is called an alligator tie clip. The name refers to the movable section of the clip that resembles the toothed jaw of an alligator. This is a very effective finding, but before putting it into use, it is necessary to consider the design of the proposed tie clip. If the bar (or entire clip) is of silver or gold, the body of the tie clip itself may comprise the main body of the finished tie clip. If this is the intention and additional decoration is planned involving hard soldering, the whole finding must be dismantled. In Figure 141 the basic piece is shown. If the two "ears" are grasped with a smooth flat pliers, and one bent up as the other is bent down, the jaw and spring will drop out. Observe the position of the spring before doing this so that it can be properly replaced. Any soldering additions are now made with no danger of spoiling the spring by high temperatures. A suitable stone may be mounted, or very effective "strip" initials may be bent and soldered onto the clip. When all such work is completed, the spring and alligator jaw may be replaced by reversing the procedure used to dismantle the original finding.

Fig. 141.

If a body larger than the one supplied with the original finding is desired, the jaw may be removed, the original body pounded out flat, and the end used as a pattern to form a similar end on a larger piece of metal.

Note that it is *not* suggested that a larger tie bar be soldered over the original. This, in the author's opinion, is not a craftsman's procedure.

Referring again to Figure 141, it will be noticed in the second drawing that a piece of tubing is laid across the "ears." In fact, the "ears" in this case have been removed. This procedure was evolved by the writer as a more effective pivot than the original. Tubing was chosen having a larger outside diameter than the hole in the "jaw" piece and soldered in place as shown. A space was cut in the center just wide enough to accommodate the movable jaw. This, with the spring, was snugly fitted into position and a pin through these parts was riveted into place. This procedure makes a fine-working, good-looking job.

If such work is planned with gold, the jaw (in gold) and spring can be purchased separately, and the body or bar of the clip can be made any size from suitable material.

16

Etching and Electroplating

Many simple effects can be obtained by etching handwrought jewelry. Bracelets consisting either of individually designed links or wide bands can be ornamented with a design etched into the surface of the metal. In enameling, the sunken field required in some forms of such work can be effected by etching. Such etched fields for enameling can be carefully delineated for clean detail with properly selected chasing tools after etching has been completed.

Etching itself is a form of controlled erosion of metal. The action of a solution of nitric acid upon a metal is involved, with portions of the work protected by a "resist." This resist, which prevents the action of the acid from taking place at selected portions of the design, is usually black asphaltum varnish, obtainable at large art supply shops or craft suppliers.

Before actually starting the work, the design must be considered. It must be decided whether a motif is to be eaten into the metal or the metal around a motif is to be etched down, leaving the motif raised or in relief. In general, the edge of a piece of work should keep its original thickness, which means that an unetched margin may be required around some designs. Figure 142 shows an example of an acid-etched bracelet and neckpiece.

Applying the Design to the Metal

Before applying the design to the metal, it is well to bring the surface of the metal to a smooth, flawless state with fine abrasive papers. Everything, including polishing, is done to remove any marks from the surface. This is done to eliminate the removal of surface metal after the etching has been completed. If this step is neglected and it is found necessary to remove bad flaws after the etching, the metal removal at this point will mean that there will be little depth to the etched design, and it may even result in its partial erasure. It is true that parts of the metal supposedly protected by the asphaltum are sometimes attacked by the acid, but if the application of the asphaltum is carefully done on a clean surface, this will not be an important factor to consider.

Clean the surface of the metal thoroughly. Coat with white tempera color. This is easily done by rubbing the paint over the metal with a fingertip. The procedure is described in detail in *Transferring the Design to the Metal*, Chapter 2. The design is traced over the paint with carbon paper and then outlined with a sharp scriber so that it will appear on the metal beneath the paint.

Wash off all traces of tempera paint and dry the metal. The black asphaltum resist can now be applied with a camel's hair brush of suitable size. The asphaltum should be thick enough to cover the metal well but thin enough to handle easily with the brush. It is thinned (and removed) with turpentine. When the design has been completely painted in, the back of the metal as well as the edges must be fully covered. Be sure the designed part is thoroughly dry before turning over the work. Test with a fingertip. Asphaltum generally dries in about an hour. If the work is immersed in acid before dry, the painted portions will peel, spoiling the work. A wide brush is used to cover the large areas on the back of the work. Clean the brushes in turpentine when finished with the painting. Errors in the painting can be scraped to correct the outline with a narrow knife blade or a physician's scalpel. If the asphaltum has a tendency to break away in fragments when attempts are made to "clean up" a design, slightly warm the work to reduce this tendency. Another way to avoid such fragmentation is to do the scraping before the asphaltum is thoroughly dry.

Preparing the Acid

The acid bath is made up of nitric acid and water. The proportions are about two-thirds water and one-third acid. The *acid* must be poured *into the water* to avoid a violent reaction. A glass tray or battery jar makes a good container. A pyrex dish may be used. Ventilation should be good. Stir the mixture for even distribution with a stick or a glass stirring rod. Keep this solution away from possible contact with small children.

When the work has been immersed in the acid bath, the formation of tiny bubbles should be seen. These will rise slowly to the top of the solution. If they do not rise, the solution is too weak, and a little acid can be stirred in. A dense, cloudy formation of bubbles rapidly rising denotes too strong a solution. To weaken it, pour water into a suitable container, *then add* the too-strong solution. This is in keeping with the safety precaution *add acid to water*. Yellowish fumes are another indication of a strong solution. Sometimes the formation of tiny bubbles that cling to the edges of the design will be noted. When these bubbles are allowed to remain in place for a long time, the resulting etching will appear ragged at the outline. Therefore, it may sometimes be necessary to gently brush over the surface of the work with a soft cotton swab to dislodge these bubbles.

Experience with etching will be necessary before one is familiar with the smoothest working solution. Time required for etching to proper depth, which is about 1/32", will range from perhaps 1 to 4 hours, depending on the metal and the strength of the solution. The author has made it a practice to have a red electric bulb illuminated at the etching tank whenever any work is in the acid. This will act as a reminder, preventing any possibility of leaving the studio for the day and forgetting the work in the acid.

To test the proper depth of etch, use a long copper tongs to remove the work, which should be immediately dipped into clean, cold water. A tray of water can be kept alongside the acid bath. Examine the work in a strong light to see depth of etch. Testing with the edge of the fingernail against the etched wall is another method.

It will be found that the cleanest and smoothest results are obtained with a relatively weak, slow-acting solution. The added time needed for such an acid bath will be more than compensated for by the excellent results obtained.

Removal of Asphaltum

When the etching process has been completed, the work can be rinsed and the asphaltum varnish removed. To do this, place the work on several thicknesses of newspaper and scrub with medium-grade steel wool well saturated with turpentine. Use fresh pieces when necessary and the removal of asphaltum will be quickly and simply accomplished. Before repolishing with the usual buffing equipment, scrub the surface of the metal clean with fine powdered pumice and hot water.

ELECTROPLATING

Electroplating is a method of depositing a layer of metal upon another piece of metal by electrochemical means. It requires certain chemical solutions, anodes (the source of metal from which the deposit originates), a heat supply—usually electric hot plates—and an electrical device to provide direct current at low voltage (usually between 2 and 8 volts and therefore harmless). The current almost universally available to the consumer from the electric company is known as alternating current and is 110 volts. This supply must be changed to DC at low voltage. The electroplating machine accomplishes this. Such plating devices, as well as the properly formulated plating solutions and accessories needed for doing this work, are available from most jewelers' suppliers. Solutions can be mixed by the craftsman, but the writer recommends purchasing such supplies ready mixed. For those doing this kind of work on a relatively limited basis—that is, plating one or two pieces at a time—the smallest models of these machines will serve nicely. Storage batteries and battery chargers, both of which supply direct current at low voltage, can also be used for electroplating, but the voltage and current flow must be adjusted properly, which requires wiring a voltmeter and an ammeter into the circuit, together with a variable control (a rheostat, or variable resistor). While this is quite simple for someone familiar with radio and related work, it is not a practical alternative for the uninitiated. Booklets giving additional descriptions of plating in all its applications are available very cheaply from those suppliers who sell the plating equipment.

Electroplating and Jewelry Design

Electroplating as an added jewelry technique is well worth considering, particularly as the cost of precious metals has become so great. Not only does it have certain economic advantages, but a whole new range of aesthetic possibilities becomes available with a comparatively modest investment.

In Figure 142, silver was used as the basic structure, with partial gold plating. The substitution of copper for the basic piece with silver-plated portions is an alternative that may be chosen, particularly in the case of a first attempt when a craftsman may have ambivalent feelings about the results. In either case the use of etching and plating will result in contrasting areas of differing metals that make for a very beautiful effect.

Designs for jewelry to be treated this way should be planned very carefully before starting the actual construction. The best procedure when silver is to be used for the basic structure is to use the recessed areas for the gold plating. As a result, the portions plated with a thin layer of gold will be relatively protected from excessive wear because the surrounding metal is higher.

When a design has been decided upon and applied to the metal as described earlier, the work should be given a somewhat deep etch. All areas that are to appear as raised silver parts of the design will be those that have been given a coating with an acid resist—asphaltum.

If the etching has been done slowly and the asphaltum originally applied to a carefully cleaned surface and thoroughly dried before the etching bath, there should be little or no need for any repairs to the asphaltum layer before going ahead to the plating procedure. Inasmuch as the areas to be plated are the same ones that have just been etched, the asphaltum will act to resist the plating just as it resisted the acid solution. Examine the work carefully. If any touch-up to the asphaltum work *is* needed, the work should be rinsed, then dried. A hair dryer, *held not too close* (no closer than a foot away), will hasten the drying. Retouch the asphaltum coating and allow it to dry. The work should then be ready for the plating process.

Fig. 142.   Bracelet and neckpiece. Etched design with gold-plated recessed areas. (Mary Ann Scherr)

Plating the Etched Work

The plating process involves suspending the work, sequentially, in *electro-cleaner*, *rinse*, and *plating solution*. Figure 143 shows three Pyrex beakers. The first, on an electric hot plate, contains a commercial electro-cleaner from the electroplating equipment supplier. This is to be used, with a stainless steel anode, at 100° F. (Usual plating temperatures are closer to 180°F, but to protect the asphaltum, the temperature has been reduced. Plating time may be somewhat longer as a result. An immersion thermometer will be helpful in checking temperature of solutions; rinse in warm running water between uses.) The second beaker holds clean, distilled water used to rinse the work. The third beaker, also on a hot plate at 100°F, holds the plating solution and the requisite anode. The anode—gold or silver depending on the kind of plating being done—is the source of the metal being deposited during the plating process. The anodes are fully immersed in their lutions.

Note the heavy bars or wires of copper resting across the first and third beakers. One bar lies across beaker No. 1. The stainless steel anode hangs from it. Two bars lie across beaker No. 3. They must not be allowed to touch each other. The left-hand bar holds the suspended gold anode. The work will hang on the right-hand bar when it is being plated.

To the left is shown a plating machine. Connect to the positive terminal a length of flexible, insulated copper wire long enough to reach the beakers comfortably. The other end of this wire should have an alligator clip attached (available at any radio or electronic supply store). A similar piece of wire, also with an alligator clip, must be connected to the cathode or negative terminal of the plater.

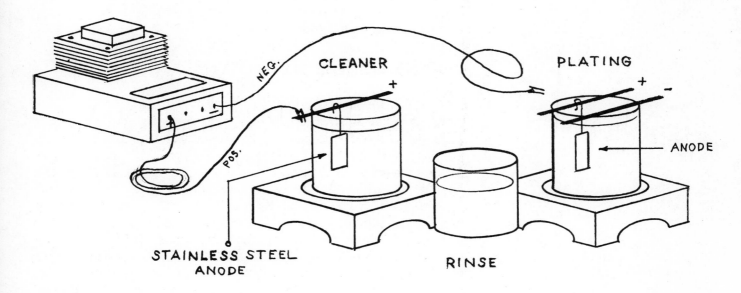

Fig. 143.

Cleaning. Connect the positive clip to the end of the anode support bar lying across beaker No. 1 and the negative clip to the wire holding the work. Turn on the plater. Move the work up and down a bit in the hot cleaning solution for perhaps 10 seconds or so. Watch the asphaltum surface carefully to avoid its being injured in the hot solution.

Remove and rinse in beaker No. 2 (cool, distilled water). Avoid touching the work with the fingers, to prevent surface contamination.

Plating. Using the wire holding the work, hang the work from the cathode bar on beaker No. 3 (plating solution). Connect the positive clip to the anode bar and the negative clip to the bar from which the work has been suspended. With the plater turned on the work can remain in the plating solution from 1 minute to about 10 minutes, depending on the depth of plating desired. Keep an eye on the asphaltum coating. Should any peeling be noticed, remove the work and rinse. The damaged asphaltum can either be repaired and the plating continued (when asphaltum is dry), or the plating can be discontinued and, if a reasonable deposit of gold has accumulated, considered completed.

After plating, the asphaltum should be removed and the metal surface carefully inspected. If the metal was cleared of all blemishes and well polished before the design was applied and etched, it should only be necessary to do a little additional polishing at this point. Some may not want to polish the etched portions, preferring the mat surface for greater contrast. It is important to understand that a plated surface will not appear polished if the metal underneath the plating was not originally polished. It must also be realized that any further polishing *after the plating process* can only be done very gently with a rouge polishing cloth by hand. This is because the plating will be extremely thin and can be partially, if not entirely, removed by the abrasive action of a polishing wheel. (Clear lacquer is sometimes used as final protection for the plating. This, of course, makes later polishing impossible unless the lacquer is removed with a lacquer solvent.)

PLATING AND THE STUDIO

Plating Safety

If a small area of one's studio is to be set aside for plating, consideration must be given to certain factors that can, if ignored, pose hazards for both craftsmen and others who may enter or occupy the area. Fortunately, common sense as well as the awareness of such hazards can easily overcome such problems.

Ventilation. Because the fumes from the chemical solutions being used during plating are harmful if inhaled, good ventilation is required. Many metallic salts are poisonous. Cyanides are particularly dangerous. An exhaust fan and a nearby window are necessary if no professional ventilation installation has been made. The hood and *vented* exhaust (not just a filter unit) usually found over a stove is an example of a good professional venting system.

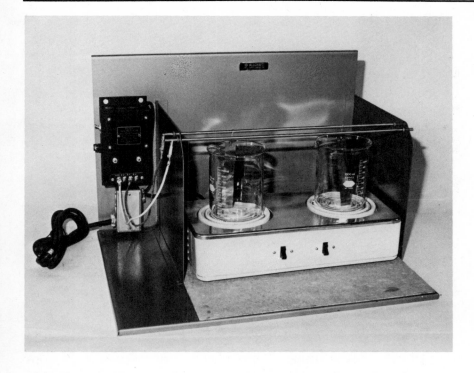

Fig. 144. Electroplating setup. Rinse beaker, not shown. (Allcraft)

Storage. Because of the poisonous nature of some solutions, plating materials must be kept safely out of the reach of children, preferably under locked conditions. Not only should dangerous supplies be labeled by name, but the notation Poison should be added.

Cleanliness. Because poisons are frequently handled—particularly when gold plating is done—good quality rubber gloves should be worn during handling. They should be thoroughly washed *before* they are removed from the hands. Avoid using common household utensils (glasses, bowls, pots) from the kitchen, as these may find their way back and cause harm. Lock the utensils used for plating in a separate locker *in the studio.*

Disposal. Having a sink nearby is a great advantage, not only when plating is to be done, but whenever chemicals are used. Cyanides are the most dangerous of the chemicals used in plating. If cyanide-bearing solutions are to be disposed of, they must not be poured down a sink drain unless the drain has been very thoroughly flushed with a lye solution. This will neutralize any acids present in the drain and thus prevent the formation of very harmful cyanide gases. Drainpipes should be flushed continuously when chemicals are being handled at the sink so that not only are the chemicals diluted and flushed away, but the pipes themselves are protected from excessive corrosion.

While all this concern over plating procedures may have an inhibiting effect on the craftsman, it must be remembered that practically all the activities in a workshop or studio contain some elements of danger. One's safety in such an environment is simply a matter of being aware of possible dangers, and through awareness, avoiding them.

17 Enameling

Enameling is the process of applying a glasslike colored substance to the surface of a piece of metal for the purpose of decoration. The enamel itself is a form of glass, highly refined and colored with different metallic oxides. This glass is crushed, applied to the metal, and subjected to intense heat. The beauty of the resulting glazed surface depends directly upon the artistic judgment employed. Transparent, translucent, and opaque enamels are obtainable, and their effective use must be preceded by a consideration of color, harmony, design, and the purely constructional elements involved in making any well-designed piece of jewelry. A carefully drawn actual-size plan using the colors of the enamels under consideration is an important preliminary.

Enamel is commonly available in prepared form—that is, it is ready ground. The mesh, or grind, may vary from 60 mesh (coarse) to 150 mesh (very fine). Enamel in this powdered form is available packaged in paper bags or in plastic jars. Quantities for craftsmen usually go up to 1-pound packages and can be purchased by the ounce. For a start, however, the 2-ounce jar is recommended. A screenlike shaker top may be supplied or can be improvised by topping the jar with a piece of tightly drawn coarse nylon stocking secured by a strong rubber band (Fig. 145). Enamels, when not in actual use, should be stored dry in containers with secure, reasonably airtight lids to prevent deterioration.

Transparent enamels are not too finely ground (about 80 mesh). To get the most brilliant and clear effects, a quantity of the ground enamel should be placed in a jar and washed. Washing is accomplished by flooding the enamel with clean, preferably distilled, water and stirring with a clean spatula. When the ground enamel has been allowed to settle, the remaining cloudy water is poured off. This is done several times with transparent enamels in order to get the most brilliant results. *One* washing will do for opaque enamels. The moist enamel is ready for use at this stage. If it is

Fig. 145.

to be stored in its container, it should be dried first by *gentle* heating and then returned to its container and capped.

The jars containing enamels should be labeled, and such information as color, fusing temperature, transparency (or opacity), and even manufacturer or supplier, recorded. (A code number for manufacturer can be devised if label space is small, and the code record kept in a notebook with any other pertinent data.)

As soon as some experience in enameling is gained and a sufficient palette of colors is on hand, it is very useful to make a set of small fused samples for each color. These chips will serve as the most valid samples if fired on the metal generally used by the craftsman. The samples, of course, should be labeled to match the data on the jars.

THE METALS

A variety of metals is used for enameling purposes. *Pure copper* sheet, usually 18 gauge, is most commonly used because it is easily worked and is relatively inexpensive. It is also available in wire and tube form.

Fine silver, considerably more expensive, is used for more important work. Sterling silver, because it may contain a small amount of zinc, is usually avoided as the zinc volatilizes during high temperatures—that is, it is transformed into a gaseous state and bubbles through the enamel as it is being fired, spoiling the work. Fine silver is also available in sheet, wire, and tube form. The melting point of fine silver (1761° F) is well above that of sterling (1640° F), another important advantage.

Gold is used in very fine enamel work and obviously is for the experienced because of its high cost. Gold is available in many different forms, karat values and colors, and it is wise to purchase it from suppliers who specialize in gold (as well as other metals) *for enamelers.* By doing this one can avoid alloys containing zinc or other metals unsatisfactory for enameling.

In general, brass, bronze, and ordinary iron or steel are unsuitable for enameling, either because of tin or zinc content or because of oxidizing qualities. Dealers in enameling supplies do, however, handle specially alloyed or plated metals and prepared steel sheet suitable for enameling and relatively reasonable in cost. Consult their catalogs.

THE FORMS OF ENAMELED WORK

When a piece of work is designed with intent to enamel a part of it, the craftsman, in considering his design, must recognize the various ways in which enamel is employed as a part of the jewelry.

Basse-taille enameling requires the execution of a design (later to be covered with a transparent enamel) in a sunken field. The area to be enameled is cut below the surface of the surrounding metal. This may be accomplished with gravers, by etching, or by

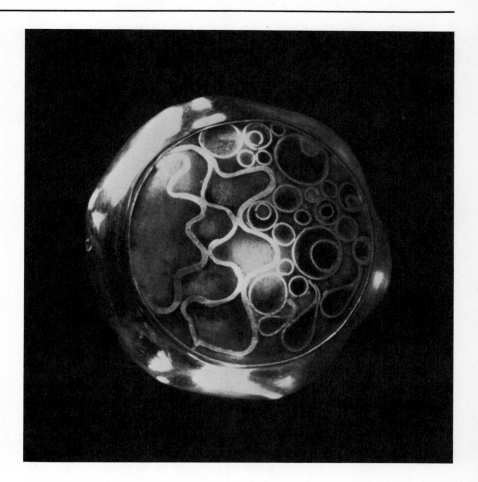

Fig. 146.   Cloisonné enamel pin. (Molly Plaster)

stamping. The resulting low area is then ornamented with some form of decoration. This may be done by carving, engraving, repoussé, stamping (embossing), or etching. The use of a hand-held vibrator tool for creating an attractive background pattern or design is another possibility. It is worthwhile experimenting with this technique using scrap copper until some expertise is developed. The work itself, if reasonably flat, may be anchored to a *solid* work space by using a double-sided adhesive tape on the underside of the work. This tape, obtainable in most art supply stores, provides an adhesive surface on *both* sides of the tape.

When the sunken area has been suitably embellished with some form of design, this area is then filled, or charged, with the transparent enamel in its powdered or granular form. When fired, or fused, the transparent enamel permits the design wrought in the sunken field to be visible through its transparency. The surface of the enamel in its final stage should be level with the surrounding metal.

Champlevé enameling is accomplished by fusing enamel into a sunken surface. The *unornamented* sunken area contains the enamel and can be made by carving with gravers, etching, stamping or sinking with flat repoussé tools. Sunken areas can also be formed by the application or overlaying of pierced sections or by a suitable casting. Opaque or transparent enamels can be used to fill these sunken "fields." In cast work, however, opaque enamels are usually preferable because of the porosity of a casting, which becomes too noticeable if transparent enamel is used. (See *Preparation,* further on.)

Cloisonné enameling is accomplished by means of cloisons, or cells. These cloisons are compartments formed by ribbons or strips of metal or flattened-wire sections soldered or otherwise adhered to the surface of the jewelry. The cloisons are formed and arranged according to the desired design. After these cloisons have been affixed in place, the resulting hollows or cells are filled with enamels of various colors, which are then fused (Fig 146).

Limoges enameling is done without the aid of separate compartmented areas or cells. Finely ground enamel is applied to the metallic surface and further applications of different colors are made in turn over the nearly dry previous applications. The enamels are then fused at one firing.

Limoges enameling can also be done in successive steps. A ground color is first fused over the metal. The design or picture is then worked out by careful application of fusible color. A second firing is given the work. A final firing lays over the whole a thin coating of a transparent, colorless enamel. Pictorial work can be done in this way, as shown on the illustrated ring in Figure 147. Additional information on this technique is given later in this chapter.

Plique-à-jour enameling resembles, to some extent, miniature stained-glass work. Forms of curved wire, cloisonnélike, are built into a design. These forms are soldered into a single unit *without* a backing. Enamel is used to completely fill each cell or compartment. After fusing, the glasslike transparent enamel transmits light, which is unimpeded by any backing. This work is best done using fine silver or gold.

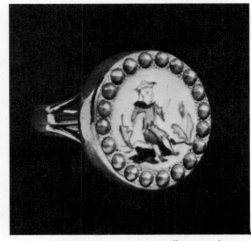

Fig. 147. Limoges enameling on ring. (L.W.)

CONSTRUCTION

Construction of Work for Basse-taille and Champlevé Enameling

For such work, a portion of the design must be sunk by one of several methods to hold enamel. The simplest method utilizes the etching action of an acid. Etching as a process has been described in detail in the chapter preceding this one. All that is necessary to repeat here is that the etched areas must be as smooth and clean-cut as possible. The depth of such areas may be from 1/32" to 1/16". The only way in which this depth can be obtained with a cleanly defined edge is by *slow* etching. A slow etching process will take as much as 6 or 8 hours. It also entails the occasional brushing aside of tiny bubbles that may cling to the outline of the design. Remember that the back of the work is to be protected in etching. Black asphaltum or prepared artist's etching ground can be used as a resist.

When the etching has been completed and the work cleaned, the additional work for basse-taille enameling can be done. This means that the addition of a carved design or chased portion is

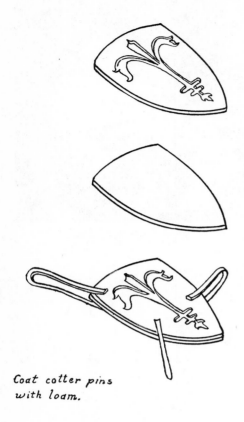

Coat cotter pins
with loam.

Fig. 148.

added to the sunken area. If repoussé is used, the highest part of the design must *not* protrude higher than the surrounding area of metal, so that *all* of the area to be enameled can be covered. Instead of repoussé work, a stamped or embossed design can be added to the sunken field. Transparent enamel is used in basse-taille work to permit the added decoration to be visible. An interesting method for achieving a basse-taille effect can be tried as follows: etch the sunken field in the usual manner. When a depth of 1/32" has been obtained, clean the work and then paint in the design in the sunken area with a resist and re-etch. The surrounding high metal is also repainted. The result will be a design in two depths. Fill the whole with enamel. The design will be visible in the sunken field at the finish.

If the champlevé technique is used—that is, the sunken area is made simply to hold enamel, opaque or transparent—nothing need be done other than etching the proper area, cleaning the metal, and applying the enamel to be fired.

A second method of obtaining a sunken field, which may be used as a basis for basse-taille work, is the chasing method. In this case the metal to be enameled is placed in the pitch bowl after the design has been laid out. The outline is then traced with a fine tracer. An "offset" chasing tool is then used to clarify the outline, and a polished flat tool finishes the sinking of the remaining area. It might be well to refer again to the chapter on chasing for a detailed discussion on the technique of chasing.

A third method used to gain a sunken field for enameling utilizes the application or overlay of a piece of pierced metal. This means that a suitable design is pierced on a piece of metal, about No. 20 gauge. This piece of metal is then sweat-soldered to a back piece. The pierced portions then become containers for the enamel (Fig. 148). In this case, the pieces of soldered metal should be tightly bound in such a way so as not to interfere with the enamel and yet keep the metal together. This is necessary because the fusing point of the solder may be lower than that of the enamel and therefore care must be taken to keep the pieces from separating during the firing process. This point will be further discussed later under *Firing.*

The final method for securing a sunken field is by casting. A ring, for example, is cast in sand. The model used has sunken areas. These areas hold the enamel. Opaque enamel is generally used because the porosity of a casting spoils the beauty of transparent enameling. This porosity, however, can be considerably minimized by carefully working over the cast surface with properly shaped chasing tools. Such flattened tools planish the cast surface, which gradually becomes smooth and dense. Cast surfaces so treated are much more pleasing in texture than if left with the original cast texture. Curved surfaces that may occur in such work may require the use of tragacanth together with the enamel. In such cases the powdered enamel is mixed with gum tragacanth solution instead of water. This procedure keeps the moist enamel in position on sharply curved surfaces. Otherwise, procedures for applying and firing enamel are similar to cloisonné work.

Construction of Cloisonné Work

Wire is used to form the cells or cloisons. This wire is, ideally, in ribbon form—that is, wire with flat surfaces or rectangular or square cross section (see cutaway view of a group of cloisons in Fig. 149). This wire can also be formed by drawing round wire of sufficient diameter through a rectangular drawplate. Wire so processed must be annealed before it can be used for forming cloisons (see *Annealing Wire*). Wire preformed especially for cloisons is available in both fine silver and gold. Check suppliers for such materials.

If no other form of wire is available, however, round wire can be used. In such a case the top of this wire is ground flat when the fired enamel piece is given its final treatment with a Carborundum stone, during which process the fired enamel is leveled off. Wire used for cloisonné work is generally not more than ⅟₃₂″ in width across the top, though it may be as *deep* as ⅟₁₆″.

The cloisons are formed using various pliers, round rods, or fingers, and then hard-soldered. They are applied as per design to a suitable backing plate and soldered at various points to this plate. The contact between the plate and the complete unit of cloisons should be as nearly perfect as possible before soldering is done. If necessary to get good contact, the soldering can be done in several successive steps, pressing the cloisons against the plate after each step. The annealing action during each soldering may make it easier to press the cloisons against the plate for closer conformity.

A word concerning the solder: hard solder of high melting temperature should be used. Solder should be used sparingly—it is not necessary to solder the cloisons to the backplate with a soldered contact along every edge. Merely tack the units at various points. Some hard solder contains zinc. This zinc may become a gas, vaporizing during the firing process. If this should occur, holes may be created in the enamel that are sometimes difficult to do away with. The holes are the result of the volatile gas seeping through the enamel. Therefore, some information concerning the hard-solder alloy is useful and should be obtained from the supplier or maker whenever possible. Gold solder is frequently used to avoid discoloration of some enamels. If used on metals other than gold, melting points should be considered, as well as the particular gold-solder alloy. Eight- or ten-karat solder usually will serve. If enameling is done on gold, a solder appropriate to the karat of the gold should be used (see *Hard Soldering*).

A good method for setting cloisons which does away with the use of solder is the following:

The plate upon which the cloisons are to be fastened is *counterenameled* on the *reverse* side and given a coat of "flux" on the *cloison* side. This flux, or "fondant" is a clear enamel used to brighten transparent colors. When the work has cooled, the shaped cloisons are dipped in a solution of gum tragacanth and positioned on the clear enamel. (If opaque enamel is being used for the piece, a suitable ground color enamel can be substituted for the fondant

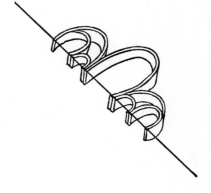

Fig. 149.

and fired in its place. Cloisons are then fixed in position as described above.)

When all cloisons are in position, the work is gently dried. This can be done in front of a warm kiln with its door open. Then the work is refired *in* the kiln so that the cloisons sink permanently into the enamel and remain there. When the work has cooled again, it can be given a quick dip in a nitric acid solution, rinsed, and the cloisons then filled, or "charged," with enamels of the desired colors.

Plique-à-jour Construction

This construction is somewhat similar to cloisonné work, the difference being that no backplate is used. This means that light may pass through the enameled piece. It also means a more delicate end product. To keep the enamel safely anchored in the cloisons, the inner surfaces of each cell are "keyed." To key a surface means to provide some anchorage for the enamel. This can be done by carving the insides of the cells with a graving tool.

A simple and effective method of keying uses wire that is rectangular or ribbonlike in cross-section. This can be made with a rectangular-hole drawplate as recommended for cloisonné work or purchased ready-made in ribbon form. Anneal the wire and draw through a round-hole drawplate, selecting a hole *slightly* smaller in diameter than the "depth" of the rectangular wire. When such wire is drawn through the proper-sized round hole, the wire is curved slightly in cross section. The leading end of the wire must be filed to a taper, of course, to start through the opening of the drawplate (Fig. 150). Procedures for assembling the piece are similar to those for cloisonné, eliminating, of course, the backplate. The hard solder used should be of the high-temperature type, sometimes referred to as IT grade. This is the kind generally used in enameling.

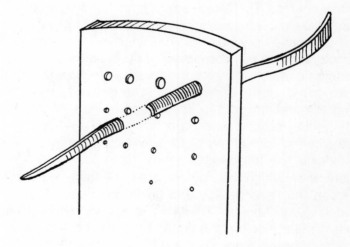

Fig. 150.   Broken view of ribbon to show section.

In a simpler form of plique-à-jour construction, the intricately pierced design is cut from a single piece of fine sheet silver, usually 18 gauge. Any necessary touch-up of shapes is done with needle files. The completed lacelike design is then ready to be filled, or "charged," with enamel and fired.

CLEANING BEFORE ENAMELING

Before going ahead with further techniques in the application of enamels it must be understood that all work to be enameled must be scrupulously clean before the enamel is applied. Loam, if used during soldering, should be scrubbed off first. Any binding wire or similar materials must be removed. The work itself is then ready for pickling. If a surface has been carved or planished with chasing tools, pickling will deaden the luster. Pickle before using these tools when possible, using the pickle described in the chapter on pickling. (Keep pickle for silver and pickle for copper separate and use appropriately.) Bright details can be restored by using a burnisher or scraper where necessary.

If a highly polished surface for transparent enamels is desired, it will be necessary to do some repolishing, inasmuch as any previous polishing will have been dulled by the pickle. Use a soft felt buff and preferably white jeweler's rouge to rebuff the pickled mat finish. Wash the polished work in clean water to which a tiny amount of detergent has been added. Some use a solution of water containing a bit of bicarbonate of soda. Rinse, finally, in clean water and avoid handling with bare hands, so as to keep oils from the skin from marking the metal surface. Cleaned work can be kept immersed in water until ready to be charged with enamel. This will delay oxidation. "Bright dips" (see *Dips and Oxidizing or Coloring Solutions*) can be used before enameling, followed by a clean rinse.

APPLYING AND FIRING

Charging and Firing Cloisonné Work

Enamel to be applied should be in the form of a damp paste. The powdered enamel must be moist enough to pack evenly but should not be so watery as to flow. The enamel should be applied with a slightly spoon-shaped spatula, patting it down very lightly with the underside of the spatula. Enamel shrinks somewhat after firing, which usually means the addition of enamel and refiring in order to fill a sunken area. One should not attempt to overcome this by too heavy an initial application of enamel, since this can cause chipping. Enamel is almost always applied as thinly as possible. Repeated firings of thin applications give greater depth and beauty to transparent colors.

Excess water should be removed when the enamel has been applied. This can be done by applying the edge of a piece of clean cloth or clean blotting paper to the edges of the enamel-bearing areas. Each time an assembled cloisonné piece is charged, it should be dried in front of the furnace before firing. This is done repeatedly until the fired cloisons are sufficiently full.

If cloisons are not full to the top (as is usually the case), they must be given additional enamel and refired. Any small holes or flaws appearing on the fused surface must be cleaned out with a sharp, pointed instrument such as a scriber or scraper, and enamel added. If bare spaces appear on the sunken portions, they must be scraped clean, and enamel must be added. For cloisonné work several successive firings are quite normal.

Work can be examined more accurately after firing if it is pickled first in a pickling solution appropriate to the metal being used. *This is done after the work has cooled.* The pickle will not affect the enamel. After pickling, the work should be scrubbed in running water with a clean, stiff bristle brush. A clean toothbrush can be used.

Excessively high cloison wire or enamel can be removed by grinding, so that enamel and surrounding cloison metal are at the same level. A medium-grit corundum or Carborundum abrasive stick should be used. The rubbing or grinding-off of the enameled surface should be done under running tap water or in a tray filled with water. The work can be rested on a flat piece of leather belting and submerged in water. It should then be rubbed with the stone until the whole surface is properly leveled. Unless a mat finish (as with an opaque enamel) is the desired effect, the work should be refired to recapture the gloss lost during stoning. The work must be washed thoroughly before this final refiring.

Final Finish Without Refiring

A good final finish on cloisonné work can be achieved without the final firing by stoning alone, or stoning and buffing.

To stone, use the Carborundum abrasive stick and water as described above. Use successively finer-grit stones and follow with Scotch stone and water. With patience, the Scotch stone finish will eliminate the fine scratches left by the previous stones. Fine-grit "wet-or-dry" paper (used wet) of about 320 to 400 grade may be used before the Scotch stone.

After all stoning, the work should be washed clean and given its final polished finish. Cerium oxide in powdered form is used wet. It is applied to the surface and rubbed by hand with a block of hard felt. A 3" hard felt buffing wheel, about ¾" thick, is useful for this. Use the flat side of the wheel. When the work has been given this treatment for a while, it can be washed off. A polished surface should result.

A substitute for the hand work with the buffing wheel is the powered buffing machine. A firmly stitched cloth wheel and a bar of tin oxide or other lapidary-type polishing compound are used at somewhat lower speed than usual in buffing and will result in a fine polish.

Charging and Firing Limoges Enameling

This type of enameling is frequently done on thin copper. In order to give the required stiffness to the work, the metal should be domed slightly. The decorative enameling can then be done on the convex surface (Fig. 151). Methods for doming are discussed elsewhere in this book.

If a flat piece must be done without doming, the metal should be *counter-enameled.* Such pictorial and generally larger work is done on somewhat thicker metal, such as 18 gauge.

Counter-Enameling

The practice of enameling the reverse side of any enameled piece is called counter-enameling. It is especially important when considerable area is involved. As little as 2 or 3 square inches can be considered in this category.

Counter-enameling is done because, after enamel has been fired, it shrinks upon cooling. If the metal that was fired was heavy gauge and moderate in area, no ill effects should result. Thus, for example, if a coat of enamel were fired over one face of a five-cent piece, counter-enameling would not be necessary. But because much work is done on thinner metals and on larger surfaces, a shrinkage of the cooling enamel would cause enough distortion of the metal so that the enamel would be likely to crack and pieces would fly from the surface.

Therefore, when the ground color for a Limoges-type object is to be applied, it is wise to counter-enamel the back of the work, using as a counter-enamel the same material used as the base coat for the front of the piece. The counter-enamel is applied first, after using a solution of *gum tragacanth,* not water, to moisten it. A spatula is used to apply the counter-enamel in a very thin coating. On large pieces, the back of the work is moistened with the gum solution and the dry, powdered enamel is dusted over the metal while wet with the solution. A shaker-type jar is used. The powdered enamel will darken with moisture as it adheres. The dusting should not proceed beyond this stage.

Charging the Front

The front of the work may be charged at this stage by turning it over carefully and resting the counter-enameled side on a piece of clean blotting paper or between the prongs of a stainless steel enameling trivet. The water-moistened fondant or ground color can be laid on with a spatula or fine camel's hair brush. This enameled surface will rest faceup in the kiln, so no gum solution is mixed in. Excessive water, if any, can be removed from the charged piece by applying a piece of lint-free cloth or blotting paper to the edge of the work. A tamp can be made from this cloth and used, if necessary, to gently press the enamel flat. If the enamel coating is still unevenly applied, a spatula can be used to spread the enamel evenly and thinly. The piece is dried *gently* in front of the open kiln before it is fired.

Fig. 151. A domed cloisonné pendant. (Young Baek)

The Gum Tragacanth Solution

Before going ahead to the firing of the enamel, the following procedure for making a gum tragacanth solution is offered:

About 1/10 of an ounce of the powdered gum is placed in a pint jar and just enough wood alcohol is added to cover the gum completely. This is allowed to stand overnight, after which time a pint of clean, warm water is added. The solution is stirred thoroughly. If a drop or two of oil of cloves is stirred into the solution, it will last without deterioration for a few months. This mixture can be used wherever a gum tragacanth solution is recommended. (Prepared solutions are sold.)

If a heavier solution is needed for any steep-sided work (bowls, vertical work) let some of the solution stand overnight and then pour off some from the top. The heavier remaining solution can then be used.

The Limoges work is now ready for firing. See *Firing Enamel— General Procedures*, later in this chapter.

Further Application of Colors on Limoges Work

When the combined ground and counter-enameled firing has been completed, the desired decorative enameling characteristic of Limoges work can be applied over the fired ground.

Colors used for painting in the design are supplied ready for use in tubes somewhat like oil paints or can be used in dry powder form specially ground for Limoges work. These are extremely fine-ground and must be kept well corked and absolutely dust-free. The vehicle for the color is an essence or oil. The supplier of the color may be best qualified for suggesting the vehicle, or an essence can be prepared for use with colors finely ground for Limoges painting, by allowing a small quantity of turpentine to evaporate in air, leaving its nonvolatile or fatty content. Add this to benzene in the proportion of 1:200.

The colors are mixed with this and painted on with a fine camel's hair brush. Another vehicle for the enamel is oil of lavender and squeegee oil. The enamel is mixed with the oil of lavender to form paste thin enough to handle with a fine brush. Only a tiny amount of squeegee oil is used as a binder. Experience will show which colors can be placed in juxtaposition for the same firing without spoiling. So many chemical reactions occur when dealing with these metallic oxides that only long practice in enameling can assure success in more ambitious undertakings in this field.

To dry these applied colors, the work must be carefully warmed until the essence is seen evaporating in a thin smoke. This may be done cautiously and intermittently over a small blue flame. The work is rested on a flat plate. When no more smoke rises, the colors will appear to be quite changed. This is normal. Place the work carefully in the kiln, which should be at firing temperature. It is generally advisable to use a long tongs which holds the support, or cradle, upon which the work has been placed. The work is brought into the kiln gradually so that it is not heated suddenly. The surface should be watched closely. After perhaps a minute, the colors will glaze. Should the work be withdrawn too soon, it can be fired further until thoroughly vitrified. True color will not appear until the work cools. If all painting has been done, the work is ready for the protective final glaze. Otherwise, additional "painting" is done on the cooled surface and another firing is given.

Final Glaze on Limoges

The final protective glaze used to cover an otherwise completed Limoges piece is a clear, colorless, transparent enamel called flux. This should be of the highest quality. Fine grind and freshness are important. When purchasing, reference should be made to its intended use. The fusing point will necessarily be somewhat lower than the previously fired colored enamels. The object to be glazed is thoroughly cleaned and carefully dried. It is then moistened with a commercially prepared gum solution called Klyr Fyr, and the powdered flux is sifted thinly but completely over the surface of the work, which is then gently dried by heat. The work is next fired in the already heated furnace and should be removed as soon as a smooth glaze appears. Do not overfire! If any additional flux or minor repair is needed, an additional flux firing will be the final step.

Charging and Firing Plique-à-Jour

When the basic metal work for a piece of plique-à-jour is clean and ready for charging with enamel, it can be placed on a piece of material to which fired enamel will not adhere. The material most often used is a specially selected grade of mica sheet, not affected by high firing temperatures, with a particularly smooth surface. Such mica is available from supply houses dealing with enamelers' materials. Sometimes specially alloyed sheets of aluminum or brass are used. The work must rest perfectly flat on the mica, which, in turn, can be placed on a heavy screen heating frame shaped like a flat, inverted **V**. Perforated sheet iron can also be used, although, whenever possible, stainless steel is the best choice.

The enamel can then be moistened with a thin solution of gum tragacanth and the openings filled with this enamel using a small spatula. The work should then be carefully dried and fired in a kiln previously brought up to firing temperature. More than one firing may be necessary to completely fill the openings.

Because the work rested on mica during firing, the result may be a slight texturing on the mica side after the mica has been removed. If the openings in the design are fairly small, such a texture can be eliminated by a final vertical firing. To do this, a piece of heavy (No. 14 or 16 gauge) nichrome wire should be erected by pushing one end into a piece of fire brick. The other end is then formed into a hook from which the work can hang vertically. The work then can be refired. Capillary action will hold the enamel in the openings if the work is done with care *and not overfired.* If the design is such that a hook cannot be used at any point, the work may possibly be wedged into a narrow groove cut into the brick with a heavy-duty hacksaw blade. It must be remembered that the remelted enamel will sag out of the vertical spaces if left in the kiln too long.

FIRING ENAMEL—GENERAL PROCEDURES

Protection of Previously Soldered Joints

Because of the fact that much enamel fuses at temperatures past the melting points of hard solders, exposed joints previously made *and having no contacts with enameled areas* should be carefully protected with loam or ochre coatings before firing the enamel. It is not practical to hard-solder such parts as ear-wires or pin-backs *after* enameling has been completed.

To repair enameled work when soldering is involved, use soft solder, as this flows at a temperature well below that of enamel. Avoid chilling!

Firing the Enamel

Three sources of heat for firing enamels are available. A gas burner of the venturi type is the simplest means. This is permissible for small objects. Care must be taken to keep the flame off the enameled surface, or discolorations will result. Only a blue flame will serve for enameling. Figure 152 shows a venturi-type Bunsen burner firing a piece of enameled work (one surface only—no counter-enameling). The heavy piece of screening called a heating frame is used to support the work and should be of stainless steel, nickel, or iron. If iron is to be used, a thin solution of loam in water must be made, into which the screen should be dipped and thus coated. This will prevent any scales of iron oxide formed during heating from flying off into the enamel. (The loam is slowly baked dry before the firing process.)

A gas furnace provides the second means of firing, and an electric furnace, or kiln, provides the third means. It is best to have a small electric furnace equipped with a pyrometer (Fig. 153) so that the exact "flow" temperatures of the various enamels to be used can be established and noted on the labels of their containers.

When placing the work in a furnace for firing, the work should first be carefully baked dry in a moderate heat near the furnace with its door open. When no more vapor rises from the enamel, the work is ready for firing.

Enamels fuse at temperatures ranging from about 1400° F to 1600° F. It is therefore important for the craftsman to make test firings of samples of the enamels as mentioned earlier. By checking with a pyrometer, the melting points of the enamels being used can be ascertained. Work should not be placed in a furnace until the furnace has reached firing temperature. The best work is done with a short, hot firing.

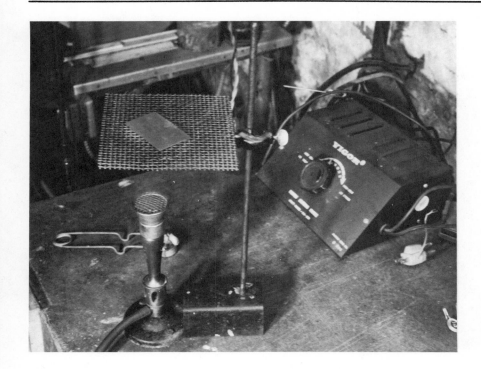

Fig. 152. The simplest method for firing enameled work.

Fig. 153. Small electric enameling furnace equipped with pyrometer. Note peephole in door. (Allcraft)

Work placed in a furnace can be supported on a screen similar to that used in the photo showing the Bunsen burner firing. If used in a furnace, shape the screen support so that it resembles a squat, inverted U with a broad, flat top and short legs to raise the work about an inch off the furnace floor. This will allow for good circulation of heat. If an iron screen is used, coat with loam as previously described. A variety of "stilts," or stainless steel trivets, are available for different kinds of setups. Consult catalogs.

When the enamel has fused, it will present a glossy surface, reflecting the glow of the incandescent interior of the furnace. This can be seen if the furnace door has been provided with a peephole, a useful feature which prevents the excessive lowering of furnace temperature when the door is opened. If no peephole has been provided, open the door as little as possible and take a quick look. If glossy, the enamel has fused, and the work may be removed for slow cooling. Protect the hands with asbestos gloves and use a special "fork" for lifting out the screen support. Keep the work near the furnace for warmth, resting it on a piece of transite until cool. If cooling should take place too rapidly, the work may crack or shatter. Transite board, which is a hard, cementlike form of asbestos, is somewhat safer than ordinary asbestos board since it has no loose particles of asbestos that can float around to be inhaled, rest on newly fired enamel, or pollute freshly charged enamel work nearby.

Removing Enamel from Work

When enamel must be removed for any reason, the greater part can be tapped out with a small steel tool. The flexible shaft machine can also be used if the Foredom hammerpiece is available. This is one of the various types of handpieces available for use with the flexible shaft. With a pointed tip inserted and the hammering pressure adjusted, it does the job quickly and effectively.

Any remaining bits of enamel can be eaten out with hydrofluoric acid. This attacks enamel or glass. To use such acid, heat a porcelain bowl containing some paraffin or wax. Swish the melted wax around in the bowl to coat the inside thoroughly. Allow to cool. A bowl so treated will safely hold hydrofluoric acid. The enameled piece must then be thoroughly coated with wax—back and front—except for the enameled part to be removed by acid. The piece can then be carefully immersed in the acid. As the action takes place, a white substance will form. To inspect the action from time to time, remove the work (use rubber gloves) and rinse under running water. *Do not inhale the acid fumes.* Eye protection and good ventilation are necessary when working with all corrosive acids.

If corrective enamel work is then decided upon, all wax should be removed, the piece scrubbed in a mixture of warm water and ammonia, and rinsed, and the usual enameling procedures followed. Remember—the hydrofluoric acid must be stored in the special container in which it was originally purchased.

POLISHING OR BUFFING ENAMEL SURFACES

If an enameled surface has had its luster dulled through wear or accident and refiring is impractical, the gloss can be reestablished by machine buffing. For an abrasive compound, use wet pumice on the work, together with a hard felt wheel. For a good final gloss, use compounds as prescribed for lapidary or glass polishing, such as tin oxide. This is available in bar form, like tripoli and rouge. Remember when doing such buffing that enamel is harder than the surrounding metal. Observe the progress of the buffing carefully in order to avoid removing an excessive amount of the metal.

MISCELLANEOUS INFORMATION

A final word on enamels: although color changes in enamels can be effected by mixing enamels that fuse at the same temperatures, better results are obtained when a color change is produced by fusing a transparent enamel of one color over an opaque enamel of another color.

A flux or fondant is the colorless vehicle for the metallic oxide that when added results in a colored enamel. This fondant sometimes is used for a preliminary firing. Transparent colored enamels following this firing will have greater brilliance. The use of fondants for a preliminary firing will result in truer colors, since metals such as copper tend to affect the color of an enamel if a fondant has not been previously applied.

When gum tragacanth is necessary to keep enamel clinging to a curved surface or to eliminate the tendency of colors to mingle, use it in liquid form and in very small quantity. The water used should be of the distilled variety rather than ordinary tap water. (This should be the case when water is used for any enameling procedures other than rinsing and clean-up.) A commercially prepared solution called Klyr Fyr can be substituted for the studio-prepared gum tragacanth. Either solution will also keep enamel on an inverted metal surface. Neither will affect the color of an enamel.

Ground enamels should be kept in well-stoppered jars that can be labeled as described at the beginning of this chapter. Dating the contents can also be helpful. If the enamel is wet, it should be gently baked dry for storage purposes, since wet enamel tends to deteriorate and should not be stored for an extended period.

A kiln with a drop-front door has an advantage in that the opened door can serve as a convenient shelf useful for drying the freshly applied enamel before it is dried inside the kiln. The kiln, of course, should be warm during this drying process. A peephole in the door is an additional convenience since it is useful for checking the progress of the work inside. If the piece being fired is in line of sight with the peephole, the glow of the red-heated elements reflected on the newly glazed enamel can be observed. The work can thus be removed at the proper moment and overfiring avoided. Shelves of transite or similar heatproof materials are available in ceramic supply houses as well as at suppliers of jewelry and enameling materials.

Kiln wash, also available at the above sources, can be mixed with water to a thin cream consistency and used to coat the kiln floor. This protects the firebrick floor of the kiln from the drippings and encrustations of glazed enamels. The interior of a kiln should be cleaned regularly—particularly before firings. After prying loose any dripped enamel, the kiln can be vacuumed. Loose scale and other detritus might otherwise find their way to enameled surfaces during firing.

Supply Catalogs

The value of catalogs from dealers in jewelry and enameling supplies cannot be overemphasized. These catalogs are informative in that they keep the craftsman in touch with the latest information on new equipment and developments in metals, tools, chemicals, and related materials. Many catalogs contain explicit, useful technical information. Craft magazines contain not only information concerning the work of other craftsmen, but advertisements of suppliers as well. Their catalogs are frequently of considerable value. Make a point of obtaining them.

Appendix

THE SHOP

Throughout the text, suggestions have been given concerning the proper care, as well as usage, of the jeweler's tools. The requirements of a suitable workbench have also been stated in the chapter on sawing.

For the sake of the craftsman who hopes to start business in a small way, photographs have been included to show how equipment can be set up as efficiently and inexpensively as is possible, without the requirement of great space. The workbench pictured (Fig. 154) seats six artisans comfortably. These workers—in the photograph, pupils—can do all sawing and filing at the bench. Soldering and heating operations are done elsewhere, as are heavy pounding operations. The unit pictured was originally designed for use in a school shop in which the jewelry craft activity was added at a later date. The unit was quite successful and required very little room. Working plans have been provided in this text so that such a workbench can be easily duplicated. A long, fluorescent lighting fixture can be mounted over the workbench if proper lighting is not otherwise provided for.

The closet pictured (Fig. 155) is one of three units housing a complete complement of hand tools. Racks are provided for all tools, and they are mounted in practical fashion, as well as with an eye towards safety. Note the guarded scriber points, as well as the needle file racks placed so that the tips of the files are rendered harmless by the overhang of other racks. Outlines of tools are painted in bright red. Surrounding area is canary yellow—chosen to provide self-illumination because of the lack of a lighting fixture. Light from an opposite window makes tool checkup a simple matter.

Nameplates are provided to identify the tools, the author having noted a tendency upon the part of the users to refer to the tools as "this" or "that" rather than by name. The tool cabinets are provided with lock-equipped doors, and all equipment can be secured as well as checked in a matter of a few moments.

Fig. 154. A convenient bench for sawing and filing designed by the author for use in a restricted space.

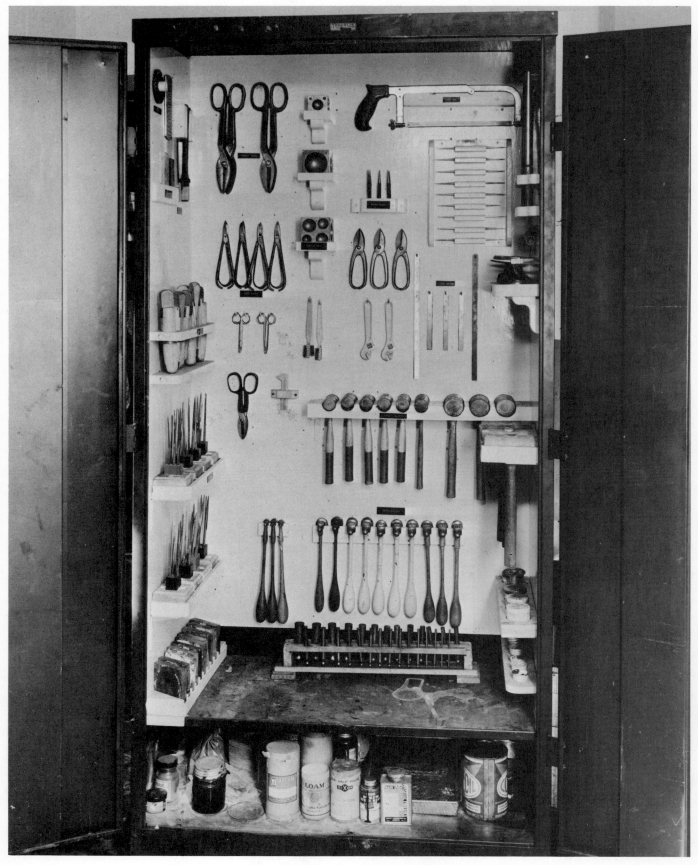

Fig. 155.   One of a set of closets for a group of twenty training craftsmen.

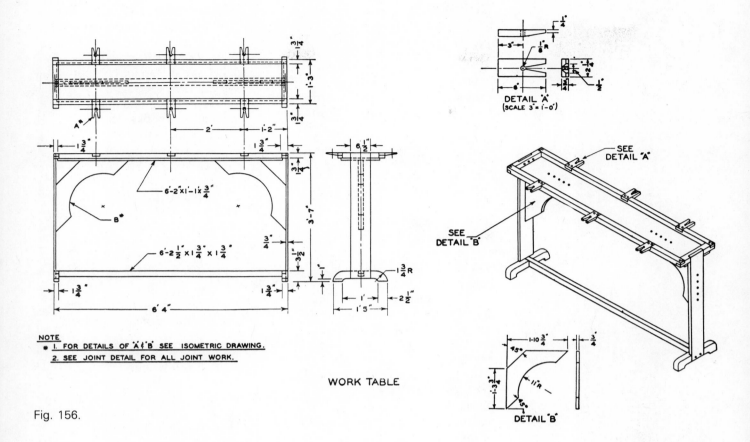

NOTE
* 1. FOR DETAILS OF "A" & "B" SEE ISOMETRIC DRAWING.
2. SEE JOINT DETAIL FOR ALL JOINT WORK.

WORK TABLE

Fig. 156.

DETAIL "A"
(SCALE 3" = 1'-0")

SEE DETAIL "A"

SEE DETAIL "B"

DETAIL "B"

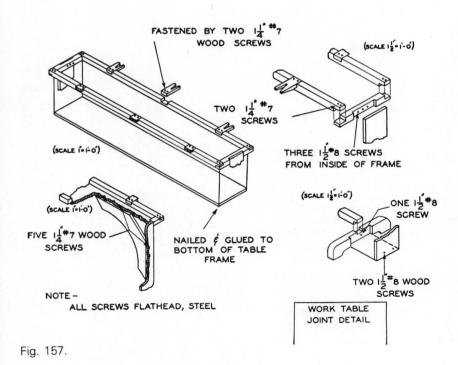

FASTENED BY TWO 1¼" #7 WOOD SCREWS

(SCALE 1½" = 1'-0")

TWO 1¼" #7 SCREWS

(SCALE 1" = 1'-0")

THREE 1½" #8 SCREWS FROM INSIDE OF FRAME

(SCALE 1" = 1'-0")

FIVE 1¼" #7 WOOD SCREWS

NAILED & GLUED TO BOTTOM OF TABLE FRAME

NOTE –
ALL SCREWS FLATHEAD, STEEL

(SCALE 1½" = 1'-0")

ONE 1½" #8 SCREW

TWO 1½" #8 WOOD SCREWS

WORK TABLE JOINT DETAIL

Fig. 157.

SUPPLIERS

The following are a selection of the many suppliers who issue excellent catalogs, from a few to over 150 pages. Most involve a moderate charge. For information write to them directly.

Allcraft Tool & Supply Co.
100 Frank Road
Hicksville, NY 11801
or
22 West 48th Street
New York, NY 10036
or
204 North Harbor Boulevard
Fullerton, CA 92632
(Tools, metals, books, findings, chemicals, enamels, kilns, plating equipment, machines)

Anchor Tool & Supply Co.
231 Main Street (Route 24)
Chatham, NJ 07928
(Tools, findings, machines, plating equipment, books, jewelry boxes)

Bourget Bros.
1626 11th Street
Santa Monica, CA 90404
(Tools, findings, metals, machines)

W.R. Cobb Co.
850 Wellington Avenue
Cranston, RI 02910
(Specialist: findings [mfrs.] tubing, silver wire)

Wm. Dixon Co.
Carlstadt, NJ 07072
(Tools, books, metals, chemicals, findings, plating equipment, machines)

D.R.S. Inc.
15 West 47th Street
New York, NY 10036
(Tools, findings, books, chemicals, machines, plating equipment, watchmakers' supplies)

James Garriti
82 Bowery
New York, NY 10013
(Stones—synthetic, semiprecious, and precious; lapidary services)

G & G's Miracle House
5621 West Hemlock Street
Milwaukee, WI 53223
(Tools, metals, findings, plating equipment, books, kilns, watch supplies)

T.B. Hagstoz & Son, Inc.
709 Sansom Street
Philadelphia, PA 19106
(Findings, tools, jewelry boxes, machines)

C.R. Hill Co.
2734 West 11 Mile Road
Berkley, MI 48072
(Tools, enamels, findings, plating equipment, casting supplies)

Kilns Supply & Service Corp.
38 Bulkley Avenue
Portchester, NY 10573
(Kilns & kiln accessories; enamels)

New York Findings Corp.
72 Bowery
New York, NY 10013
(Specialist: findings)

Rodman & Yaruss Refining Co.
17 West 47th Street
New York, NY 10036
(Specialist: findings & precious metals)

C.W. Somers & Co., Inc.
387 Washington Street
Boston, MA 02108
(Tools, findings, books)

Swest, Inc.
Dept. GJ
10803 Composite Drive
Dallas, TX 75220
(Tools, machines, metals, findings, plating equipment)

Myron Toback, Inc.
23 West 47th Street
New York, NY 10036
(Specialist: findings, precious metals, jewelry boxes)

BOOKS

Several books of considerable interest are listed here. They contain not only beautiful illustrations and history but are wonderful sources for design inspiration as well. They also contain technical details concerning ancient methods that are surprisingly useful today. The museum books, issued in very limited numbers, may be available in your library.

Aldred, Cyril. *Jewels of the Pharaohs.* New York: Praeger Publishers, 1971.

Bray, Warwick. *The Gold of Eldorado.* New York: Harry N. Abrams, Inc., 1979.

Vilímková, Milada. *Egyptian Jewellery.* London: Paul Hamlyn, 1969.

Walters Art Gallery. *Jewelry: Ancient to Modern.* Edited by Anne Garside. New York: Viking Press, 1979.

Winlock, Herbert E. *The Treasure of el Lahun: Metropolitan Museum of Art.* New York: Arno Press, 1972.

Winlock, Herbert E. *The Treasure of Three Egyptian Princesses.* New York: Metropolitan Museum of Art, 1948.

MAGAZINES AND JOURNALS

Four magazines of interest to jewelry makers are listed below. Only the *Goldsmiths Journal* is concerned primarily with work in metal. The other three regularly contain some material devoted to jewelry but treat other craft fields also.

American Craft
American Craft Council
22 West 55th Street
New York, NY 10019

Goldsmiths Journal
The Society of North
American Goldsmiths
8589 Wonderland, N.W.
Clinton, OH 44216

Lapidary Journal
P.O. Box 80937
San Diego, CA 92138

Ornament
Ornament, Inc.
1221 South La Cienega
Los Angeles, CA 90035
(quarterly)

TESTS AND TABLES

Testing Silver and Gold

Sometimes a piece of metal scrap or a metal object must be tested to ascertain whether or not it is gold or silver. Some pure nitric acid and a glass stirring rod are all that are needed for these tests.

To test for silver, file a notch deep enough to penetrate any possible plating and apply the nitric acid with the glass stirring rod. Sterling silver will show a reaction in the form of a cream-colored cloudy froth. If the metal is coin silver, the reaction will produce a foam tending to blacken. Silver of low grade—750 and lower—show different greens, darker as the lower content silver is tested. Comparative checking with silver of known content will aid in identifying these.

To test gold, a notch is filed as described previously. If the acid is applied to gold over 10 karats, there will be very little reaction, if any at all. Gold of 10 karats will show a slight reaction. If gold has been plated over silver, the reaction will be creamy pink. If plated over a base metal, bright green will result.

Jewelry supply houses sell a kit consisting of the proper acids and a rubbing stone for testing precious metals.

RULES RELATING TO CIRCLES AND OVALS

1. A circle is .7854 times as heavy as a square of the same size, i.e., the loss in cutting a circle from a square is .2146 of the weight of the square.
2. The area of an oval is the longest diameter × the shortest × .7854.
3. The area of a circle is the diameter × itself × .7854.
4. The circumference of a circle is the diameter × 3.1416.
5. The diameter of a circle is the circumference multiplied by .31831.

TABLE OF MELTING POINTS (°F)

Aluminum	1218
Antimony	1166
Bismuth	520
Brass, also called "gilding metal" (copper 95, zinc 5)	1949
Brass, casting	2075
Brass, common (copper 65, zinc 35) also called "high brass"	930
Brazing metal (copper 50, zinc 50)	1616
Bronze (copper 80, tin 20)	1868
Copper	1981
Gold	1945
18 K green	1810
18 K red	1655
18 K white	1730
18 K yellow	1700
14 K green	1765
14 K red	1715
14 K white	1825
14 K yellow	1615
10 K green	1580
10 K red	1760
10 K white	1975
10 K yellow	1665
Iridium	4260
Iron	2795
Lead	621
Nickel	2645
Palladium	2831
Platinum	3200
Silver (fine)	1761
Silver (sterling)	1640
Silver (coin)	1615
Tin	450
Zinc	787

Circles and Squares

Circumferences and Areas

Size in Inches	Circumference of ○ in Inches	Area of ○ in Square Inches	Area of □ in Square Inches	Size in Inches	Circumference of ○ in Inches	Area of ○ in Square Inches	Area of □ in Square Inches
¼	.7854	.0491	.0625	10¼	32.20	82.52	105.06
½	1.571	.1964	.2500	10½	32.99	86.59	110.25
¾	2.356	.4418	.5625	10¾	33.77	90.76	115.56
1	3.142	.7854	1.000	11	34.56	95.03	121.00
1¼	3.927	1.227	1.563	11¼	35.34	99.40	126.56
1½	4.712	1.767	2.250	11½	36.13	103.87	132.25
1¾	5.498	2.405	3.063	11¾	36.91	108.43	138.06
2	6.283	3.142	4.000	12	37.70	113.10	144.00
2¼	7.069	3.976	5.063	12¼	38.48	117.86	150.06
2½	7.854	4.909	6.250	12½	39.27	122.72	156.25
2¾	8.639	5.940	7.563	12¾	40.06	127.68	162.56
3	9.425	7.069	9.000	13	40.84	132.73	169.00
3¼	10.21	8.296	10.56	13¼	41.63	137.89	175.56
3½	11.00	9.621	12.25	13½	42.41	143.14	182.25
3¾	11.78	11.04	14.06	13¾	43.20	148.49	189.06
4	12.57	12.57	16.00	14	43.98	153.94	196.00
4¼	13.35	14.19	18.06	14¼	44.77	159.49	203.06
4½	14.14	15.90	20.25	14½	45.55	165.13	210.25
4¾	14.92	17.72	22.56	14¾	46.34	170.87	217.56
5	15.71	19.64	25.00	15	47.12	176.72	225.00
5¼	16.49	21.65	27.56	15¼	47.91	182.65	232.56
5½	17.28	23.76	30.25	15½	48.69	188.69	240.25
5¾	18.06	25.97	33.06	15¾	49.48	194.83	248.06
6	18.85	28.27	36.00	16	50.27	201.06	256.00
6¼	19.64	30.68	39.06	16¼	51.05	207.39	264.06
6½	20.42	33.18	42.25	16½	51.84	213.83	272.25
6¾	21.21	35.78	45.56	16¾	52.62	220.35	280.56
7	21.99	38.48	49.00	17	53.41	226.98	289.00
7¼	22.78	41.28	52.56	17¼	54.19	288.71	297.56
7½	23.56	44.18	56.25	17½	54.98	240.53	306.25
7¾	24.35	47.17	60.06	17¾	55.76	247.45	315.06
8	25.13	50.27	64.00	18	56.55	254.47	324.00
8¼	25.92	53.46	68.06	18¼	57.33	261.59	333.06
8½	26.70	56.75	72.25	18½	58.12	268.80	342.25
8¾	27.49	60.13	76.56	18¾	58.91	276.12	351.56
9	28.28	63.62	81.00	19	59.69	283.53	361.00
9¼	29.06	67.20	85.56	19¼	60.48	291.04	370.56
9½	29.85	70.88	90.25	19½	61.26	298.65	380.25
9¾	30.63	74.66	95.06	19¾	62.05	306.36	390.06
10	31.42	78.54	100.00	20	62.83	314.16	400.00

Sheet Metal

Weight Per Square Inch by B & S Gauge

B & S	Thickness in Inches	Fine Silver	Sterling Silver	Coin Silver	Fine Gold	10 K Yel. Gold	14 K Yel. Gold	18 K Yel. Gold	Platinum	Palladium
		Ozs.	Ozs.	Ozs.	Dwts.	Dwts.	Dwts.	Dwts.	Ozs.	Ozs.
1	.28930	1.60	1.58	1.58	59.0	35.3	39.8	47.5	3.27	1.83
2	.25763	1.43	1.40	1.40	52.6	31.4	35.5	42.3	2.90	1.63
3	.22942	1.27	1.25	1.25	46.8	28.0	31.6	37.7	2.59	1.45
4	.20431	1.13	1.12	1.11	41.7	24.9	28.1	33.6	2.30	1.29
5	.18194	1.01	.996	.992	37.1	22.2	25.1	29.9	2.06	1.15
6	.16202	.899	.887	.883	33.1	19.8	22.3	26.6	1.83	1.02
7	.14428	.800	.790	.786	29.4	17.6	19.9	23.7	1.63	.912
8	.12849	.713	.704	.700	26.2	15.7	17.7	21.0	1.45	.812
9	.11443	.635	.627	.624	23.3	14.0	15.8	18.8	1.29	.723
10	.10189	.565	.558	.555	20.8	12.4	14.0	16.7	1.15	.644
11	.09074	.503	.497	.495	18.5	11.2	12.5	14.9	1.03	.574
12	.08080	.448	.443	.440	16.5	9.85	11.0	13.3	.913	.511
13	.07196	.399	.394	.392	14.7	8.77	9.91	11.8	.813	.455
14	.06408	.356	.351	.349	13.0	7.81	8.82	10.5	.724	.405
15	.05706	.317	.313	.311	11.6	6.96	7.86	9.37	.645	.361
16	.05082	.282	.278	.277	10.4	6.21	7.00	8.35	.574	.321
17	.04525	.251	.248	.247	9.23	5.52	6.23	7.43	.511	.286
18	.04030	.224	.221	.220	8.22	4.90	5.55	6.62	.455	.255
19	.03589	.199	.197	.196	7.32	4.38	4.94	5.89	.406	.227
20	.03196	.177	.175	.174	6.52	3.90	4.40	5.25	.361	.202
21	.02846	.158	.156	.155	5.81	3.47	3.92	4.67	.322	.180
22	.02534	.141	.139	.138	5.17	3.09	3.49	4.16	.286	.160
23	.02257	.125	.124	.123	4.60	2.75	3.11	3.71	.255	.143
24	.02010	.112	.110	.110	4.10	2.45	2.77	3.30	.228	.127
25	.01790	.0993	.0980	.0976	3.65	2.18	2.45	2.94	.202	.113
26	.01594	.0884	.0873	.0869	3.25	1.94	2.19	2.62	.180	.101
27	.01419	.0787	.0777	.0773	2.89	1.73	1.95	2.33	.160	.0897
28	.01264	.0701	.0692	.0689	2.58	1.54	1.74	2.08	.143	.0799
29	.01125	.0624	.0616	.0613	2.29	1.37	1.55	1.85	.127	.0711
30	.01002	.0556	.0549	.0546	2.04	1.22	1.38	1.66	.113	.0633
31	.00892	.0495	.0489	.0486	1.82	1.09	1.23	1.46	.101	.0564
32	.00795	.0441	.0435	.0433	1.62	.969	1.09	1.31	.0898	.0503
33	.00708	.0393	.0388	.0386	1.44	.863	.975	1.16	.0800	.0448
34	.00630	.0350	.0345	.0343	1.29	.768	.868	1.03	.0712	.0398
35	.00561	.0311	.0307	.0306	1.15	.684	.772	.921	.0634	.0355
36	.00500	.0277	.0274	.0273	1.02	.610	.689	.821	.0565	.0316
37	.00445	.0247	.0244	.0243	.908	.543	.613	.731	.0503	.0281
38	.00396	.0220	.0217	.0216	.808	.483	.545	.650	.0448	.0250
39	.00353	.0196	.0193	.0192	.720	.430	.486	.580	.0399	.0223
40	.00314	.0174	.0172	.0170	.640	.383	.432	.516	.0355	.0199

NOTE: Sterling silver stock is supplied in annealed (soft) state, although it may be supplied otherwise if so specified in ordering.

Troy and Avoirdupois Weight Equivalents

Troy weight:* 24 grains = 1 pennyweight (dwt.). 20 dwt. = 1 ounce (oz.)
12 oz. = 1 pound (lb.)

Ounces Troy to Pounds and Ounces Avoirdupois						Avoirdupois Ounces and Pounds to Ounces Troy					
Ozs. Troy	Lbs. & Ozs. Avoir.	Ozs. Troy	Lbs. & Ozs. Avoir.	Ozs. Troy	Lbs. & Ozs. Avoir.	Avoir. Ozs.	Troy Ozs.	Avoir. Lbs.	Troy Ozs.	Avoir. Lbs.	Troy Ozs.
1	1.1	39	2-10.8	77	5- 4.5	1	.9115	21	306.250	61	889.583
2	2.2	40	2-11.9	78	5- 5.6	2	1.823	22	320.883	62	904.167
3	3.3	41	2-13.0	79	5- 6.7	3	2.734	23	335.417	63	918.750
4	4.4	42	2-14.1	80	5- 7.8	4	3.646	24	350.000	64	933.333
5	5.5	43	2-15.2	81	5- 8.9	5	4.557	25	364.583	65	947.917
6	6.6	44	3- 0.3	82	5-10.0	6	5.469	26	379.167	66	962.500
7	7.7	45	3- 1.4	83	5-11.1	7	6.380	27	393.750	67	977.083
8	8.8	46	3- 2.5	84	5-12.2	8	7.292	28	408.333	68	991.667
9	9.9	47	3- 3.6	85	5-13.3	9	8.203	29	422.917	69	1006.250
10	11.0	48	3- 4.7	86	5-14.4	10	9.115	30	437.500	70	1020.833
11	12.1	49	3- 5.8	87	5-15.5	11	10.026	31	452.083	71	1035.417
12	13.2	50	3- 6.9	88	6- 0.6	12	10.937	32	466.667	72	1050.000
13	14.3	51	3- 8.0	89	6- 1.7	13	11.849	33	481.250	73	1064.583
14	15.4	52	3- 9.1	90	6- 2.8	14	12.760	34	495.833	74	1079.167
15	1- 0.5	53	3-10.2	91	6- 3.9	15	13.672	35	510.417	75	1093.750
16	1- 1.6	54	3-11.3	92	6- 5.0			36	525.000	76	1108.333
17	1- 2.7	55	3-12.4	93	6- 6.1			37	539.583	77	1122.917
18	1- 3.8	56	3-13.5	94	6- 7.2	Avoir. Lbs.	Troy Ozs.	38	554.167	78	1137.500
19	1- 4.9	57	3-14.6	95	6- 8.3			39	568.750	79	1152.083
20	1- 6.0	58	3-15.7	96	6- 9.4			40	583.333	80	1166.667
21	1- 7.1	59	4- 0.8	97	6-10.5	1	14.583	41	597.917	81	1181.250
22	1- 8.2	60	4- 1.9	98	6-11.6	2	29.167	42	612.500	82	1195.833
23	1- 9.3	61	4- 3.0	99	6-12.7	3	43.750	43	627.083	83	1210.417
24	1-10.4	62	4- 4.1	100	6-13.8	4	58.333	44	641.667	84	1225.000
25	1-11.5	63	4- 5.2	200	13-11.5	5	72.917	45	656.250	85	1239.583
26	1-12.6	64	4- 6.3	300	20- 9.2	6	87.500	46	670.833	86	1254.167
27	1-13.7	65	4- 7.4	400	27- 6.9	7	102.083	47	685.417	87	1268.750
28	1-14.8	66	4- 8.5	500	34- 4.6	8	116.667	48	700.000	88	1283.333
29	1-15.9	67	4- 9.6	600	41- 2.3	9	131.250	49	714.583	89	1297.917
30	2- 1.0	68	4-10.7	700	48- 0.0	10	145.833	50	729.167	90	1312.500
31	2- 2.1	69	4-11.8	800	54-13.8	11	160.417	51	743.750	91	1327.083
32	2- 3.2	70	4-12.8	900	61-11.5	12	175.000	52	758.333	92	1341.667
33	2- 4.3	71	4-13.9	1000	58- 9.2	13	189.583	53	772.917	93	1356.250
34	2- 5.4	72	4-15.0	2000	137- 2.3	14	204.167	54	787.500	94	1370.833
35	2- 6.4	73	5- 0.1	3000	205-11.5	15	218.750	55	802.083	95	1385.417
36	2- 7.5	74	5- 1.2	4000	274- 4.7	16	233.333	56	816.667	96	1400.000
37	2- 8.6	75	5- 2.3	5000	342-13.8	17	247.917	57	831.250	97	1414.583
38	2- 9.7	76	5- 3.4			18	262.500	58	845.833	98	1429.167
						19	277.083	59	860.417	99	1443.750
						20	291.667	60	875.000	100	1458.333

*Precious metals are weighed by troy weight.
NOTE: Silver—sold by the troy ounce. Gold—sold by the pennyweight.

Round Wire

Weight in Pennyweights or Ounces Per Foot in B & S Gauge

B & S Gauge	Thick-ness in Inches	Fine Silver	Sterling Silver	Coin Silver	Fine Gold	10 K Yel. Gold	14 K Yel. Gold	18 K Yel. Gold	Plat-inum	Palla-dium
		Ozs.	Ozs.	Ozs.	Dwts.	Dwts.	Dwts.	Dwts.	Ozs.	Ozs.
1	.28930	4.38	4.32	4.30	161.0	96.2	109.	130.	8.91	4.99
2	.25763	3.47	3.43	3.40	128.	76.3	86.1	104.	7.07	3.95
3	.22942	2.75	2.72	2.70	101.	60.5	68.3	81.5	5.61	3.14
4	.20431	2.18	2.15	2.15	80.3	48.0	54.2	64.6	4.45	2.49
5	.18194	1.73	1.70	1.70	63.6	38.0	43.0	51.2	3.53	1.97
6	.16202	1.37	1.36	1.35	50.5	30.2	34.1	40.6	2.80	1.56
7	.14428	1.09	1.07	1.07	40.0	23.9	27.0	32.2	2.22	1.24
8	.12849	.863	.852	.848	31.7	19.0	21.4	25.6	1.76	.984
9	.11443	.685	.676	.673	25.2	15.1	17.0	20.3	1.39	.780
10	.10189	.543	.536	.533	20.0	11.9	13.5	16.1	1.11	.619
11	.09074	.431	.425	.423	15.8	9.46	10.7	12.7	.877	.491
12	.08080	.341	.337	.335	12.6	7.50	8.47	10.1	.695	.389
13	.07196	.271	.267	.266	9.96	5.95	6.72	8.01	.552	.309
14	.06408	.215	.212	.211	7.89	4.72	5.33	6.36	.437	.245
15	.05706	.170	.168	.167	6.26	3.74	4.23	5.04	.347	.194
16	.05082	.135	.133	.133	4.97	2.97	3.35	4.00	.275	.154
17	.04525	.107	.106	.105	3.94	2.35	2.66	3.17	.218	.122
18	.04030	.0849	.0838	.0834	3.12	1.87	2.10	2.51	.173	.0968
19	.03589	.0674	.0665	.0662	2.48	1.48	1.67	1.99	.137	.0767
20	.03196	.0534	.0527	.0525	1.96	1.17	1.33	1.58	.109	.0609
21	.02846	.0424	.0418	.0416	1.56	.931	1.05	1.25	.0863	.0483
22	.02534	.0336	.0331	.0330	1.23	.738	.833	.994	.0684	.0383
23	.02257	.0266	.0263	.0262	.979	.585	.661	.789	.0543	.0304
24	.02010	.0211	.0209	.0208	.777	.464	.524	.625	.0430	.0241
25	.01790	.0168	.0165	.0165	.616	.368	.416	.496	.0341	.0191
26	.01594	.0133	.0131	.0131	.489	.292	.330	.393	.0271	.0151
27	.01419	.0105	.0104	.0103	.387	.231	.261	.312	.0214	.0120
28	.02164	.00835	.00825	.00821	.307	.184	.207	.247	.0170	.00952
29	.01125	.00662	.00653	.00650	.243	.145	.164	.19ᴜ	.0135	.00754
30	.01002	.00525	.00518	.00516	.193	.115	.130	.155	.0107	.00598
31	.00892	.00416	.00410	.00409	.153	.0914	.103	.123	.00847	.00474
32	.00795	.00330	.00326	.00325	.122	.0726	.0820	.0978	.00673	.00377
33	.00708	.00262	.00259	.00258	.0964	.0576	.0651	.0776	.00534	.00299
34	.00630	.00208	.00205	.00204	.0763	.0456	.0515	.0614	.00423	.00236
35	.00561	.00165	.00162	.00162	.0605	.0362	.0408	.0487	.00335	.00188
36	.00500	.00131	.00129	.00128	.0481	.0287	.0324	.0387	.00266	.00149
37	.00445	.00104	.00102	.00102	.0381	.0228	.0257	.0306	.00211	.00118
38	.00396	.000820	.000809	.000806	.0302	.0180	.0204	.0243	.00167	.000934
39	.00353	.000652	.000643	.000640	.0240	.0143	.0162	.0193	.00133	.000742
40	.00314	.000516	.000509	.000507	.0190	.0113	.0128	.0153	.00105	.000587

Index

(Boldface numbers indicate a major entry.)